To Mel Jackson
friend and scholar, best wishes.
John Parker Carol Clemens

THE AMERICAN REVOLUTION:
A HERITAGE OF CHANGE

The James Ford Bell Library
Bicentennial Conference
University of Minnesota

edited by
John Parker and Carol Urness

ASSOCIATES OF THE JAMES FORD BELL LIBRARY
Minneapolis, 1975

Contents

iii

Preface

The James Ford Bell Library Conference on the American Revolution was held May 2, 3, 4, 1973 at the University of Minnesota. Its purpose was instructive: to bring together for discussion leading scholars who would share with students, teachers, and laymen their ideas and insights on the American Revolution as the United States approaches its bicentennial anniversary.

The Conference was supported with financial grants from the Associates of the James Ford Bell Library and the James Ford Bell Foundation. It was their concern that the proceedings of the Conference receive the widest possible distribution, and this volume is published with that concern in mind.

Assisting with the Conference were the following scholars who presided over the individual sessions: Clarke A. Chambers, University of Minnesota; Carl M. Chrislock, Augsburg College; Louis G. Geiger, Iowa State University; and Robert P. Wilkins, University of North Dakota. We wish to express our gratitude for their participation. For promptness and cooperation in the preparation of their papers both for oral and published presentation we commend our Conference speakers. We owe special debts of gratitude to Boyd Shafer for suggestions in planning the Conference; to J. Harold Kittleson, Irv Kreidberg, and Judy Hendricks for assisting with publication arrangements; to Wendy Wettergren, Janeen Morey, and Jeanette Erickson for typing the manuscript; and to Vicki Zobel and Steve Kemmerer for proofreading.

All notes to the text refer to items in the bibliography for the entire work which is at pages 158-173.

Minneapolis

John Parker
Carol Urness
For the Associates of the
James Ford Bell Library

Introduction

JOHN PARKER and CAROL URNESS

In 1701, a little more than half way along history's road from Jamestown to Concord Bridge, an anonymous author who simply styled himself "an American" published *An Essay upon the English Plantations on the Continent of America* in which he stated that the first necessity for happiness in the American colonies and for good relations with their mother country was "a good constitution of government." It was a point of view that found increasing acceptance in the following decades. The search for a satisfactory government for the colonies and an empire policy conducive to both harmony and economic success became major Anglo-American concerns in the period before the outbreak of armed conflict.

The American Revolution is too often thought of as a series of military confrontations eventually confirming this nation's independence. The battles were the rebellion, an aspect of a revolution that began long before Lexington and continued after Yorktown. It is the nonmilitary aspect of this movement toward democracy and the founding of a new nation that are the concern of the eleven essays presented here. Nowadays such a revolution might be called a "battle for the hearts and minds" of a people. At a time when it is no longer easy for Americans to include armed rebellion as a means to "a good constitution of government" it is worthwhile to examine the hearts and minds of Americans who made the Revolution, to understand the complex set of social, political, philosophical, and economic developments on both sides of the Atlantic Ocean that sent the quest for just and effective government in the direction of the battlefield.

Born of the European power struggle of the seventeenth century, the English presence in the New World provided an outlet for the ambitious and the discontented, seekers for both opportunity and freedom. Ideas migrated with them: Whiggish notions about restraints upon the power of kings, dissenting passion for liberty of conscience, Enlightenment beliefs that reason would—if allowed to operate—produce equitable government. These philosophical seeds, planted in the fields and forests of the New World, grew beside the pragmatic necessity of creating local governments that would handle everyday concerns which could not come before Parliament in London. There were other necessities to be provided locally: food, clothing, schools, churches, militias; and in providing them the colonists inevitably developed a sense of independence and of differentiation from Englishmen, even as they sought to copy closely English institutions and ways.

A developed talent for local government, often functioning in close relationship to local economic interests, could not but raise the question of outside control inherent in the imperial situation. A pamphleteer in 1775 asked by what reasoning it could be justified "that five hundred and fifty-eight men in a little tiny Spot, in one Corner of Europe, should at this time have the Lives, Liberties, and Properties of three millions of People...at a distance of three thousand miles from them exclusively at their disposal." The volumes of Locke and Blackstone stood ready at hand for those who chose to intellectualize the argument over the powers of rulers and the rights of subjects. But a very large degree of local control over local affairs made very good sense to those who had become accustomed to it and who had local economic interests to protect.

However, the argument that distance diminished the right to dominate had unsettling possibilities in America, where the underrepresented farmer or frontiersman cared little whether it was London or Philadelphia and Charleston that was deaf to his concerns. The Revolution thus intruded into local politics as a search for a home grown "good constitution of government." Blacks, landless poor, artisans, women, all had a stake in changing their condition of powerlessness. Innovation threatened by these groups produced some very strong practical reasons why some Americans could fear the Revolution, try to avoid it, or even seek to supress it.

The termination of British authority in the Thirteen Colonies necessitated an intensification of creative thinking with respect to American society and its government. The war of national liberation was over, but independence did not automatically install the liberty and justice so loudly contended for by leaders of the movement. There were property rights challenged by newly assumed political right. There was the truth of Samuel Johnson's remark, "we hear the loudest yelps for liberty among drivers of negroes." There was no turning back from Thomas Jefferson's lofty lines about life, liberty, and the pursuit of happiness as ends of government, which for most Americans are the noblest words of statecraft, yet the search for their fulfillment had far to go.

Indeed, the search continues, and the approach of our national bicentennial anniversary seemed an appropriate time for the James Ford Bell Library to sponsor a sharing of recent scholarship for the better understanding of the origins and early development of this quest. We address ourselves to the citizen as well as the specialist, to the student as much as to the professor. We hope with these essays to create understanding and to suggest further inquiry into our country's adventure with democracy.

Motivations and Aspirations for Colonial Settlement in North America

LOUIS B. WRIGHT

In considering the reasons that prompted the colonization of North America, we must deal with two levels of motivation: official and political, and unofficial and personal. These reasons were more complex than we are usually led to believe and perhaps are worth a brief recapitulation, even at the risk of repeating much that is an old story to specialists.

At the official and political level it should be emphasized that European power politics in sixteenth-century Europe had a profound influence upon the settlement of North America. If we sometimes wonder why England was so dilatory about claiming a portion of the New World, it is because we forget the nature of relations between Spain and England for the first three quarters of the sixteenth century. Because of the dramatic episodes of the last twenty-five years of that century, particularly the English intervention in the Low Countries in behalf of the Dutch rebels against Spain followed by the coming of the Spanish Armada, we are likely to believe that England and Spain were traditional enemies. On the contrary, the two countries for long periods had been friends and allies, both suspicious of the ambitions of the French monarchy. Henry VII, the first Tudor, could think of no better marriage for his heir than a union with Catharine of Aragon, daughter of Ferdinand and Isabella. Henry VIII's daughter Mary, who came to the throne in 1553, married Philip of Spain. After Mary's death Elizabeth toyed with the idea of marrying her late sister's husband, then reigning as King Philip II. During the years when Spain was founding an empire in the New World that soon extended from Tierra del Fuego to Texas, relations with England were intimate and close. This traditional friendship with Spain explains the early Tudors' hesitancy to embark upon any American enterprise. Even by the middle years of

1

Elizabeth's reign, when it had become obvious that friendship with Spain could not be much longer maintained, the sheer military power of the Iberian colossus kept the English cautious. Furthermore, English merchants had developed a profitable trade with Spain and did not want their profits threatened.

France, on the other hand, with raids on Spanish shipping and the exploring expeditions of Giovanni da Verazzano in 1524 and Jacques Cartier in 1534, indicated no willingness to concede the New World to Spain, particularly its northern regions. But in the south and southwest there was no serious challenge to Spain's ambitions. Hernando de Soto, who landed at Tampa Bay on May 18, 1539, led his expedition as far north as the Carolinas, thence across the Mississippi River into Arkansas, and back into northern Louisiana where he died. While De Soto was wandering through the southeast, Francisco Vasquez de Coronado was searching through the southwest as far as western Kansas for the mythical seven cities of Cíbola and Quivira. Disappointed at his failure to find another hoard of gold, Coronado finally gave up in 1542 and returned to Mexico. But he made good the Spanish claim to a vast region that included present-day Arizona, New Mexico, and Texas.

Even with Spain firmly established in the south and France determined to hold Canada, the English might still hope to gain a foothold somewhere between Florida and Maine. A few regions in South America, claimed by Spain or Portugal but not yet occupied "by any Christian prince," would also tempt English adventurers. But political disagreements among Queen Elizabeth's officials would delay effective action.

By the 1570s a violently anti-Spanish faction of English Protestants, later to become known as Puritans, had become deeply concerned over Spain's continued expansion overseas. They feared that England would soon be shut out of the New World unless efforts were made to checkmate Spain. Furthermore, they pointed out, Spain's military strength, the greatest in Europe, was made possible by gold and silver from American mines, which poured into her coffers. Until that stream of wealth could be blocked the Spanish would retain the power to threaten the peace and freedom of all Europe. If England could set up bases at strategic points in the New World and settle colonists there, Spain's lifeline of treasure ships might be cut. Thus their argument ran.[1]

This anti-Spanish faction was led by the Queen's Principal Secretary, Sir Francis Walsingham, and her favorite, the Earl of Leicester. Others in the group included Sir Humphrey Gilbert, Sir Walter Raleigh, and Richard Hakluyt, preacher and compiler of voyage literature, an ardent propagandist for overseas expansion. Walsingham had been English ambassador to France at

1. L. Wright, "Elizabethan Politics," 254-269.

the time of the Massacre of St. Bartholomew's Day, August 24, 1572, and he never forgot this demonstration of the terrifying influence of Catholic Spain, even upon France. Though a man of prudence, Walsingham no longer was willing to appease Spain. By 1576 he was supporting secret aid to the Dutch rebels, an action opposed by Queen Elizabeth's other great counselor, the Lord Treasurer, Sir William Cecil (created Baron Burghley in 1571).

Lord Burghley was the leader of a group who sought to maintain peace with Spain, not because they approved of Spain's policies but because they believed it imprudent to incur the enmity of so strong a power. A man of infinite caution, Burghley's policy was to encourage trade, build up England's economic and political strength, and bide his time. He never let his emotions sway his judgment, and though he doubtless shared Walsingham's distrust of Spain, he had no intention of letting England lead a Protestant crusade if he could help it. And he did not encourage efforts to encroach on Spanish claims in America.

Queen Elizabeth, respecting both Walsingham and Burghley, tried to steer a middle course between them. For years she had sought to avoid risk of open war with Spain, but by early 1577 even she began to doubt that appeasement of Philip II could long continue. For one reason, her suspicions had been aroused by rumors that Philip was secretly plotting to aid her rival, Mary Queen of Scots. Taking advantage of the Queen's concern, Walsingham proposed that she give secret encouragement to English corsairs eager to raid Spanish shipping. To enumerate specific targets, Walsingham called in Francis Drake.

John Cooke, author of a contemporary account of Drake's voyage, reported Drake's reaction: "Walsingham did come to confer with him (Drake) and declared unto him that her Majesty had received divers injuries of the King of Spain for which she desired to have some revenge." Walsingham produced a map and asked Drake to mark in his own hand places where the King of Spain "might be most annoyed." This Drake refused to do because "if it should please God to take her Majesty away, it might be that some prince might reign that might be in league with the King of Spain, and then will my own hand be a witness against myself."[2] Drake was wise; Raleigh, for his enmity to Spain, lost his head when James I came to the throne. But Drake agreed to tell the Queen of a plan to attack the Spaniards from the Pacific and to raid the west coast of South America. His audience with the Queen resulted in Drake's circumnavigation of the globe between 1577 and 1580, lucrative raids on Spanish shipping, the claiming of New Albion (California) for the English crown, and the knighting of Drake on the deck of the *Golden Hind*—a clear signal to Philip that appeasement was over.

2. Corbett, I, 207-208.

Concerning this audience, Drake reported that "her Majesty did swear by her crown that if any within her realm did give the King of Spain to understand hereof (the proposed raid on the west coast), as she suspected too well, they should lose their heads therefor." Drake added: "Her Majesty gave me special commandment that of all men my Lord Treasurer (Burghley) should not know of it." The Queen knew that her cautious counselor would try to thwart so dangerous an affront to Spain.

Propaganda for overseas expansion was now becoming more insistent. While Drake was preparing to sail on his great expedition, Sir Humphrey Gilbert, half brother of Sir Walter Raleigh, was writing two reports in which he proposed that he should lead an expedition to seize the Spanish, Portuguese, and French fishing fleets off Newfoundland and then join with other privateers to take Cuba and Santo Domingo.[3] Such an action clearly would have annoyed the King of Spain, not to mention the King of France, but, if successful, it might have dealt a fatal blow to the Spanish empire. For Queen Elizabeth, however, Gilbert's proposal was too overt and she contented herself with surreptitious aid to Drake.

As early as 1580, Richard Hakluyt, the most vigorous propagandist for colonial enterprise, prepared a paper entitled, "A Discourse of the Commodity of the Taking of the Strait of Magellanus." In it he argued that without "great charge and without open war" England might cripple Spain by fortifying the passage to the Pacific. He also suggested seizing a base on the hump of Brazil. To avoid antagonizing Spain the government might quietly send a pirate to settle the base at the Strait of Magellan with a quota of English convicts, plus slaves and half-breeds rescued from Spanish colonies. In 1582 Hakluyt published *Divers Voyages*, his first compilation, which contained arguments for colonization. In 1584 he had an audience with Queen Elizabeth and presented a long report whose title conventionally has been shortened to "A Discourse of Western Planting."

This "discourse" summarized the motivations that inspired Hakluyt and other Protestant advocates of expansion. The princes of the reformed religion, of whom Queen Elizabeth was the leader, he asserted, had an obligation to see that the heathen of the New World were not allowed to become a solid Catholic bloc. It would not be sufficient to send a few Protestant missionaries to compete with the Catholics overseas. The salvation of the heathen must be a concomitant of colonization. Hakluyt then painted a glowing picture of the profits to English merchants and the enrichment of the English crown from the commodities of the New World which Spain then monopolized. Spain, he insisted, was vulnerable and was less powerful than the public had been led to believe. King Philip's pride would be brought low, he predicted, if Englishmen

3. Quinn, I, 33-40.

were to launch a determined attack on the outposts of his empire.[4] These arguments were shrewdly designed to appeal to Queen Elizabeth's vanity, greed, and patriotism. The presentation of the paper coincided with efforts already being made by both Gilbert and Raleigh to send out colonies to America.

It will be observed that Hakluyt emphasized religion as one of the primary motives for colonization overseas. A modern reader is likely to dismiss this argument as pious hypocrisy, for in our non-religious age it is hard for us to comprehend the intensity of religious motivations in the sixteenth and seventeenth centuries—both Catholic and Protestant.

Most of the Spanish conquistadors who laid the foundations of empire in the New World were motivated not only by greed for gold, but by a sincere belief that they were carrying out the will of God. Long conditioned to fight under the banner of the Cross in their efforts to drive the Moors out of Spain, they carried this religious intensity to America early in the sixteenth century. The Spaniards, it is true, saw no inconsistency in enslaving the Indians whom they converted. In their eyes a heathen made a good bargain if he exchanged, however unwillingly, present liberty for future bliss. If he died from overwork in the mines, he had at least been baptized and could hope to ascend to heaven. This was not hypocrisy but sincere if misguided faith on the part of the conquerors.

Protestants, whose views were reflected in Hakluyt's writings, were also concerned about their religious responsibility overseas, but they differed from the Spaniards in emphasis and purpose. Though they too recognized an obligation to carry the Gospel to the heathen, they were even more concerned to prevent the spread of "Popish" Catholicism. Their motives, therefore, were political as well as religious.

In trying to comprehend this religious motivation of Protestants, we should bear in mind their genuine fear of Catholic domination. They remembered the fires at Smithfield during the reign of "Bloody" Queen Mary when Protestants were burned at the stake for their beliefs. Even more recent in memory was the Massacre of St. Bartholomew's Day of 1572, when thousands of French Protestants were murdered in cold blood. They also could cite as proof of the iniquity of Spanish Catholics a book from a Spaniard's pen: Bartolomé de las Casas' *Brevissima relación de la destruycion de las Indias*, translated into English in 1583 as *The Spanish Colony*, which magnified "Spanish cruelties and tyrannies perpetrated in the West Indies." Here for all the world to see was a Spaniard's own testimony of what would happen if Spanish Catholicism were allowed to take over all the New World. The Spanish text of this work, which Las Casas saw through the press in

4. See also L. Wright, *Religion and Empire*; L. Wright, *Gold, Glory and the Gospel*.

1552, was soon translated into other European languages, and became a potent weapon in the hands of anti-Spanish propagandists.

When the Protestant powers in Europe, however, seized the initiative for expansion into the New World, they were inspired by motives similar to those of the Iberians. They wanted new areas for trade and they hoped to find gold and silver such as the Spaniards had captured in Mexico and Peru. They also hoped to cut Spain's financial lifeline and block that nation's further expansion. Spain, the world's paramount military power, dominated by a zeal to impose its religion on the rest of the world, aroused great fear in other European nations.

As the dream of quick riches from the discovery of gold and silver faded after the initial explorations by Englishmen in North America, England came to the sober realization that prosperity would depend upon trade and commerce. Captain John Smith was one of the first to point out the potential value of fish and furs. In the first quarter of the seventeenth century, the fisheries of New England and Newfoundland and the fur trade with the Indians assured settlers in America and merchants in London of continued prosperity. In 1614 John Rolfe sent from Virginia his first shipment of tobacco, a commodity that would in time prove more valuable than all of the gold and silver of Peru.

The value of raw materials from colonies in America confirmed the mercantilist views of English economists. Henceforth they would be motivated by a desire to insure their sources of tobacco, furs, fish, grains, meat, rice, indigo, timber, spars, rosin, and turpentine within a closed imperial system. The colonies would provide a continually expanding market for goods of English manufacture. So the Navigation Acts of the mid-seventeenth century were designed to maintain this economic framework; and, contrary to popular opinion, these Navigation Acts were not altogether bad. But that is another story.

Up to this point we have been concerned principally with the political and official motivations that prompted England to seek a portion of the New World. But what made individuals willing to endure incredible hardships and dangers to settle in the wilderness?

Just as religion supplied an impelling reason for the nation to try to expand overseas, so religious motives account for much individual emigration. The new land offered havens for the persecuted of many faiths. When Sir Humphrey Gilbert tried to colonize Newfoundland in 1583, he proposed to create a refuge for English Catholics. Though he himself was a Protestant, his scheme was intended to provide religious liberty for an oppressed group in England, free the country of a dissident element, and perhaps enrich Gilbert by peopling his "plantation" with steady workers. His plan came to naught but it gave Sir George Calvert, Lord Baltimore, the idea for a Catholic colony, first in Newfoundland and later in Maryland.

The story of the Puritans who came to Massachusetts Bay seeking a place apart where they might worship as they pleased has been so often told that it needs no repetition here. We also have heard, perhaps too often, the story of the Pilgrim Fathers, although William Bradford's *History of Plymouth Plantation* is a noble piece of prose worth frequent reading. Nor do we need to emphasize again the appeal that William Penn's proclamation of religious freedom made to countless Europeans. The liberty to worship as any sect wished brought thousands of Quakers, Mennonites, Lutherans, Huguenots, Scotch Presbyterians, Welsh Baptists, Moravians, and others to Pennsylvania and helped to insure the immediate prosperity of that colony. But what of countless men and women not inspired by deep religious motives?

Too often we have neglected to remember one of the prime motives in any age for exploration and settlement in a strange land: the sheer love of adventure. There is no reason to believe that our ancestors in the sixteenth century had less of this spirit than man of later periods. The desire for personal glory was a heritage from the Renaissance that persisted in the cultural consciousness. Many men were willing to undertake a voyage to the New World merely to show their mettle, to see the wonders, and to acquire wealth if fate ordained; if not, so be it; it was an adventure worth the risk. If mere adventurers had not so cluttered the passenger list of the first supply of settlers at Jamestown, Captain John Smith would have had less trouble and the colony might have prospered sooner. From Jamestown to California during the Gold Rush, many of the adventurers went for excitement as much as for gain. This is a motive that gets too little emphasis in appraising the quality of the early emigrants to North America.

Another neglected, even forgotten, motivation was the hope of finding a healthier climate. A long sea voyage, then and later, was often prescribed for the ailing. Despite the numbers who died in the early days of settlement in Virginia and New England, the belief was widespread that the new land could provide cures for all the ailments of the Old World. A Spanish physician, Dr. Nicolás Monardes, published an influential work on the medical products of America, which John Frampton brought out in an English version in 1577 and entitled *Joyful News out of the New Found World*. Monardes commended tobacco as a sovereign remedy for most of man's ailments. This book and others that followed it helped to fix the idea that miraculous cures could be found overseas.

How many emigrants came in search of curative drugs and a healthful climate, no one knows, but the number must have been considerable. Some of the promotion literature was aimed at this audience. The Reverend Francis

Higginson in 1630 sent back from Salem in the Massachusetts Bay Colony a little tract commending, among other things, the wholesomeness of the climate. Published under the title, *New England's Plantation, or, A Short and True Description of the Commodities and Discommodities of That Country,* the little book had a chapter "On the Air of New England with the Temper and Creatures In It" which extolled the healthfulness of the climate. "The temper of the air of New England," Higginson asserted, "is one special thing that commends this place. Experience doth manifest that there is hardly a more healthful place to be found in the world that agreeth better with our English bodies. Many that have been weak and sickly in old England by coming hither have been thoroughly healed and grown healthful and strong." Higginson testified that he himself had been cured of sundry ailments and concluded: "I think it a wise course for all cold complections to take physic in New England, for a sup of New England's air is better than a whole draft of old England's ale." Unfortunately for proof of his theory, Higginson died of tuberculosis in August of the year in which his commendation of the climate was composed.

Idealism was also an important motive in the settlement of North America. From early times one of the aspirations of many Europeans was to create in the New World an Utopian society. In actual fact, More's *Utopia* was adapted in the sixteenth century by a Spanish bishop as the basis for government in the province of Michoacan in New Spain. The unlimited space and freedom to experiment without too much interference from tradition-bound authorities was a temptation to idealists of many sorts. The impetus of the humanitarian movement in the eighteenth century accounts for many Utopian schemes. Oglethorpe's dream of making Georgia a refuge for distressed debtors is evidence of the impact of the movement.

One of the most colorful projects was the brain child of a Scottish baronet, Sir Robert Montgomery of Skelmorly, who published in 1717 *A Discourse Concerning the Designed Establishment of a New Colony to the South of Carolina in the Most Delightful Country of the Universe*, a territory including most of the present state of Alabama and extending to the Pacific.

This land Montgomery named Azilia, "our future Eden," and he declared "that Nature has not blessed the world with any tract which can be preferable to it, that Paradise with all her virgin beauties may be modestly supposed at most but equal to its native excellencies." Montgomery envisioned a principality that would produce all the exotic products that the mercantilists had not yet been able to find within the closed empire: silk, lemons, oranges, wine, coffee, tea, dates, raisins, almonds, currants, cochineal, "and a great variety of still more rich commodities which we are forced to buy at mighty rates from countries lying in the very latitude of our plantations." Unluckily the collapse of the South Sea Bubble ruined Montgomery and his fellow promoters and the vision of the prosperous commonwealth of Azilia faded.

Another Scot, Sir Alexander Cuming of Coulter, even more visionary than Montgomery, proposed to create in the back country of South Carolina a new Zion for 300,000 distressed European Jews. His wife had dreamed, Cuming said, that he should make a trip to South Carolina to negotiate with the Indians for the Promised Land. Perhaps Lady Cuming hit upon this ruse to procure a little peace at home, but whatever the reason, Cuming set out in 1729 for Carolina; on March 13, 1730, he left Charleston for the Cherokee country where he described to marveling Indians the power and glory of King George II, had them swear allegience to the King—with him as viceroy—and persuaded six Cherokees and another stray Indian to return to England with him. The red men were received by King George and were the sensation of London but Cuming's Zion failed to materialize.

For reasons not altogether clear, visionary projects for Utopian colonies in the South appealed to Scots. In 1763 Archibald Menzies of Megerny Castle, Perthshire, devised a plan to people Florida with Armenians, Greeks, and Minorcans, who would achieve prosperity for themselves and become an asset to the British by producing silk and growing olives and wine grapes.

Nothing came of this but four years later Dr. Andrew Turnbull, another Scot, and two English associates formed a partnership to send Greeks, Italians, and Minorcans to Florida. They actually made a settlement at New Smyrna on the coast below St. Augustine, but quarreling and fighting among the colonists ruined the enterprise.

It was left for a sentimental and mystical German from Saxony, Christian Gottlieb Priber, to plan the most idealistic Utopia of them all, a communistic state among the Cherokees that combined concepts from Plato's *Republic*, current doctrines of humanitarianism, and a foreshadowing of Rousseau's idea of the noble savage. His efforts to teach the Indians to resist the knavery of white traders aroused the antagonism of colonists in Georgia who arrested him in 1743 and kept him a prisoner until his death a few years later.[5]

The vision of America as a site for ideal communities persisted through the centuries and indeed has never died. The nineteenth century saw many such groups settled throughout the country from New York State to California. Their story has been the theme of many books and more need to be written.

Among emigrants whose coming gets little emphasis are the involuntary settlers: convicts, remittance men, and black slaves. These were the *un*motivated ones, however strong were the motivations of those responsible for their arrival on these shores. English authorities from time to time unburden-

5. See L. Wright, *The Colonial Search for a Southern Eden.*

ed the jails by sending the inmates to America. A sardonic historian once commented that if Virginians would quit looking for their ancestors in Burke's *Peerage* and start searching the calendars of Newgate Prison they would have better luck. The grim truth is that not many of the convicts survived to reproduce themselves. Weakened by jail fever, unable to endure hard work in the fields, the majority sickened and died. But the effort to unload convicts on the colonies was a cause of numerous protests to the authorities in London. Convicts were a nuisance and a danger unwanted in any colony. Even Oglethorpe's plan to make Georgia a refuge for debtors failed in that purpose, for few debtors came.

By persuasion or command, a considerable number of younger sons who had no future in England were shipped off to the colonies. In this lot were a fair number of ne'er-do-wells whose families were glad to rid themselves of an embarrassment by sending them overseas. Thomas Morton, author of *New English Canaan* (1637), who scandalized the Puritans by setting up a Maypole at Merrymount and selling guns and liquor to the Indians, may have been one of this type.

Of the involuntary emigrants the most tragic were the black slaves from Africa who became more numerous from the 1670s onward. The Royal African Company found them a profitable commodity and pushed their sale in the colonies. New England shipmasters also discovered that they could make a fat profit by trading rum on the west coast of Africa for captives brought in from the interior by local African kings. Thus the nefarious trade flourished and bequeathed to North America a problem that would remain unsolved.

The motivation that brought the greatest number of settlers to America of course was economic. Even John Winthrop and many of his fellow Puritans in Massachusetts Bay came not only to find a place where they could worship as they pleased but to better their economic condition, for England in the 1630s was in the depths of a depression. Not only England but other countries of Europe suffered periodic depressions. The Thirty Years' War left much of the Rhineland devastated, and no country was free of distress. For that reason William Penn found it easy to attract thousands of German and Swiss settlers. Religion, to be sure, played a part in the desire of Mennonites and other pacifists to emigrate, but economic opportunities as described in Penn's advertisements were irresistible. For hordes of Germans, French Huguenots, and Scots, Philadelphia became the gateway to hoped-for prosperity.

The opportunity to buy land and become freeholders provided an incentive to English and other emigrants that was intense and persistent, not only in the colonial period but long afterward. Land was the key to status and freedom. A landowner was his own master. From time immemorial the possession of land marked a man as above the common run of humankind. Large landed estates indicated wealth and position. Even the small plot of a yeoman farmer raised the owner in the social scale.

Yet land in England, as elsewhere in Europe, was scarce, expensive, and hard to come by. No laborer by the sweat of his brow could hope to earn enough to acquire even a tiny farm. But in America in the early colonial period, by merely paying the cost of ocean passage, he could get a headright of fifty acres for himself and each member of his household. With a little capital an emigrant could acquire an ample estate, and, if luck was with him, he could look forward to taking his place as a member of a rising aristocracy. In the agrarian colonies, particularly in Virginia, Maryland, and South Carolina, landed proprietors consciously or unconsciously modelled themselves on the English country gentry. The aspiration of many an English emigrant, regardless of his birth, was to get enough land to become a gentleman in the technical sense. In New York, great proprietors with immense estates in the Hudson Valley exercised the prerogatives of Old World aristocracy. Virginia developed one of the most distinguished bodies of landowners. Whether they were aristocratic in their origins makes little difference. Once in possession of land and power, they soon exercised rights and privileges similar to those of the landed gentry they had known in England. The ease with which land was obtained in America provided the opportunity for the growth of aristocratic proprietors who gained immense power. Thus was the ambition of many an emigrant satisfied.

Attainable land was the attraction that brought the greatest number of settlers to America, in the colonial period and later. Land insured independence, and even the small landowner was fierce in defense of his rights, whether from marauding Indians or from what he considered interfering neighbors, unjust traders, or tax-gatherers. For three centuries and more the rural landowners, the American farmer, symbolized the acme of freedom and independence.

The aspiration of most colonial emigrants and those who came later was to improve their status and rise in the world. English-speaking North America offered the broadest opportunities of any region on this side of the Atlantic. Whatever may have been the limitations in this or that colony, in one period or another, by and large the English colonies guaranteed the greatest freedom to the individual to be found anywhere in the world. Some of this freedom was not by legislative fiat but by "natural right" that the settler seized. Dwellers in the wilderness were frequently beyond the reach of either sheriff or tax collector.

The liberty to which colonial Americans became accustomed, either those in long established communities or those on the frontier, made them sensitive to any encroachment by governmental authority. They were jealous of their freedom. Hence, England found the colonies recalcitrant when she tried to tax them in the 1760s. To officials in Whitehall the rebelliousness of Americans seemed evidence of willful stubbornness and ingratitude. But the aspirations of generations of Americans had been achieved, and they would not willingly surrender any jot of their freedom to an authority across the seas.

What Makes a Revolutionary?

CAROLINE ROBBINS

Rebels and revolutionaries are not commonly made by taking Algernon Sidney's *Discourses* off the shelf, studying John Locke's *Two Treatises*, or poring over Emmerich de Vattel's *Law of Nations*. The Devil can quote Scripture, but its teaching has not yet converted him. A lifetime of reading the ancient and later republicans, and of delving into the history of the rise and fall of empires, has produced a conservative as often as a potential reformer. An indisputable lesson derived from history is that single explanations of attitudes, catastrophes, or noticeable progress are not only unreliable, but unsatisfactory. The historian's speculation must always be circumscribed by the event, the moment of time, and circumstance. The attraction of concentrating upon the economic situation, the racial origins of a given group, or on the legal and education systems current is often very powerful, but must be withstood. Examination of all factors on the other hand, is of course, beyond the competence of an individual. Selection of emphasis is determined by personal predilection or prejudice, and command of material. In this brief paper, Benjamin Franklin's dictum "that it is prodigious the quantity of good that may be done by one man, if he will make a business of it," shall be kept in mind, and its obvious reverse.[1] "It is by individuals in a certain sense, not numbers," wrote Thomas Hollis, of Lincoln's Inn, one of the few English republicans of the reign of George III, to two friends in 1766, "that societies, communities, nations flourish, or are brought low."[2] A few people active in the revolutionary years will serve, perhaps, to illustrate the making of rebels in that era.

1. Franklin, *Writings*, IX, 103-5.
2. Blackburne, I, 294; Hollis Papers, f. 91-2.

Yet a study, limited to the heritage, education, reading, occupation, religion and associates of the fifty-six signers of the Declaration of Independence and half a dozen of their closest allies, reveals at once the difficulties of generalization. Thomas Hutchinson, the royal governor of Massachusetts, like John Adams, was of Puritan descent, educated at Harvard and a lawyer by training, yet their politics were diametrically opposed: Hutchinson saw safety only within the British orbit, and parliamentary supremacy as unquestionable; Adams began to think security possible without imperial protection, and believed that the rights of Englishmen could legitimately be claimed above legislative authority. George Mason, author of the Virginia Declaration of Rights of May, 1776, was of cavalier ancestry; Benjamin Harrison, another Virginian and a signer, was proud of a possible connection with a regicide officer; but if anything, Mason was a more dedicated supporter of the rebel cause. Two famous teachers, Francis Alison and John Witherspoon, disagreed over the tenets of the presbyterian creed they professed, but both supported the Revolution. Episcopalians in Virginia advanced, after a later start, as quickly, or even at times more precipitately towards independence, than the Congregationalists of New England. Charles Carroll of Carrollton, a Catholic, once determined, never faltered. John Lovell, master of Boston's Latin School, taught Samuel Adams, Robert Treat Paine, John Hancock, among signers, but Andrew Oliver the loyalist also studied with him. Lovell himself died in loyalist exile: his son remained in New England as an advocate of the American cause. Harvard, Yale, William and Mary, the Colleges of Philadelphia and New Jersey trained some signers, but the self-educated, who had had but a few months in the common schools were also, like Roger Sherman of Connecticut, among the number of signers. Early biographers indeed liked to write of the rise of one or another of these founders of a nation from cabin boy to supreme bench, or shoemaker to statesman.[3]

The suggestion occasionally made that Americans educated abroad were more oriented towards a national than a state's rights position needs more careful documentation: its relevance is greater to later constitutional debates, than to those leading to independence. One thing about travel at home or overseas seems clear: it cannot be credited with decisive motivation. Charles Carroll's experience at St. Omer did not make him a Jesuit propagandist. The many who studied in England at schools like Eton and Hackney, colleges at Cambridge, and the Inns of Court, were not on the whole made Anglophiles by their training. Anglo-American contacts in the field during the French and Indian Wars, or in London and elsewhere in the British Isles, as often brought about bad feeling, as any warmth of allegiance. Richard Stockton, a New Jer-

---

3. See J. Sanderson and Walm; Lossing; Grigsby; Rush, *Autobiography*, for information about signers.

sey signer, discovered a vast ignorance of American affairs in England, though his personal relationships there seem to have been unusually cordial. Thomas Heywood of Virginia, Thomas Lynch of South Carolina, and William Williams of Connecticut in differing ways, found English hauteur, patronizing manners, and general disdain for colonials, even those with whom they fought a common foe, very distasteful. They were anti-English before the troubles of the sixties began. Personal pique accounted for similar prejudice in others. William Henry Drayton was quite a vigorous loyalist until he discovered that as a native of South Carolina he was not likely to get the legal position he sought. Who knows what would have happened in Benjamin Franklin's case had he been made governor of Pennsylvania instead of being called a thief before the Privy Council by Alexander Wedderburn. The policies of the age of George III affected Americans personally in many ways other than by direct attacks upon the pocketbook, or by threats to establish bishoprics in the colonies.

Revolutionaries often develop by the company they keep. Some of the signers were, according to Lossing and Sanderson, their biographers, early disposed to what were called "levelling" and republican ideas. Loyalists, both before and after exile, believed the revolution to be the work of republican conspirators long anxious to overthrow the established order. They of course pointed to the prominent like Samuel Adams, but later memorialists suggest that among signers, George Clymer, a Pennsylvania merchant; Abraham Clark, surveyor; Elbridge Gerry of Rhode Island; and Francis Lewis, a Welsh New Yorker, were long-time republicans. Benjamin Rush, one of the few well-documented cases, became a convert to republicanism while studying medicine in Edinburgh, through the exhortations of John Bostock who introduced the American to Sidney's work, changing his political philosophy forever.[4] Samuel Adams learned his republicanism at home. He found his father's brewing business less to his inclination than the associates with whom he mixed in the Boston caucus. Politics always fascinated him. The return of Louisburg to the French in 1748, and the writs of assistance of 1761 issued for the enforcement of the Sugar Act, simply increased a disaffection to English rule long nourished by discussion in his circle. Ministerial policy thereafter kept their indignation near the boiling point. Occasional concessions by government followed by new regulations provided the pamphleteers with a fine field for the exercise of their talents, the orators for their arts. In their speeches and tracts familiar reading recalled eloquent quotations buttressing argument, stirring sentiment, appealing to precedent: all of it if a Whig complexion. How far this Whiggishness affected developing republicanism is open to question; that it supported revolutionary claims is certain.

4. Rush, *Autobiography*, 45-6.

"Let us ransack history," the philosopher and historian James Wilson once exclaimed.[5] And, of course, by history he meant much beyond that English history which Jefferson explored, to prove how little money had been spent in colonial establishment and maintenance.[6] The ancient world was examined for appropriate lessons. Plutarch taught more than one reader to love liberty.[7] Cicero encouraged patriots to die for their country. The rise and fall of the Roman Republic, much written about and widely studied, afforded food for thoughtful comparisons. The Abbé Vertot, a historian, not only wrote two popular volumes on this topic earlier in the century, but also dealt with other revolutions, in Sweden and Portugal. His talent was envied by Edward Gibbon.[8] Machiavelli's *Discourses* on Livy proved a well of moral precepts for statesmen. Adams and Jefferson read it. The fifteenth paragraph of the Virginia Declaration, prepared by George Mason, echoed one of its most commonly quoted precepts as it admonished Americans to preserve liberty by a firm adherence to justice, moderation, temperance, frugality and virtue, and by "frequent recurrence to fundamental principles."[9]

Classical history was well known. The federations of the ancient world praised by Montesquieu were to be scrutinized for their possible relevance to Confederation and Republic. But, as Jefferson told the Philadelphia journalist William Duane, English history enjoyed a special precedence. "Our laws, language, religion, politics and manners are so deeply laid in English foundations that we shall never cease to consider their history as a part of ours."[10] When in England Jefferson visited the battlefields of the English Civil War, but he did not share Adams's nostalgia for the English constitution so much admired before corruption had destroyed its virtue. He was certain that the developing American system was entirely different and infinitely better. He felt uneasy and out of place in London as Adams, in spite of snubs and affronts, never did. He continued to admire profoundly Edward Coke, Sidney, and Locke. And he studied parliamentary manuals of procedure, regarding them as an invaluable aid for all Americans.

English history in the seventeenth and eighteenth centuries it was felt went back to the classics. Tacitus, translated by Thomas Gordon, lamented the luxury and decayed virtues of Rome as he saw them, and described by way of exemplary contrast, the simple manners of the free Germans. The Saxon myth, the belief that English forebears in the German Woods enjoyed great liberty, was widely held. This liberty not only accompanied Saxon migration from those woods to England; centuries later, according to the myth, it sur-

5. Colbourn, *Lamp of Experience*, 127.
6. Jefferson, *Complete Jefferson*, 5-19.
7. Blackburne, I, 5.
8. Gibbon, 67, 111.
9. Thorpe, vol. 7, 3814.
10. Jefferson, *Life and Writings*, 605.

vived the vicissitudes of another voyage to take on new strength in America. In the century or so before the American Revolution politics determined historical perspective. Roundheads supported and cavaliers mocked claims for Saxon parliaments. Whig history dwelt upon the early freedom enjoyed as a priceless heritage: Tory chroniclers emphasized the absurdity of such pretensions.[11] Americans enjoyed David Hume's elegant *History*, but deplored its Tory distortions. Indignation was high in the colonies when the Scottish historian Sir John Dalrymple in his *Memoirs of Great Britain and Ireland*, 1771, revealed that French money was received by Whig heroes and martyrs in the age of Charles II.

Americans read English history in authors like Paul Rapin de Thoyras and White Kennett, and searched the great collections of John Rushworth, covering the period of English history 1618-1648,[12] and John Thurloe, whose papers describing the Protectorate were consulted by the relatively untutored Stephen Hopkins, governor of Rhode Island.[13] Franklin or some other wrote a widely circulated epitaph to John Bradshaw, the presiding judge at the trial of Charles I. Others boasted of forebears who had sheltered three regicides who escaped overseas. Everyone knew the story of the opposition to Charles I and Archbishop William Laud, and of John Hampden's brave refusal to pay ship money, as well as the course of events in the 1680s leading to the flight of James II to France, and William and Mary's acceptance of the Bill of Rights. Trevor Colburn's *The Lamp of Experience* has told us much about American reading of history, especially Whig history. Jonathan Mayhew's famous sermon on the centennial anniversary of the execution of Charles I dwelt upon a topic fully appreciated by most of its audience.[14]

A related study pursued by more than half the signers was law—only merchants compete with this category. The historian Hugh Blair Grigsby in an address of mid-nineteenth century, declared that lawyers "leant to liberty." Towards the end of his life, Jefferson writing to James Madison about the desirable qualifications for a law professor, reminded his friend that "our lawyers were then, that is before the Revolution, all Whigs," brought up on Sir Edward Coke or Sir Thomas Littleton. "A sounder Whig" than Coke, he said, never wrote, "nor of profounder learning." He lamented the change from the great Jacobean's "uncouth but cunning" erudition, to the "honeyed Mansfieldism of Blackstone."[15] In his youth to be sure, Jefferson had found Coke "a dull old scoundrel,"[16] but as he looked back on the pursuit of learning, he found in him a man whose principles he approved. The

---

11. Colbourn, *Lamp of Experience*, appendix I,194-8.
12. Jefferson, *Papers*, I, 106.
13. J. Sanderson and Walm, I, 356-7.
14. Bailyn, *Pamphlets*, 218-47.
15. Jefferson, *Life and Writings*, 726.
16. Jefferson, *Life and Writings*, 353.

legal decisions of the first half of the 17th century provided convenient support for the Americans against the administration of George III. The decision in Calvin's Case of 1606 to test whether a man born after the accession of Scotland's James VI to the throne of England as James I, enjoyed equally citizenship north and south of the border, could be applied to the American claim to the rights of Englishmen even though born and resident overseas. This claim had been disputed after 1688, not entirely resolved, and boldly argued before 1776. It was fiercely denied by English proponents of parliamentary sovereignty over all colonies and dependencies.

Calvin's case was not Coke's in the sense that was Bonham's case of 1610. Dr. Thomas Bonham had practiced medicine without the certificate required by the Royal College of Physicians. That body secured his imprisonment. He brought suit and Coke defended him on the basis of the belief that where a privilege or act of parliament or imposition was against Common Law, right reason, or repugnant, or impossible to be performed, the Common Law will control or amend it. Since the College collected half of every fine imposed for infractions of their rules, they were a party to every process, and should not therefore have power to judge. When in 1765 James Otis declared the Stamp Act invalid as being against the provisions of Magna Carta and the rights of Englishmen, he was following Lord Coke's dictum that unreasonable enactments were by their nature null and void.[17]

Famous decisions were not Coke's only contribution. In the *Institutes* he wrote that subsidies or taxes could not be imposed save at the instigation of the Commons. Opponents of virtual representation believed that even a vote of the lower House, considering the existing state of the distribution of the franchise, was insufficient. No man, declared the Petition of Right in 1628, could be compelled to make or yield a gift, loan, benevolence, tax, or such charge, without common consent. This was the basis of John Hampden's refusal in 1637 to pay ship money, and this idea was incorporated into a clause in the Bill of Rights pronouncing illegal the levying of money to the use of the Crown by pretense of prerogative. The colonist of 1765 believed that history and law were on his side: he was not represented in the Parliament voting the hated impositions. George Read, Delaware lawyer and signer, like Jefferson, found Coke the authoritative voice on the relation of parliamentary enactment to natural or common law. About 1780 he urged a young inquirer to read Coke, re-read him, and read him over again. "For," he said, "this is the well whence you must draw your knowledge of the law."[18]

Jefferson's scorn of Blackstone was unjust, conservative though the *Commentaries* might seem compared to Coke's *Institutes*. Professor Gerald

17. Bailyn, *Pamphlets*, 408-82, 580, 554, 579, 669-91.
18. Read, 571.

Stourzh in "William Blackstone, Teacher of Revolution," points out that the *Commentaries* justify revolution when unconstitutional oppressions, even of the sovereign power, "advance with gigantic strides." Mankind will not be reasoned out of the feelings of humanity; if a future king should endeavor to subvert those statues by breaking the original contract, "the throne would thereby be vacant." Elie Halévy also pointed out the resistance rights implicit in Blackstone's writing.[19]

All this serves to illustrate the difficulty of finding in the eighteenth century, outside of a few pulpits, proponents of passive obedience and a divine right theory of submission, if need be, to tyranny. Order, obedience, authority were all stressed, but men did not forget the stand taken against their monarch in 1688, by seven bishops of a church committed to these doctrines. There never was, John Joachim Zubly once said, an American Jacobite[20] and though the southern preacher exaggerated, Jacobites in the colonies were certainly rare birds. Even less common, in spite of wild statements by loyalists, were arguments like those of the levellers of mid-seventeenth century against the tyrannical rule, not merely of kings and magistrates, but of arbitrary parliaments. Such thoughts were to develop in the colonies as a result of the exercise of royal, ministerial and parliamentary power in coercive and "intolerable" acts. An appeal was now to be to the people, rather than to the people in Parliament assembled. This marks the great divide between American constitutional thinking and that of contemporary British theories.

The question must be asked, since influences upon the colonists are being considered, how many besides those public-spirited lawyers and statesmen, and even what proportion of them, read the tedious black-letter type in the early editions of Coke, or the many pages of Blackstone. The answer must be found in a glance at a couple of compilations circulating more cheaply, and more widely than the learned treatises studied by Adams, Jefferson, and Read: *English Liberties*, attributed to the radical editor, Henry Care, and published in a small octavo of 288 pages sometime about 1682, and *The Judgment of Whole Kingdoms and Nations, concerning the Rights, Power, and Prerogative of Kings, and the Rights, Priviledges, and Properties of the People*, written by John, Lord Somers, or possibly by Daniel Defoe. This had been issued in 1709 as *Vox Populi, Vox Dei*, and appeared with the longer title in 1710. *English Liberties* was reprinted "with larger additions, by W. N." in 1719; and in Boston by James and Benjamin Franklin in 1721. The fifth edition, issued in London by Edward and Charles Dilly in 1766 as *British Liberties*, acknowleged a debt to Henry Care's design, but increased the 1719 edition from 356 to 396 pages, adding a 79-page introduction and

19. Stourzh, "William Blackstone...," 184-200; Halévy, 131.
20. Zubly, 24.

observations upon the British constitution including references to a wide range of authorities, Continental and British. A Providence edition appeared in 1774. *The Judgment* went into eleven editions before 1714, and was brought out by presses in Boston, Newport, New York, and Philadelphia in 1773-1774. Both compilations were readily available in England and America before 1776.

The earliest edition of *English Liberties* was the briefest; it declared that by their rights Englishmen were bound by no laws but those to which they had given their consent. Nor could Englishmen be tried by any court without the presence of a jury of their peers. Among documents printed in *English Liberties* were: Magna Carta, Coke's discourse upon the antiquity and character of Parliament, and his opinion on the famous *De Tallagio non concendendo*. Other enactments such as the 1628 Petition of Right and the Habeas Corpus Statute of 1679, were included. The jury system was explained, and an account given of Bushel's case, deciding the independence of jurymen. Henry Care's "directions concerning the choice of members to serve in Parliament" and his warning against electing officers or pensioners, non-residents, men of ill-repute, debtors, men who took bribes or gave recompense for a vote, men in the service of foreign powers, made clear whom voters should avoid. This was included in the 1719 edition and again in 1766. Without listing all of its contents, enough has been given to show that *English Liberties* provided a convenient guide to the laws so frequently cited guaranteeing rights, and to Whiggish interpretation of both legal system and constitution. With even the smallest format in hand, an American could readily pontificate upon these matters without recourse to the black-letter Coke.

The Judgment was brought out originally in defense of the settlement of 1689, against Dr. Henry Sachaverell's support of divine right and passive obedience. Government, it declared, was instituted by God to secure the welfare, safety, and prosperity of the governed. Even when a compact had been made, it would not be binding if it enlarged the power of the ruler beyond reasonable limits. All legal governments have their origins in compacts, stipulations, compromises, and agreements. Ancient authorities such as Andrew Horn, Randulf de Glanville, and Henry de Bracton were cited, along with Coke, on the laws under which English kings ruled. The Great Charter, though sometimes ignored, was, *The Judgment* maintained, a ratification of privileges long claimed. Aristotle and Holy Writ were drawn into service. The similarities between the assemblies, diets, *cortes*, and parliaments of states enjoying the Gothic free policy were remarked. Tacitus, with others such as François Etudes de Mézeray, bolstered descriptions of Saxon freedom; Hugo Grotius provided 17th century arguments for natural rights. The terms imposed on William and Mary were summarized. Examples of the dethronement of monarchs and ejection of magistrates added strength to refutations of the doctrine of passive obedience. Many addresses and petitions of the period of the Glorious Revolution were reproduced. No American reading *The Judgment*, a rather disjointed but powerful work, could fail to see in the story of the English Revolution, reflections of the problems facing them in their own day.

Much admiration was accorded the English Settlement both at home, in the colonies and plantations, and on the European continent. Travelers to England described not only the buildings and people of its countryside, but also detailed the London Law Courts, Parliament, and the extraordinary liberty enjoyed by all inhabitants. The only parallel to the English achievement was to be found in the Roman Republic. The two constitutions were compared, studied, and admired from 1689 until after the creation of the American constitution in 1787. Voltaire, Montesquieu and the Swiss jurist Jean de Lolme were prominent among European Anglophiles; John Adams and Alexander Hamilton, in the new United States. But by the time the latter two men were, unjustly in one case at least it appears, accused of wanting to establish a monarchy after the English pattern in America, there had been a considerable diminution of Anglophilic attitudes. This could be illustrated by reference to travelers' comments in mid-century, and the reflections of political philosophers like the Marquis D'Argenson.[21] More familiar to Americans were the criticisms of Englishmen themselves, and their analysis of the sorry state into which they thought their country had declined. There were quite a few jeremiads, but less than half a dozen need be noticed here. In them can be found attacks on the maintenance of a standing army in time of peace, on the continued intolerancy of the episcopacy, on the growing corruption in public life, and on the decline of public morals and virtue.

Controversy over a standing army raged after the Glorious Revolution when the Peace of Ryswick, little more than a truce as it transpired, was signed in 1697. Walter Moyle, also author of an *Essay on the Roman Republic*, and John Trenchard published *An Argument showing...a Standing Army ...Inconsistent with a Free Government*. It was perhaps the most popular of the tracts of the 1690s and remained so throughout the eighteenth century. Parts of it and of kindred pieces were used to great effect in the orations commemorating the Boston Massacre, as well as in many debates on earlier occasions in both England and America.[22]

Not more famous, but more varied in approach were a series of occasional papers or essays appearing from 20 January 1720-4 January 1721, and almost immediately reprinted as a collection called *The Independent Whig*. This

21. Argenson, 23-6.
22. Robbins, 84-133.

came out in Philadelphia in 1724 and 1740, and in a free translation into French by Baron d'Holbach in Amsterdam in 1767. There were at least seven printings in London by mid-century. Its violently anti-clerical authors, Thomas Gordon and John Trenchard, prompted by the controversy raging over a sermon by Benjamin Hoadley on the spiritual nature of the church, reviled the worldly hierarchy and pointed out the evils that sprang from the pride and power of churchmen. Oppositionist writers had produced much in this vein since the Restoration reestablished the Episcopal Church and passed a severe series of laws enforcing uniformity. In 1698 Cotton Mather in his *Eleutheria*, narrating the story of the Protestants since the Reformation, had quoted long and bitter passages about the intransigence of the bishops from Andrew Marvell's famous *Rehearsal Transpros'd*, a defense of relaxation of uniformity. Benjamin Hoadley in his "Bangor" sermon of 1717 had suggested that the kingdom of Christ was not of this world. In *The Independent Whig*, and in Jonathan Mayhew's anniversary sermon of 1750 this idea was echoed. Americans, many of whom of course had fled from the restrictions put upon dissent by Archbishop Laud, continued to oppose any extension of episcopal authority overseas. Even those colonies where members of the English established church had settled, were by no means enthusiastic about control of their worship by authorities in London. Professor Bridenbaugh has traced the anxiety about the "mitre" as one of the major causes of colonial unrest in the sixties and seventies. *The Independent Whig* continued to express much with which Americans were in whole-hearted sympathy.[23]

A standing army and apprehensions about the appointment of American bishops were not the only threats to liberty detected. *Cato's Letters*, the second of the series published by Trenchard and Gordon, appeared from November 1720 to December 1723 in *The London Journal*, were reprinted first as a selection and then in four volumes in 1724. These four were reprinted in at least six editions in England. No American imprint of the whole collection has been found, but the letters were readily available.[24] In Boston, *The New England Courant*, and in Philadelphia, *The Mercury* published individual numbers in their pages. Such "letters" as those "On freedom of Speech," on "The right and capacity of people to judge governments," on the effects of "general corruption," taken by Cato from Sidney's *Discourses*, on standing armies, and two at least on "Parties," were all widely read and quoted.[25] David Ramsay in his *History of the American Revolution* noticed the importance of "Cato" who was cited by Philip Livingston, John Dickinson and many others.[26]

23. Bridenbaugh, *Mitre and Sceptre*.
24. Rossiter, 141; Jacobson, ed.; Séguin.
25. De Armond.
26. Ramsay, *History of the American Revolution*, vol. 1, 30.

Cato's Letters began as an indictment and exposure of the supposed promoters of the South Sea Bubble, the great economic disaster of the eighteenth century. Much attention was paid to policy concerning trade and finance. The famous number 106, "Of Trade and Plantations," though not reprinted in *The Mercury* or *The New England Courant*, was inserted in the London Press in 1765 by the Whiggish Thomas Hollis, at the suggestions of American correspondents. This "Letter" described a model England might have done well to follow, and conveyed a message appropriate to the crisis. These essays and tracts by Trenchard and Gordon, widely read in England, had their greatest effect overseas.[27] To their criticisms of the Establishment were added those of Henry St. John, Viscount Bolingbroke, in *The Craftsman, Essay upon History*, and *A Dissertation upon Parties*, brilliantly censorious of the ministries of George II.

Bolingbroke, out of power since his flirtation with Jacobitism in 1715, was free to write his thoughts, though not to hold office. He was often more Whiggish than those orthodox and stalwart Whigs who held the reins of power from 1714 to 1761. He attacked Walpole's monetary policy, in defense of the old squirearchy, the independent country gentry. This image of a landed class presented to men like Jefferson an idealized and rapidly disappearing way of life in England, and, for that matter, in America. Avarice, the pursuit of wealth, and the power its corrupting use could bring were vividly portrayed. Bolingbroke was read and re-read five times by John Adams, though the sage of Braintree, while praising the inimitable and original style found more fiction than truth in much of what St. John wrote. The thirteenth letter in *A Dissertation upon Parties* was, Adams thought, a "jewel." Many of the ideas about the English constitution were correct; lamentation for the decline of "old English" liberty justified; attitude to party and corruption well documented. Adams found less to praise in *The Spirit of Patriotism*, another of Bolingbroke's political *jeu d'esprit*, and twice reprinted in America, one of these editions coming from Franklin's house in Philadelphia. Isáac Kramnick has plausibly suggested that, whatever reservations may be held about Bolingbroke's sincerity, there can be no doubt that he gave to opposition politics a role later developed by Edmund Burke. His style, skillful use of the older Whig interpretation of English liberties, and detection of the shortcomings of Walpole's administration, commended him to Adams, Jefferson and others of their countrymen.[28]

Perhaps the most gloomy criticism of England's situation came out on the eve of her greatest imperial triumph. John Brown, vicar of Newcastle-on-Tyne, commentator on the Earl of Shaftesbury's *Characteristics*, author of two

27. Hollis, Diary, 18 October 1765; 24 February 1769.
28. Kramnick, 56-83, 137-87, 156; Haraszti, 53.

plays already produced, brought out in 1757 *An Estimate of the Manners and Principles of the Times.* The two volumes went into many editions, the seventh at Boston in 1758. Brown found that, since the beginning of the Seven Years War (the French and Indian War), and the death in 1754 of Henry Pelham, who had served as Chancellor of the Exchequer and Prime Minister, both foreign and domestic affairs were confused. Luxury and effeminacy had replaced England's old martial vigor. Wealth had corrupted religion and banished frugality and diligence. Morality was poor. New leaders were necessary. There was need, he urged, for a spiritual regeneration. Americans reading his *Estimate*, the reflections of earlier polemicists, and of contemporary travelers prognosticating disaster if deterioration of English morals were not arrested, scarcely needed the experiences of the sixties to realize that the famed English liberties were declining, or had almost vanished from the mother country.[29]

In 1765 opponents of English policy found in their reading, traditions, folk-law, and in rather widely articulated views of the contemporary scene, all the support they required. John Adams maintained that it was at that time that the true revolution took place, rather than during the wars.[30] In the sense that Americans then suffered a more violent disillusionment about their relationship with England he was right. They suffered real hardships, even if they sometimes exaggerated them, and expressed themselves with immoderate demonstrations. By the time Thomas Paine published *Common Sense*, early in 1776, its teaching found a ready echo in sentiment prepared by the events of a decade. Independence was well on the way. Yet Adams perhaps overstressed the significance of those fateful years, and the changes they wrought.

It would, I think, be possible to trace antagonism between colonists and English administrations all the way back to the beginning of settlement. Colonists might refer to England as "home," but a sea-change rapidly developed. Whenever a question of definition came up, a difference in attitude was to be found in policies suggested in London, and in measures sought by colonists. Even at the time of the Glorious Revolution of 1688, though some relief from the authoritarianism of the later Stuarts was achieved, not much, for example, of what Increase Mather wished to obtain was conceded. Later disagreements over the Molasses Act of 1733, or over the concession made at the peace of 1748, did not produce exceptions comparable to 1765, nor was ministerial policy as firmly pursued. What was lacking in the early years of American history was the occasion for separation; I suspect the potential was always there.

29. Robbins, 308-10, *passim.*
30. Adams, *Adams-Jefferson Letters*, II, 455.

Thomas Jefferson writing about 1821 declared "Before the Revolution we were all good English Whigs, cordial to their free principles, and in their jealousies of their executive magistrates."[31] Note the adjectives "good" and "free." Those Whigs protested prerogative, and justified, under certain circumstances, revolution. Adams writing to Jefferson modified the statement cited earlier. "In my opinion" he declared, "the Revolution began as early as the first plantation of the country." Independence of church and parliament was as fixed a principle "of our Predecessors in 1620" (Adams was hopelessly New England in approach) as it was of Sam Adams and Christopher Gadsen in 1776.[32] In other words, Whig influence, that is the influence of lawyers, historians and of the Commonwealthmen, was all pervasive in the free frontier, and in the traditions of the early settlers. Over the years the ruling Whigs of England tended to forget anything revolutionary in their background, though reminded of it occasionally by oppositionist writers, or by the needs of political oratory against a Tory opponent. The gulf between these Whigs and the Americans widened. When circumstance and occasion made the difference apparent, Americans found, ironically enough, support in older English tradition, as well as in their colonial experience, for achieving the freedom of the New World.

31. Jefferson, *Life and Writings*, 83.
32. Adams, *Adams-Jefferson Letters*, II, 525.

The Growth of Political Stability: An Interpretation of Political Development in the Anglo-American Colonies, 1660–1760

JACK P. GREENE

No aspect of Anglo-American colonial life has been any more thoroughly studied than the political. In contrast to the situation in France,[1] history in both Great Britain and the United States has been—and continues to be—pre-eminently the history of politics and public life. Equipped with an increasingly sophisticated conception of political history as not only the narrative of public events and institutional development but also the study of social context, structure, culture, process, and function, scholars of early America have produced, especially over the past twenty years, an impressive collection of monographs and specialized works on the several political systems of the colonies.[2] The vast majority of these studies have, however, been local and segmental in nature, and there have been relatively few attempts to bring their conclusions together in an effort to discern general patterns in the direction and character of change over time. The best general analysis presently available[3] provides us with a *static* model of the colonial political process. What is required is a *developmental* model capable of calling attention to and revealing the interaction among the entire range of political activities within and among the several colonial societies. Such a model also will need to take into account the relationship between the social and the political system, process as well as structure and content, and spatial and temporal variations throughout colonial political life. This short paper is obviously not the place to undertake an assignment of such magnitude. But it does provide a vehicle for exploring some tentative hypotheses about the nature of political develop-

1. Le Goff, 1-4.
2. J. Greene, "Changing Interpretations...," 151-184.
3. Bailyn, *Origins of American Politics.*

ment in colonial America with particular reference to the growth of colonial political resources and changing patterns in the structure, semiology, and character of politics during the period 1660 to 1760. Although illustrations will be drawn from many of the colonies, the hypotheses will be based largely upon the experiences of five of the largest and/or economically most important colonies: Virginia, Massachusetts, Pennsylvania, South Carolina, and New York.

Such an exploration should begin with a clear recognition of the importance of those basic properties or features of the political systems of the colonies that underlay and characterized political activity throughout the colonial period. Certainly among the most significant was the *colonial* status of the colonies. The fact that they were colonial rather than *independent* meant that they were socially and economically truncated, that the highest echelons of the economic and social systems to which they were tied lay in the parent state.[4] It also meant that the apex of authority—political, legal, moral, and cultural—rested there as well. The relationship between colonies and metropolis was thus of crucial significance. It bound the colonies within a system in which the ultimate determination of policy lay largely beyond their control. But it also gave them access to resources—to markets, credit, manufactures, staples, shipping, technical skills, military and naval protection, political rewards and preferment, status, and, perhaps most important of all, normative standards and models of behavior and an intimate connection with a "great" metropolitan tradition—which none of them could have commanded on their own.[5] Finally, the relationship also guaranteed, as J. G. A. Pocock has recently emphasized, that the colonies would be "subcultures within a single Anglophone world."[6] For colonial political life, this meant that institutions of government, systems of law and justice, and patterns of behavior and perception would be, to one degree or another, clearly derivative from those of the mother country.

A second, and equally important feature of colonial political life was that each colony constituted an almost wholly separate political environment. Many colonies were to some extent offshoots of older colonies: Maryland and North Carolina of Virginia; Rhode Island, Connecticut, New Hampshire, and Nova Scotia of Massachusetts Bay; the Leeward Islands, Jamaica, and South Carolina of Barbados; and Georgia of South Carolina. As such, they exhibited important similarities in political structure and culture to the colonies that had spawned them. Yet, because each colony had its own distinctive patterns of economic activity, social and ethnic composition,

---

4. Hobsbaum, 40-41.
5. J. Greene, "Uneasy Connection," 45-56.
6. Pocock, "Virtue and Commerce," 122.

religious organization, and urban development as well as its own peculiar body of traditions, custom, and experience, it manifested its own characteristic configurations of political activity. This individuality was reinforced by the fact that at least until the Seven Years' War and really until the pre-revolutionary crises there was virtually no common political life among the colonies. Political contact among colonies was largely transitory and tangential to the central concerns of politics, and the political involvement of each colony with the metropolis was considerably greater than that with its neighboring colonies. Not even the metropolis had sufficient power to erode the peculiarities of the political systems of individual colonies, however, as metropolitan influences were received, modified, ignored, or discarded according to their relevance to local circumstances and their correspondence with local traditions.

A third characteristic of basic significance was that the political system itself was almost everywhere highly circumscribed in its operation. Because of the exigencies common to such new communities, provincial governments, as Bernard Bailyn has pointed out, engaged in a much wider range of activities than did the central government in Britain. They performed all of the normal functions of government: the *symbolic* function of affirming—and embodying—through actions and laws the values of society; *regulative* functions such as establishing the ground rules directing the allocation of land and the process of settlement, setting forth prescriptions governing individual conduct, and enforcing the law; and the *protective* functions of guaranteeing security of liberty and property and contributing to defense against alien attacks. But they also assumed responsibility, first, for the initiation of a wide range of social services and for conferring a variety of privileges, benefits, and exemptions upon groups or individuals charged with the provision of those services, and, second, fostering the economic well-being of the citizenry through regulations for improving the production of old staples or for establishing incentives to encourage the development of new ones.[7]

However wide the range of government activity in the colonies in comparison with that in Britain, by any modern standards, as Robert Zemsky has recently underlined in regard to early eighteenth-century Massachusetts, the colonists expected remarkably little from government, which was a minuscule, almost a shoestring, operation. Budgets—and taxes—were low; paid full-time public officials few (Massachusetts had six); civil, judicial, and police establishments small, part-time, and unprofessional; and, prior to the Seven Years' War, military establishments never large and usually temporary. Because most of the responsibility for maintaining order, enforcing laws, mediating conflicts, handling routine litigation, and performing public ser-

7. Bailyn, *Origins of American Politics*, 101-104.

vices devolved upon agencies of local government in counties, towns, and parishes, colonists had considerably more contact with formal components of the political system at the local level than with the small establishments at the provincial. But at most times and places government weighed lightly upon the vast majority of colonists, whose usual involvement with the political system was limited largely to the payment of normally light taxes, the occasional performance of public service obligations such as road maintenance or militia musters, and no more than annual participation in elections, and, in New England, town meetings. The results were that the political systems of the colonies both provided a rather small scope for the active involvement of citizens in the formal agencies of government and, as Zemsky has argued, "had in many respects become an archetype of the classical economic state." They placed a few constraints on individual behavior, the public sphere was relatively small, and the private sphere was exceptionally large.[8]

A fourth important feature of the political systems of the colonies was that they were all basically exclusivist in their assumptions and operation. That is, full rights of participation in political society were denied most of the inhabitants, including women, children, servants, slaves, Catholics, Jews, non-naturalized aliens, non-property holders, and, in many cases, even long-term tenants and older sons still living with their parents. Partly this wide exclusion derived from the traditional conception that, just as membership in a corporation should be restricted to those with a full legal share, so citizenship in a polity should be limited to those with a permanent attachment in the form of property.[9] More fundamental, however, and as yet insufficiently appreciated, was the assumption that full participation should be restricted, in the words of John Locke, to those people not "depending upon the wills of any other man" in ordering "their actions" and disposing "of their possessions, and persons as they think fit, within the bounds of the law of nature."[10] Those without property—which was equated with and thought to be requisite for independence—and those who because of religious, legal, or familial obligations were subject to the wills of others simply did not have the degree of autonomy necessary for full rights of participation. A corollary of this assumption, one that required the exclusion of women, minors, and slaves, was that groups with presumed emotional, physical, or "natural" disabilities were incapable of controlling themselves and, for that reason, also lacked the competence to be accorded full civil status in society.[11]

None of these basic properties of the colonial political systems—not their colonial status, their separation into largely discrete political environments,

8. Zemsky, 1-9.
9. Pole, 25-26, 31, 36-37, 47-49, 53-56, 84, 88, 136-138, 143-147.
10. Laslett, *The World We Have Lost*, 190.
11. Zuckerman, *Peaceable Kingdoms*, 195-196.

the circumscribed nature of their operations, nor their exclusivist character—remained wholly constant over time. Of the four, however, only the first varied in sufficiently important ways to produce major repercussions in colonial political life prior to the 1760s. Indeed, the changing intensity in the degree of colonial involvement with the parent society was one of three crucial variables affecting the character of colonial political development. In two sectors—the economic and the cultural—the direction of change in imperial-colonial relations was virtually linear. Although the rate of change was obviously not constant over time and the extent of change was not uniform throughout the colonies, between the middle of the seventeenth century and the middle of the eighteenth there was a powerful movement in both the economic and cultural realms toward an ever more intense involvement. From the initial implementation of the navigation system in the 1650s and the 1660s, the tendency everywhere—among the mainland colonies and in the Caribbean—was toward a closer involvement with the economy of the home islands until by the middle of the eighteenth century the economies even of the non staple producing New England colonies had become closely integrated with that of the metropolis.[12] This growing involvement, together with an increasing volume of contacts among individuals and the improved communications that accompanied it, drew the colonists ever closer into the ambit of British life during the eighteenth century, provided them with easier and more direct access to English, Irish, and, increasingly, Scottish ideas and models of behavior, and tied them ever more closely to metropolitan culture.[13]

By contrast, in the political and military sectors, there was no linear movement from lesser to greater involvement between colonies and metropolis. The degree to which the latter imposed upon the former ebbed and flowed over time according to the amount of imperial energy and attention applied to colonial supervision, and that depended upon a wide assortment of international and domestic, as well as colonial, considerations. After the Restoration, of course, levels of political involvement never sank below those of the first years of colonization. But two long periods of more or less intensive and systematic efforts by the imperial government to impose stricter controls on the political systems of the colonies—one lasting from mid-seventeenth century to about 1710 and the other from 1748 to 1783—were separated by a period characterized by a much more casual posture toward the colonies.[14] Militarily, the mainland colonies were involved with

12. Bruchey, 16-73; Zemsky, 66-67; Daniell, 3-33.
13. Clive and Bailyn, 200-213; J. Greene, "Search for Identity...," 189-220.
14. J. Greene, *Great Britain and the American Colonies*, introduction; Steele; Henretta, *"Salutary Neglect."*

the metropolis to a substantial degree only during the Seven Years' War between 1754 and 1763 and to a considerably smaller extent during the earlier intercolonial wars between 1689 and 1713 and 1739 and 1748. Even during periods of most intense imperial political activity, however, the extent to which the imperial political system imposed upon those of the colonies varied enormously from place to place according to the political vulnerability of each colony. The degree of a colony's vulnerability was in turn a function of several different local factors, including how dependent it was upon the mother country for external and internal defense; the longevity, strength, and character of local charters, traditions, customs, and institutions; the autonomy and self-consciousness of local leaders; the integration of the social with the political system; and the degree to which it was incorporated into the imperial patronage system. Together, these many local considerations, as they changed over time, were thus themselves a second crucial variable in determining the character of political development and patterns of political activity in individual colonies.

The third, and in many respects, the most important of these crucial variables was the changing social and economic circumstances of each colony. With the colonies, as with all societies, the ethnic, cultural, and religious composition of the population, the demographic and social structure, the organization of the system of production, the strength of community attachment, and the degree of social integration as they changed over time inevitably affected in profound ways the nature and direction of political development. And changes in many of these areas in most colonies came particularly rapidly as the colonists had to adapt themselves and their societies, first, to the conditions of the New World and, then, especially after about 1710, to the new problems and opportunities created by the extraordinary and sustained growth in population, agricultural production, overseas exports, buying power, and extent of settled territory. This tremendous expansion obviously was not uniform over the whole of the colonies. It proceeded at differential rates and produced varying effects. But it was everywhere one of the most salient features of colonial life between 1710 and 1760 and brought rapid and extensive changes in its wake. By enlarging the size of the polity and the pool of potential leaders and politically relevant members of the population; by stretching institutional structures; by increasing social stratification and occupational differentiation and thereby either undermining or reinforcing the degree of social integration or strength of community; and by significantly enlarging the range and level of colonial aspirations, the remarkable expansion of the colonies affected both the character of the political systems of the colonies and the rate and thrust of their political development. As I shall argue at greater length later, these changes were by no means always—or perhaps even usually—disruptive or destabilizing. Perhaps because this process of growth seems, at least through its early and middle stages, to have been characterized by a major expansion in mobility opportunities, the increase in social aspirations that accompanied it did not lead to deep or widespread social frustration and political and social mobilization,[15] though in a few cases, as will be indicated later, it did create either social contenders for power who resorted to open political conflict to achieve their ambitions and/or an acute sense of political deprivation and discrimination among some aspiring segments of the population.

Within the context established by the basic properties discussed above, these three crucial variables—the degree of colonial involvement with the parent society, the specifically local circumstances of politics, and the changing conditions of social and economic life—interacted to shape colonial political development. Because there were considerable differences in the nature and operation of these variables from one political environment to another, there were significant variations in the form and character of that development among the several colonies. Despite these many important variations, it is the contention of this essay that the political development of each of the major colonies followed a generally similar pattern with a relatively long period of drastic, almost chronic, political disorder and flux, which, in most cases, began early in the period of settlement[16] and lasted through the first decades of the eighteenth century, being followed, beginning in the 1720s and 1730s, by an era of extraordinary political stability and in some places even relative public tranquility that continued at least into the 1750s and 1760s in most colonies.[17]

15. Huntington, 53-55; Laslett, *The World We Have Lost*, 166-177; Tully, chapters 1 and 2.

16. Massachusetts is, of course, the only exception among the major colonies. There, a long period of stability preceded a relatively short period of flux beginning in the 1680s and lasting until the 1720s.

17. The widespread and largely uncritical use of the concepts *political instability* and *political stability* in recent literature on early American politics (e.g. Bailyn, *Origins of American Politics*, 59-105; Michael Kammen, *People of Paradox: An Inquiry Concerning the Origins of American Civilization* [New York, Knopf, 1972], 57-78; and Patricia U. Bonomi, *A Factious People: Politics and Society in Colonial New York* [New York, Columbia University Press, 1971]) strongly underlines the need for some attempt at definition. J. H. Plumb has developed an apparently satisfactory definition for England in *The Origins of Political Stability, England 1675-1725* (Boston, Houghton Mifflin, 1967), xvi-xviii. But it is clearly not sufficient simply to adapt a series of specifications derived from the experience of an older, far more complex and structurally differentiated political society. Social and political conditions in the colonies differed radically from those in England, and the character and conditions of political stability differed accordingly. My contention, which will hopefully be refined by future discussion and consideration, is that for colonial America the concept of political stability may be used to characterize any situation in which the following seven conditions obtained: (1) ordinarily low levels of collective violence and civil disorder; (2)

The history of Virginia, Britain's oldest, largest (in terms of both territory and people), and, on the mainland, economically most important colony in America, is the most graphic example of this general pattern of development. Throughout the seventeenth century, the public affairs of that colony had been riven with strife and discord, the stable situation that obtained under Governor Sir William Berkeley between the Restoration in 1660 and Bacon's Rebellion in 1676 being only the exception which proved the rule. The endless struggles for ascendancy in an extremely fluid social and economic environment that had characterized political life prior to the Restoration was supplanted, following Bacon's Rebellion, by a series of recurrent conflicts arising out of the Crown's efforts to assert tighter controls over the economic and political life of the colony. These conflicts both split the gentry—the leading tobacco magnates and the colony's political elite—into warring factions and led to the expulsion or removal of one governor after another for the next fifty years. Only at the end of the second decade of the eighteenth century when Lieutenant Governor Alexander Spotswood reached an accommodation with local leaders was this pattern finally broken. By carefully cultivating local leaders as well as the new Walpolean emphasis upon harmony and cooperation among all branches of government, Spotswood's successors, Hugh Drysdale and, particularly, Sir William Gooch, who administered the colony from 1727 to 1749, managed both to extirpate "all Factions" and to achieve a new political stability that lasted for the remainder of the colonial period. Pragmatic politicians both, Drysdale and Gooch carefully avoided transgressing local interests and cherished customs and traditions. In the process, they managed largely through the force of their own moral and political leadership and with almost no utilitarian resources at their disposal to achieve a situation in which the vast majority of legislators routinely supported the administration and thereby, in one of the very few instances in the whole of the colonial experience, actually exhibited habits of obedience to the Crown similar to those displayed by the "average, uncorrupted or little corrupted M.P." in Britain, whose normal posture was one of support for the administration. With the exception of Robert Dinwiddie

the absence or muting of longstanding issues that polarize or deeply divide the nation; (3) the routine acceptance by political society of existing institutional and leadership structures; (4) the regularization of relations among the several branches and levels of government; (5) low rates of turnover among leaders; (6) the orderly transfer of authority or leadership through constitutional challenges without serious disruption of the polity; and (7) the reduction of factional or party strife to levels at which it becomes either unimportant and no longer dysfunctional or routinized and functional. Political stability does not require: (1) social and/or political inertia; (2) complete public tranquility or the absence of rivalry and contention within the political system; (3) permanency of membership in political factions or party groupings, a high degree of cohesiveness of solidarity among the political elite, or a monopoly of power by a single group within the elite.

during the first years of his tenure in the early 1750s, subsequent governors, including Francis Fauquier and Norborne Berkeley, Baron de Botetourt, obtained similar results by following the successful examples of Drysdale and Gooch.[18]

In forging this new stability, Drysdale and Gooch were, of course, aided by the new concern of imperial authorities after 1720 to achieve peace and order in the colonies, no matter what the cost, and by the fact that, in contrast to the situation in earlier years, Virginia was no longer tied so closely into the British patronage system. They were helped as well by a fortunate set of circumstances within Virginia, where a generally favorable economic situation, a homogeniety of economic and social interests among all regions and all social categories among the free population, a high degree of social and religious integration, and a community of political leaders so large as to make it impossible for a single group to monopolize political power discouraged sharp political divisions. Virginia politics during these years provides a classic example of what Samuel P. Huntington has described as a situation of "traditional stability" in which, in the absence of large or important urban centers, the countryside was dominant and the rural elite governed unchallenged by endogenous groups with the tenantry and yeomanry assuming a passive or only marginally active political role and the weak intermediate class tending to ally itself with the dominant elite.[19]

A slightly different configuration of forces produced a very similar pattern of development in South Carolina, with the exception of Maryland the colony on the continent whose socio-economic life was most like that of Virginia and, after 1746, probably the Crown's wealthiest and most thriving (in terms of the per capita wealth of free citizens) possession on the continent. Settled over six decades after Virginia, South Carolina was the scene of violent political strife for much of its first fifty years during which merchants were arrayed against planters, immigrants from the West Indies against those who came directly from England, Britons against French

18. See Bernard Bailyn, "Politics and Social Structure in Virginia," *Seventeenth-Century America: Essays in Colonial History* (ed. James Morton Smith, Chapel Hill, University of North Carolina Press, 1959), 90-115; John C. Rainbolt, "The Alteration in the Relationship between Leadership and Constituents in Virginia, 1620-1720," *William and Mary Quarterly*, 3d ser. 27 (1970): 411-434. The generalizations about developments under Drysdale and Gooch are taken from the early chapters of an unpublished and partially written volume Keith B. Berwick and I have been preparing on Virginia political culture during the eighteenth century. The quotations are from a speech of Sir John Randolph, speaker of the House of Burgesses, August 6, 1736, in Greene, ed., *Great Britain and the American Colonies*, 247, and Paul Lucas, "A Note on the Comparative Study of the Structure of Politics in Mid-Eighteenth-Century Britain and Its American Colonies," *William and Mary Quarterly*, 3d ser., 28 (1971): 301-309.

19. Huntington, 76.

Huguenots, Churchmen against Dissenters, town against countryside, and local political leaders against the proprietors. This discordance culminated in the overthrow of the proprietors in 1719, but royal government did not immediately put an end to the political turmoil. A demand for an increase in paper money, stimulated by a severe depression during the late 1720s, brought renewed chaos, the provincial government broke down completely, and the colony came dangerously close to civil war. Only after the permanent implementation of royal government in 1730 was this tumultuous pattern of politics broken.[20]

In contrast to the situation in Virginia, however, the moral leadership of the royal governors was not an important ingredient in the new era of public stability that began to take shape during the 1730s and continued to characterize the political life of the colony until the regulator troubles of the late 1760s. Although the prospects for this new stability were enhanced by the lack of pressure emanating from the imperial government during the 1730s and 1740s, it was built primarily upon the gradual integration of hitherto competing and disparate interests and groups during the "ever-increasing prosperity" enjoyed by the colony through the middle decades of the eighteenth century. With prosperity came not only the muting of earlier religious and ethnic differences but also what Robert M. Weir has referred to as an homogenization of economic interests. The common pursuit of profit in this bustling staple economy drew merchants and planters, town and country, into a symbiotic relationship and led to the development of close ties of consanguinity, a "consciousness of shared economic interests," and a consensus about values and social and political priorities among the colony's emergent elite, which included a rising professional class of lawyers as well as merchants and planters. Reinforced by a growing sense of the need for the colony's small white free population, which was composed of a relatively large elite and a comparatively small yeoman and artisanal class, to present a solid front against a burgeoning African slave majority and by a series of minor crises during the late 1730s and early 1740s that underlined the necessity for internal political unity, this new unanimity "suffocated factionalism." After 1750, the multiplication of the number of English placemen in executive offices and on the royal council and the renewal of pressure from the imperial government created tensions between the local elite and imperial representatives in the administration. But these tensions, and the few open conflicts they generated, took on the character of "a contest between the united representatives of one society and the representatives of an outside power" and did not again split the colony's leaders into factions. What South Carolina politics represented after 1730 was thus a stable town-

20. Sirmans; Waterhouse.

country alliance in which a tightly interlocked urban-rural elite with a common vision of socio-economic and political goals governed without challenge
from inside the society and with remarkable social and political harmony.[21]

A variation of the South Carolina pattern can be found in the experience
of Pennsylvania, the newest of the five major continental colonies and, by
the 1720s, already one of the most dynamic centers of demographic and
economic growth in the whole of the Americas. Like South Carolina, Pennsylvania was fraught with social and political turmoil for most of its early
history. Disagreements between Proprietor Thomas Penn and Quaker leaders
in the colony over a variety of issues, the vigorous antiauthoritarianism of
the predominant Quaker majority, and "the erosion of a sense of community among the Quakers" early split the colony's inhabitants into warring
factions and established a pattern of political instability that persisted for
almost a half century. No sooner did an antiproprietary clique composed
largely of leading "Philadelphia Quaker merchants and their country allies"
wrest power from Penn's supporters than they found "themselves challenged
from below" by a coalition of lesser men organized into a loose "country
party" under the leadership of David Lloyd. Although the first decade of
the eighteenth century found Lloyd and his group in the ascendancy, "a new
determination on the part of the leading merchants and land owners to put
an end" to the disruptive activities of Lloyd along with improving economic
conditions and the gradual development of a sturdier set of governing institutions opened up the prospect for the establishment of political peace after
1710. But two unfortunate choices as governor—Charles Gookin and Sir
William Keith—and bitter disagreements over proprietary power, conditions
of land tenure, and paper currency kept the fires of faction alive for another
fifteen years.[22]

Only after 1725 did this pattern finally begin to disappear. The tactful administration of Patrick Gordon for a decade after 1726, the disappearance of
the old political issues, the death of Lloyd, and the emergence of Andrew
Hamilton, a proponent of cooperation with the proprietor, as the colony's
leading political leader, all worked to set the stage for a new era of stability in
public life and the virtual extinction of factional politics. During the 1730s
the failure of the proprietor to exploit favorable conditions for the development of a strong proprietary political interest left the "Quaker party," a
tight coalition of city and country leaders which controlled the powerful
Assembly, in a dominate position in Pennsylvania politics. This position
was strengthened by the failure in 1740-1742 of a strong proprietary challenge led by Governor George Thomas over the issue of the Quakers' re-

21. Weir, "The Harmony We Were Famous For," 473-501.
22. Nash, 110-111, 168-169, 179-180, 274-276, 305-308.

fusal to support the war effort against Spain, and for the next twelve years "conditions of peace and stability" prevailed as Quaker control of the Assembly went unchallenged. After 1750, the growth of a powerful proprietary interest—composed mainly of a growing body of wealthy Anglican merchants and proprietary officeholders in the city and some of the leaders of the Presbyterian and German settlers in the backcountry—along with the proprietor's attempt to shore up executive authority, secure exemption from taxation of proprietary lands, and gain financial support for the British war effort against the French again brought factional politics to Pennsylvania in the mid-1750s, and the contention lasted for a decade. Significantly, however, the new factional competition did not produce the same sort of bitter and endemic conflict, civil disorder, and political breakdown that had marked the early years of Pennsylvania politics.

As in the case of South Carolina, the new stability in Pennsylvania depended quite as much upon socio-economic as upon political developments. Unparalleled commercial and agricultural prosperity both turned the attention of the middle and lower strata away from the political to the economic realm and helped the nascent elite of merchants and landholders to consolidate its position in Pennsylvania society. The result, as Gary B. Nash and Alan Tully have argued, was that after 1725 "control of the political process slowly" passed to a tightly integrated group of wealthy Philadelphia merchants and country landholders. Unchallenged by a weak proprietary interest, this stable town-country alliance, sharing a remarkable consensus about political goals and socio-economic priorities, monopolized political power and created a stable political environment, characterized by "a little contention and much good harmony."[23]

In Massachusetts, the oldest and largest of the New England colonies, a similar pattern of development is observable. The relatively unified dominance of the old Puritan leadership and the stable political world it provided were seriously undermined after 1670 by the combined efforts of imperial authorities, who hoped to expand English authority in New England, and a rising group of merchants in the coastal towns, who were unhappy with restraints imposed by the traditional Puritan leadership and wanted closer political ties to cement the economic alliances they were forming in the English mercantile world. For fifty years after 1680, conflict, intense and deeply divisive, was endemic to Massachusetts politics, conflict over the repeated attempts by royal governors Sir Edmund Andros, Joseph Dudley, Samuel Shute, and William Burnett, usually with the support of the Boston mercantile community if often only with token backing from the Crown, to extend their prerogative powers against the determined opposition of the

23. Tully, *passim*; Nash, 335; J. Greene, "Changing Interpretations...," 168-169.

country party in the House of Representatives. And there was conflict as well over the governors' insistence upon preserving the Crown's monopoly of mast trees in the New England woods (to the direct economic disadvantage of the two Elisha Cookes, who headed the country party), the desirability of a land bank and an inflationary monetary policy, and a plethora of other issues.[24]

As Robert Zemsky has recently shown, however, the quarter century beginning in 1730 "was one of basic political stability" in Massachusetts. The contest "over the royal prerogative quickly abated" following a de facto constitutional compromise during the late 1720s which "granted a measure of independence" to both the governor and the Assembly. In addition, the old rural-urban antagonism that had underlain much of the earlier factional strife became much less pronounced as representatives from the rural towns increasingly acquiesced under the leadership of a small, socially prominent elite from the maritime east—as long as it served the interests of the rural, agricultural majority. By working within and respecting this delicate balance of political forces, a governor could count on cooperation from the legislature and, from the point of view of local leaders, a successful administration. That he did not proved the eventual undoing of Jonathan Belcher. Despite a taste for compromise, he was unable during the land bank controversy in 1740-41 to walk the narrow line between the inflationary forces in the colony and their opponents in Massachusetts and London. His successor, William Shirley, who governed the colony from 1741-1757, operated in this new political milieu far more successfully. With strong connections in Britain and a talent for conciliation, he made skillful use of the limited local patronage at his command as well as the many contracts and offices at his disposal as a result of the military operations in the northern colonies during King George's War to attach many of the colony's leading men to the administration and to gain their support for his legislative programs. This administrative machine evoked fears of a "Robinarchical" corruption among his opponents and, by the 1760s, after Shirley's departure, had become sufficiently narrow and restrictive as to call forth widespread charges of "oligarchy" from those who were not a part of it, charges that took on additional resonance from the perspective of the Revolutionary controversy. But it was never so strong as to be able to ignore the wishes of the rural majority. The urban-rural alliance in Massachusetts, which, like those in South Carolina and Pennsylvania, was crucial to the achievement of stability during the years from 1730 to 1760, was thus based less upon a homogenization of interests, as in South Carolina, or the workings of an interlocking elite which brought town and country together in pursuit of shared economic, political, and religious goals,

24. Breen, 87-269; J. Greene, "Changing Interpretations...," 165-167.

as in Pennsylvania. Rather, it was an alliance born out of the necessity for compromise, in which, despite an occasional lack of congruence of interests or social goals, rural votes joined with eastern expertise to fashion a stable political environment.[25]

Of the five major continental colonies, New York deviates most sharply from the pattern exhibited by the four colonies discussed above. From its very beginning, Patricia U. Bonomi has written, echoing a general consensus, New York politics was "peculiarly unstable and factious," and the tumultuous politics of the early years seem never to have given way to a period of stability. The "Leislerian conflict and its twenty-year aftermath, the commercial-landed rivalry of the 1720s, the Morris-Cosby dispute, the court-Assembly struggle of the mid-century years, and the rancorous campaigns of the 1760s"—all exhibited "a steadily rising intensity of competition among concerted factions for a share of public authority." Marked by ethnic, religious, economic, and sectional diversity, New York society was never able to achieve the same levels of socio-economic and cultural integration that characterized Virginia and South Carolina. Despite ties of consanguinity, the split between the mercantile elite in the towns and the Hudson River landlords—between the commercial and the landed interest—was too deep to permit the development of the kind of close-knit elite that bound town and country so tightly together in Pennsylvania. Never a large colony, New York, unlike Massachusetts, was not forced by the sheer complexity of social and economic circumstances to develop a differentiated political system that by consent of all parties placed power in the hands of an identifiable and responsive elite in the capital. More closely tied into the British patronage system than any of the other four colonies, including even Massachusetts, the political life of New York was always less self-contained and always more subject to the vagaries of British politics than those of the other colonies. In New York, moreover, politics seems to have continued to be looked upon as a source of economic gain for a much wider segment of the political leadership and for a much longer time than was the case in the other four colonies. Clearly, New York seems to have been an exception to the general pattern represented by the other important mainland colonies.

The question is what kind of exception. To be sure, New York never achieved, except perhaps for a brief period in the early 1740s, the diminution of factional strife that characterized the experiences of the other four colonies for much of the period between 1730 and 1760. But the political historian's understandable and traditional emphasis upon conflict and change, an emphasis that is especially apparent in the historiography of

25. J. Greene, "Changing Interpretations...," 166-167; Bailyn, *Origins of American Politics*, 114-117; Zemsky, xii and *passim*; Murrin, "From Corporate Empire to Revolutionary Republic..."

colonial New York politics, tends to obscure basic regularities and continuities in the political process, and the blatant factionalism of New York politics may have been less destabilizing than has been conventionally supposed. Indeed, Bonomi's work suggests that following the settlement of the Morris-Cosby dispute in the mid-1730s, New York politics may have moved slowly toward a less brittle state: the multiplicity of "interests" in the colony had become too great and too many interests had become too powerful and too assertive ever again to permit a governor to purchase political calm by systematically. cultivating one interest at the expense of all others, as Governors Robert Hunter and William Burnett had done between 1715 and 1730. What seems to have developed beginning in the late 1730s was a new mode of politics that may perhaps best be described as a model of tension within a broad framework of consent. The central feature of this new mode was the vigorous—and functional—rivalry of this multiplicity of interests within clearly defined—and agreed upon—political boundaries, a rivalry that routinized and, through the eventual creation of loose parties, institutionalized competition at the same time it discouraged or diminished the possibilities for explosive open conflict, civil disorder, and political disruption. Moreover, this rivalry gave expression to occasional apologies for parties as legitimate agencies for the expression of interests in society, a development that is not found elsewhere for another half century. If these surmises turn out to be correct, then faction, in a complex political society such as that of New York, may thus have operated as a necessary precondition for stability and even New York may have fashioned out of its own exceptionally diverse cultural and economic materials a peculiar but appropriate form of political stability during the middle decades of the eighteenth century.[26]

The new stability that characterized the political life of Virginia, South Carolina, Pennsylvania, Massachusetts, and, perhaps in a somewhat different way, even New York after 1725 depended upon a number of interacting variables: the general relaxation of pressures from the imperial government, unparalleled prosperity for most sectors of the free populations of most colonies, and, to one degree or another, the functional integration of socioeconomic and political life within each of the colonies. But it was the result as well of a major development of political resources, a development that both defined or characterized the new political stability and, by stimulating changes in the structure and culture of politics, contributed to a significant increase in the capabilities of the colonial political systems. In the pages that follow, this process will be discussed as it was manifest in five principal areas: elite articulation, institutional development, configurations of political consciousness, patterns of relations between the elite and other politically relevant segments of society, and the expansion of the public realm.

26. Bonomi, 55, 59, 133-134, 143, 280-286, *passim*; Katz.

Stable, coherent, and acknowledged political and social elites were slow to emerge in the colonies. Of the five colonies under consideration, only Virginia and, to a much lesser extent, Massachusetts had what might with some semblance of credibility be described as reasonably thoroughly articulated elites by the beginning of the eighteenth century. Elsewhere, the elites were unstable and inchoate and contained, as James Logan wrote in 1713, few "men of Parts & Learning."[27] In this situation, political leadership fell to men who were at best only partially equipped for their tasks. Not that they were all so ill-suited as the boisterous and ignorant assemblymen parodied by Governor Robert Hunter in *Androboros* in 1714.[28] But, as the historian William Smith, Jr., later complained in commenting on the character of the members of the Assembly in the early days of New York, they were mainly "plain, illiterate, husbandmen whose views seldom extended farther than to the regulation of highways, the destruction of wolves, wildcats, and foxes, and the advancement of the other little interests of the particular counties, which they were chosen to represent."[29] And those few men of accomplishment who were available for public life had, as Logan remarked, to be "furnished with an Exteriour suited to take with the common humours of the Crowd."[30] Smith was correct to emphasize the parochial and basically utilitarian or bread-and-butter orientation of most politicians. From the beginning, colonial politics had been expressive of a fundamental preoccupation with the protection and facilitation of group and local interests and individual enterprise. The colonists, Gooch wrote, assumed they had "a Natural Liberty of pursuing what may promote their own benefit," and they expected political society to encourage—or at least not to inhibit—them in that pursuit. Men went into public life in large part because it provided them with direct economic and social benefits in the form of easier access to land, special business or professional advantages, lucrative public offices, or higher social status.[31]

But the character, quality, and orientation of political leadership changed markedly during the first half of the eighteenth century. By the 1730s and 1740s, the nascent elites had, in all of the important colonies, achieved considerable success in the "struggle...to establish" themselves "at the center of colonial life."[32] By European standards, they were, in many respects, peculiar elites. At their core was to be found, in every case, a group of first families or descendants of first families who, having successfully established themselves during the first or second generations after settlement, managed

27. Logan to Josiah Martin, 4 August 1713, quoted in Nash, 286.
28. Hunter.
29. Wm. Smith, Jr., I, 259.
30. Logan to Josiah Martin, 4 August 1713, quoted in Nash, 286; Rainbolt, 411-434.
31. Gooch, II, 230; J. Greene, "Uneasy Connection," 56-58.
32. Nash, viii.

to retain their wealth and social standing in the discordant years of the late seventeenth and early eighteenth century. But, especially in South Carolina, which experienced an extraordinary economic boom after 1740, and Pennsylvania and New York, where rapid commercial prosperity opened up widespread new opportunities in trade and the professions, the elites were, in some significant part, nouveau riche in composition; and even in older colonies like Virginia and Massachusetts there was always room for the talented newcomer or upstart who managed to pull himself up the economic ladder. Membership in the elite thus depended at least as much upon achievement and merit as upon traditional ascriptive criteria such as family or inherited status. As Bonomi has remarked in the case of New York, with such origins and with no "legally sanctioned sphere of influence," colonial elites, unlike their English model, never developed an exclusive function or that well-developed and secure sense of identity that derive from longevity and the illusion of permanence it creates.[33] To a large extent, the colonial elites remained loose categories and never developed into sharply defined corporate groups. But if the world lost by seventeenth-century Englishmen could not be recaptured in all its details in eighteenth-century America, these emergent elites did acquire a high degree of coherence and visibility in their respective societies. Through intermarriage and personal and social ties, they early developed those close family and personal relationships and "informal, inter-elite communications patterns" that characterize elites in every society and, like their great estates and closer connections to metropolitan culture, helped to set them apart from men in other social categories. Like those of the English gentry, the imposing (by American standards) houses they built in increasing numbers through the first half of the eighteenth century in the country and in the towns expressed "in monumental form" so all could see their accomplishments and standing.[34]

These cohering elites, spreading, as William Knox once remarked, in size and influence as the colonies became more wealthy,[35] provided a growing reservoir of political leaders. The progenitors of these elites—the men who between 1640 and 1720 had established and consolidated the positions of the elites in colonial life—had fulfilled themselves by acquiring estates, obtaining status in the community, and enhancing the family name. But their extraordinary success meant that their heirs who were just coming into manhood during the 1720s and 1730s—members of the second generation in South Carolina and Pennsylvania and of the third generation in Virginia, Massachusetts, and New York—had to look elsewhere to find a suitable outlet

33. Bonomi, 7-8; Zemsky, 76; Waterhouse, *passim*; J. Greene, "Foundations of Political Power...," 485-506; Rothermund, 140-141; Tully.

34. Laslett, *The World We Have Lost*, 179-181; Almond and Powell, 32-33.

35. Knox, 64-74.

for their energies and talents. For men whose wealth and security of position provided them with the necessary leisure to direct at least part of their attention into non-economic channels, politics, as Bonomi has suggested, provided "the most satisfying"—the most exciting, challenging, and (psychologically and publicly) rewarding—opportunities in the mid-eighteenth century colonies. Many men—for the most part first generation *arrivistes* like the Massachusetts merchant Thomas Hancock—still entered public life primarily "to advance their economic or material well-being, their income, their property, [or] their economic security." For a significant proportion of the established elite, however, and even many of the more thoroughly socialized among the new men, politics was becoming a primary activity, in many ways a profession. Within a decade on either side of 1730, the elite in each of the five colonies had, as Zemsky has shown in the case of Massachusetts, "transformed itself into a community of professional politicians," who, in contrast to men like Hancock, "enjoyed the power," "savored the responsibility," and "reveled in the opportunity" they found in the political arena. Twentieth-century Americans customarily think of professional politicians as devoted to the pursuit of "self-serving ends" which, in some measure, "deny the primacy of state and community." But in the eighteenth century colonies, the ethic—the self-image—as well as the public definition—of the professional politician was quite something else. The prevailing—almost universal—suspicion of men who hungered after power and office required that individual and particularistic goals be subordinated to, filtered through, and disguised by the predominant ideal of the public servant as the dedicated exponent of the common weal. Of course, the new professional elements in colonial politics pursued their own self-interest. Like most men, they can scarcely be supposed to have been exempt from the widespread tendency to interpret the common good in terms of individual ends. But the professional ethic, an ethic to which the professionals themselves were no less deeply committed than the members of the body politic at large and by which they interpreted their role and conduct for themselves quite as much as for their constituents, stressed the pursuit not of power or party goals or individual rewards but of the public welfare as it might best be discovered through accommodation, persuasion, debate, and manipulation amid the cross-pressures and inevitably uncertain world of day-to-day politics.[36]

The majority of men in government—at both the local and, except perhaps in the case of the comparatively small South Carolina, New York, and Pennsylvania assemblies, the provincial levels—continued to be "men of narrower experience and vision whose interests and influence had only a limited

36. Bonomi, 281; Zemsky, 39-98; Tully, *passim*; Waterhouse, *passim*. Quotations from Zemsky, 67, 209, 212. See also Kammen, "Intellectuals, Political Leadership, and Revolution."

sphere."[37] But the influence of the "professionals" was far out of proportion to their numbers. Everywhere, even when they were divided by personal or factional rivalry, as was especially true in New York, they belonged
to "a remarkably close-knit community, a specialized group of men with
remarkably similar social backgrounds and political interests." Exhibiting
attitudes and values that were "peculiarly a product of the [special inside]
roles they played within the political arena," they represented a world that
to the outsider "was indeed mysterious, employing as it did its own rules,
language, and measures of success." The source of their influence with back-
benchers in the legislatures and men of lesser rank and knowledge in the
localities was the expertise and connection that came from this tight little
world: they were able to convert that expertise into actual power because
they alone had the influence and ability to "give concrete form to ideas
favored by a rank and file majority."[38] Within the provincial governing
structure, the professionals provided a conduit of information between the
administration and the legislature, just as the legislators served as mediators
between the provincial government and the localities, where, at least in the
older settled counties and parishes in the colonies from New York to South
Carolina and in the more dynamic and larger towns in Massachusetts, the
elites helped to achieve political stability by providing the same sort of
responsible, informed, and energetic leadership they offered at the provincial
level. The emergence of the colonial elites with a solid nucleus of men with a
primary and professional commitment to politics thus led to a significant
differentiation and specialization of roles within the colonial political systems
and represented an important example of political development in the most
technical sense of that term.[39]

The appearance of these communities of professional politicians also produced important changes in the character of existing institutions. Although
the royal and proprietary councils and even the judiciary were in most places
through the first half of the eighteenth century local institutions in the sense
that a large number of their members were drawn out of the colonial elites,
the largest and most dynamic of the institutions at the provincial level were
the lower houses of assembly. By the 1730s some of these bodies were a
century old. The early colonists, as Michael Kammen has pointed out, had
"acquired the *legal* right to representative forms of government from the
Crown; but in actual practice they had discovered those forms anew for
themselves." Absolute government, Herman Merivale declared in commenting
on this development in the early nineteenth century, was "a thing quite

37. Bonomi, 9, 37-38; Zemsky, 10-38; Tully, *passim*; Waterhouse, *passim*; J. Greene,
"Foundations of Political Power...," 485-486; Cook, 586-608.
38. Zemsky, 43-44, 60, 63-64, 169-170.
39. Almond and Powell, 22.

contrary to the genius of our old colonial system, as well as to the spirit of British institutions." From the beginning, the assemblies were aggressive and simple institutions. Most of them displayed a marked tendency "to imitate the House of Commons in London and insist upon every jot and title of parliamentary privilege" during the closing decades of the seventeenth century, and their role in the colonial political systems was augmented by the demands of the first two intercolonial wars between 1689 and 1713. But some of them still lacked the independence, guarantees of regular meetings and frequent elections, and the intense self-consciousness that characterized the British House of Commons after, if not in large part also before, the Glorious Revolution.[40] Under the guidance of the new political professionals through the early and middle decades of the eighteenth century, the lower houses consolidated their position in the colonial governments and acquired greater autonomy as the growing complexities of the political process made them indispensable to the functioning of the colonial political systems. In their eagerness to cultivate metropolitan social models, the professionals in each colony sought to turn their lower house into an "epitome of the house of Commons." In the process the lower houses developed a much more articulate sense of their corporate rights, defined their procedures more clearly, and otherwise sought to give substance to the ideal that the lower houses, as the sole givers of internal public law and as the presumed equivalents of the British House of Commons, were endowed with charismatic authority and held in trusteeship all of the sacred rights and privileges of the public.[41]

Other political institutions at both the provincial and local levels presumably underwent a similar process of corporate definition and consolidation of authority, especially in the localities, which with the rapid growth of the colonies during the eighteenth century seem to have assumed an ever higher burden of responsibility for maintaining social order.[42] In few colonies, however, does the accompanying process of rationalization or secularization seem to have been so extensive as it was in Rhode Island.[43] In the area of specialized political infrastructure, the colonial political systems were relatively undeveloped. There were embryonic parties in New York and Pennsylvania, but they had no systematically cultivated base of popular support and only rudimentary organizations. Elsewhere, political groups, as in the case of Massachusetts, were "invariably small, close-knit

40. Kammen, *Deputyes and Libertyes*, 10, 57, 62-65; Merivale, 74, 96.
41. J. Greene, *Quest for Power*; J. Greene, "Political Mimesis...," 337-360; J. Greene, "Uneasy Connection...," 36-37; Murrin, "Myths of Colonial Democracy...," 65-66. Quotation from *The Privileges of the Island of Jamaica Vindicated...* (London, 1766), 33-34.
42. Tully; Waterhouse; Zuckerman, *Peaceable Kingdoms*; Zemsky, 332.
43. James, "Colonial Rhode Island...," 165-185, 275-279.

and ephemeral." Even in New York, where an interest theory of representation was more thoroughly developed, there were no well defined or reasonably permanent pressure groups, public associations, or other organizations to process demands and proposals from the citizenry.[44] The absence or rudimentary character of such an infrastructure meant, of course, that the political institutions of the colonies were not highly developed in modern terms. But they were as developed as necessary to cope with ordinary conditions of life in the colonies.

Within the context of the new political stability and under the influence of the new community of professional politicians, traditional configurations of political consciousness also underwent important changes as a result of a shift in those "agreed upon and unquestioned" premises that shape patterns of political perception, provide guidelines for acceptable political behavior and a moral basis for political action, and determine the "underlying propensities" of the political system.[45] Although political consciousness was not the exclusive preserve of the elite, it was concentrated in and most fully developed among that group. In the colonies, as in most societies, it was the elite, as Zemsky has recently underlined, who best understood and most consistently based its actions upon the "generally accepted" beliefs and values of the political systems.[46] Increasingly under the early Stuarts, Peter Laslett has written, politics in England began "to include the politics of intellectual difference, of argument about theory or something approaching it" with the result that there was a new "appreciation of political and constitutional issues in something like intellectual terms."[47] This appreciation—which revolved around a conception of political life as a perpetual struggle between prerogative and privilege, between a grasping and arbitrary monarch and a beleagured House of Commons fighting valiantly to preserve the rights of the people—was transferred to the colonies in the seventeenth century, where it was given additional power and a continuing hold on the minds of colonial legislators because of "the Crown's exaggerated claims for prerogative in the plantations."[48] In Britain under the later Stuarts and increasingly during the first half of the eighteenth century, fears of prerogative were increasingly supplanted by anxieties about corruption: "Court Influence or Ministerial Corruption," a "hydra-headed monster" whose heads were the standing army, "Placemen, Pensioners, National Debt, Excise, and High Taxation," came to be set in opposition against the ideal of the virtuous, uncorrupted, and independent (preferably landed) proprietor whose economic independence,

44. Bonomi; Zemsky, 21-22; Almond and Powell, 46-47.
45. Quotations from Almond and Powell, 23, 59.
46. Zemsky, 249.
47. Laslett, *The World We Have Lost*, 175, 177.
48. J. Greene, "Political Mimesis...," 337-355.

active patriotism, and sense of civic responsibility were both the primary
bulwarks against the subversion of liberty by the minions of corruption and,
ideally, the prerequisites for the exercise of a voice in the political system.[49]
For an aspiring political elite whose major claim to social position rested
upon the amount of property at its command and for many of whom pro-
pertied independence was an undeniable reality, the appeal of this conception of politics was irresistible. But the ideal of the vigilant independent
and patriotic landholder struck far greater resonances—and had a deeper and
more lasting impact upon colonial political consciousness—than did the fears
of corruption. With no standing army and such a small civil establishment,
without sinecures, pensions, secret service funds, or, indeed, much patronage,
colonial administrations simply lacked the means for effective corruption in
the style of Sir Robert Walpole. As Richard Bushman has shown in the case
of Massachusetts, colonial political leaders did indeed worry about corruption, but it was the more primitive form of corruption arising from the evil
and avarice of individual governors and royal officials and not corruption
deriving out of court or administrative "influence." Only in those places
like Shirley's Massachusetts or proprietary Maryland, where the governors
did have some patronage, did the fears of "Ministerial Corruption" seem to
have achieved some widespread appeal or frequency of expression.[50]

But there was an additional reason why this newer conception of politics
as an adversary relationship between virtue and corruption did not yet
achieve yet wider acceptance and why the older notion of politics as conflict between privilege and prerogative lost some of its appeal through the
middle decades of the eighteenth century. With the gradual relaxation of
pressure from London beginning in the 1720s, colonial politics, under the
accommodative ministrations of men like Gooch, Shirley, Gordon, James
Glen in South Carolina, George Clarke in New York, and Edward Trelawny
in Jamaica, came to be seen more as a cooperative and less as an antagonistic
process. No longer faced with claims for excessive prerogative power from
governors, many of whom were becoming increasingly domesticated, a rising
community of professional politicians could feel free to cultivate a pragmatic
concern for compromise and for accommodation with the executive in the
pursuit of the public welfare. In Virginia and Massachusetts, where, for somewhat different reasons, political stability lasted for several decades, there
even developed a vital tradition of such cooperation along with a habit of
following executive leadership that was not too dissimilar from the tradition
among the English parliamentary elite of routine obedience to the Crown.

49. Pocock, "Virtue and Commerce," 119-124; Pocock, *Politics, Language, and
Time*, 120-145; Kramnick.
50. Weir, "Bolingbroke," 267-273; Zemsky, 21-22, 52-54; J. Greene, "Political
Mimesis...," 355-359; Bushman, "Corruption and Power...," 63-91; Breen, 240-276.

With the revival of prerogative claims, first in New York during the late 1740s and then in Pennsylvania and South Carolina in the 1750s, such a tradition was seriously undermined. But to the extent that traditional attitudes gave way to a more rational, analytical, and pragmatic orientation during the period of stability in the mid-eighteenth century, the political systems of the colonies may be said to have gone at least part way through the developmental process referred to by political scientists as political secularization.[51]

These changes in the character of leadership, institutions, and consciousness were accompanied by an alteration in the relationship between the leaders and their constituents, an alteration that was manifest in a change from an essentially aggressive and participatory stance toward the political process on the part of the constituents to one that was much more passive and deferential. Between 1675 and 1725, the deferential behavior that had formerly characterized Puritan Massachusetts and Berkeley's Virginia gave way to a political style in which the electorate played a large role and the relationship between leaders and the people, as John C. Rainbolt has said of Virginia, "was one of familiarity...[among] all orders and frequent subservience [on the part of the leaders] to the sentiments of the common planters." In the newer political societies of Pennsylvania, South Carolina, and New York, deferential attitudes had never been strong, while popular involvement and the responsiveness of the leadership had always been rather high.[52] One of the most conspicuous features of the new era of political stability after 1725 was the contraction of the role of the electorate. Suffrage remained high. Within the limits imposed by the exclusivist assumptions on which they were based, colonial political systems were extraordinarily inclusive: in comprehensiveness, they were "not approached by any other society then in existence."[53] The new relationship did not result from the systematic exclusion by the leadership of any portion of the traditional electorate; many voters merely withdrew from or neglected to participate in elections. Unless a vital public issue was involved, voters simply did not turn out to the polls in large numbers. As Nash has pointed out in the case of Pennsylvania, as long as "government did not threaten burdensome taxes, military duty, or religious restrictions" (and the issues varied with other colonies), "most of the people found no need to engage actively in politics." "The strength of the middle and lower strata, then," Nash argues, "was passive, consisting simply of the ability to thwart any political faction which might be so care-

51. Almond and Powell, 24; Lucas, 304-307; Zemsky, 68-70; J. Greene, "Uneasy Connection," 65-74.
52. Rainbolt, 411-434, especially 412; Nash, *passim*; Bonomi, 17-102.
53. Bonomi, 281; J. Greene, "Changing Interpretations...," 156-159; Williamson, *American Suffrage*.

less as to formulate programs which ignored the fundamental requirements of the people."[54]

There was a similar development with reference to office holding. The steady spread of settlement, growth of population, and creation of new political units meant that in absolute numbers more people had access to and actually held office. But it was a declining proportion of the total political population. Moreover, the extension of political jurisdictions meant that of those people in peripheral areas only those with connections to the provincial capital did not live in a geographical isolation that effectively excluded them from access to office at the provincial level. In addition, growing social differentiation created a great social and "technical gap" between the elite and the rest of society, who lacked the expertise—and social prerequisites—for high office. The result was that a smaller and smaller percentage of the whole society could expect to hold important offices at either the provincial or local levels. Because this development was gradual, however, because the political societies of the colonies sank slowly rather than fell precipitously into it, few seem to have felt any serious sense of relative deprivation.[55]

The acquiescence of the broad body politic represented by the low level of participation in elections and the acceptance of the legitimacy and good policy of a more and more elitist leadership structure must be seen in part as the "result of political contentment or of satisfaction" with the government provided by the new professional politicians. This satisfaction was also revealed in the scope of support which the constituency regularly extended to the political system through the payment of taxes, obeying laws, and otherwise manifesting respect for and attachment to the political community and its symbols, institutions, and leaders. But the new acquiescence must also be seen as an indication of a growing degree of political socialization on the part of all segments of the free community, as they each found their place within and became increasingly more integrated into the political systems of the colonies.[56]

This satisfaction and degree of political socialization along with the revival of deferential behavior that came with them suggest, of course, that the colonial political systems under the new professionals were performing the tasks assigned to them extremely well. They were, as several scholars have argued for different colonies, both effective and responsive to the needs and wishes of the respective societies.[57] They had also developed a capacity to

54. Nash, 335-339; Zemsky, 39, 248; Bonomi, 115, 133, 162; Robert E. and B. Katherine Brown, 136-240; Tully; Waterhouse.

55. Laslett, *The World We Have Lost*, 183-185.

56. Nash, 335; Almond and Powell, 24-27, 64-69; Shils, "Political Development...," 387.

57. Almond and Powell, 27-30, 63-64, 247; Zemsky, xii-xiii, 251-252; Tully; Sydnor.

avoid or resolve conflicts. As in Britain, the localities were the primary "conflict arenas," and a variety of potentially explosive issues were raised and resolved at that level. At the provincial level, rivalry among leaders and the push and pull of politics were perpetual, but civil disorder became extremely rare. After 1715, it tended to break out only in certain specific kinds of situations: 1) where the government failed to perform its expected functions as in the South Carolina revolt against the proprietors in 1719; 2) where a government acted against the wishes of a large segment of the population as in the New Jersey land riots of the late 1740s and early 1750s; 3) where the controlling leaders suffered a loss of public confidence because of a failure to act on an issue of great moment to some significant segment of the population as in Pennsylvania during the exclusion crisis of 1756 or the Paxton uprising in 1764; 4) where the political machinery had been stretched too far to provide adequate government, as in the case of the North Carolina Regulators; 5) where a deadlock between more or less equal contending forces resulted in a serious breakdown of government as in the representation controversies in North Carolina and New Hampshire during the late 1740s; or 6) where the traditional rights and privileges of the community were thought to be threatened by an "external power" as in the impressment riots in Boston in the 1740s. The colonial political systems had difficulty in dealing with such irregular occurences, but neither the volume nor the range of such phenomenon were very great. The susceptibility of the political systems to demands, the general level of political trust of the leaders by their constituents, and a new level of civility in the political arena all helped to avoid or routinize conflict and to promote a conception of politics as an accommodative, rather than a discordant, process in which the broad body of the people normally deferred to the leadership and decisions of a highly professional and competent political elite with confidence in its capacity to govern.[58]

A final area in which there were significant developments during the long period of stability was in the improvement of the instruments of communication and the emergence of non-governmental institutions that provide political training and disperse political knowledge. These included a relatively vigorous, if not always entirely autonomous, press; a growing and increasingly sophisticated and competent legal profession; schools, including more institutions of higher learning; voluntary associations such as coffee house groups, clubs, chambers of commerce, and professional societies; and expanding networks of trade. Along with an increase in travel, literacy, and books and other printed materials, these developments contributed to erode much of the tra-

58. Laslett, *The World We Have Lost*, 166-171, 194-195; Almond and Powell, 17-18, 54-56, 186; Shils, "Political Development," 383-387; Maier, *From Resistance to Revolution*, 3-26.

ditional localism of rural America, to provide easier access to metropolitan knowledge and technical skills, and to encourage the rapid development of human capital—in sum to widen the cognitive map and augment the political potential of the colonists. More directly, despite the low level of participation in elections and the declining proportion of the population who could hold public office, men at all levels of society routinely engaged in "an extraordinary number of public and private transactions," including land grants and litigation that involved contact with politics. These transactions gave the colonists "a range [and depth] of political competence that was elsewhere unknown" and helped to create a relatively broad and informed citizenry.[59]

But the political implications of the enormous expansion of the public realm represented by these developments remained largely latent prior to the 1760s. The emergence of a "public" and an increased participation in public affairs became much more manifest beginning with the Stamp Act crisis. Thereafter, the politicization of the colonists increased at an exponential rate, as British officials, an anonymous pamphleteer complained in London in 1774, "impoliticly kept [the colonists] in a state of continual training for nine successive years. Their Orators," he lamented, "have been furnished with topics for popular harangues, and the mass of the people have been taught politics, and the mode of being troublesome to Government."[60] The potential for such broad and deep politicization had been growing rapidly over the previous generation. But in the stable political world that obtained in the major colonies for much of the period between the 1720s and the early 1760s nothing occurred to bring it to full flower.

The stability that characterized the major colonies over much of the period from 1725 to 1760 obviously did not extend to all of the colonies. A case can be made that Maryland achieved a considerable degree of stability over that period of a type that was similar in some respects to that of Pennsylvania and in others to that of New York. The more primitive political societies of North Carolina, New Jersey, and New Hampshire were rarely free of tumult or contention during these years, and, when New Hampshire did achieve some political harmony after 1752, it was a harmony that was much more akin to that experienced by Virginia under Berkeley almost a century earlier than to that of contemporary Virginia, South Carolina, or Massachusetts. In Connecticut and Rhode Island, where the Crown did not intrude so thoroughly into provincial affairs at the end of the seven-

59. Shils, "Political Development," 385-386; Shils, "Concentration and Dispersal of Charisma," 19; Laslett, *The World We Have Lost*, 209; Almond and Powell, 244-246; Bonomi, 281; Kammen, "Intellectuals, Political Leadership, and Revolution," 588-589; Cremin, 519-520, 548-549, 553, 555-556.

60. Cremin, 545; Rothermund, 83; *A Letter to a Member of Parliament*, 7.

teenth century, the direction of development seems to have been precisely opposite from that found in the predominant pattern, as the relatively stable political structures that existed at the end of the seventeenth century and during the early decades of the eighteenth century were shattered by religious divisions, disagreements over monetary policy, and exigencies created by rapid expansion between 1730 and 1750.[61] Even the political stability achieved by the five leading colonies began to crack after 1750 under pressures created by the Seven Years' War, a renewal of effort by the imperial government to impose tighter controls over the colonies, and a variety of internal stresses and strains.[62]

But the extensive political development that had taken place during earlier decades, development in leadership, institutions, political consciousness, the socialization of the electorate to their political systems, and instruments of communication and non-governmental political training institutions, was irreversible. And it had provided the political systems of the colonies with increased capabilities and resources that would prove indispensable in coping with the challenges that lay beyond 1760.

61. Barker; Kemmerer; Daniell; Bushman, *From Puritan to Yankee*; Lovejoy, *Rhode Island Politics*; J. Greene, "Changing Interpretations...," 159-172.
62. J. Greene, "Uneasy Connection," 65-80.

A Different "Fable of the Bees": The Problem of Public and Private Sectors in Colonial America

MICHAEL KAMMEN

Because my subject is a difficult one to define, I want to begin in an unorthodox fashion by illustrating it even before trying to define it. I rationalize this reversal of protocol by declaring that that is how I first stumbled on to the topic several years ago: I repeatedly ran across examples of a phenomenon, and wondered what they meant. The cases kept coming, from all of the colonies and from both the seventeenth and eighteenth centuries. Their insistent configuration clearly demanded some pattern of explanation; and that is precisely what I am about here—the configuration and consequences of public and private sectors in colonial America, culminating in the Age of the American Revolution. Some illustrations first.

Item: When New Netherland first needed to be provisioned in 1626, livestock was sent over not by the Dutch West India Company itself but in ships privately owned by Company commissioners, who thereby profited personally from their public roles despite protests from the "contrary minded."[1]

Item: When the people of New Netherland sent home a Remonstrance in 1649, they remarked that the Directors in New Amsterdam "looked close to their own advantage. They have always known how to manage their own affairs handsomely, with little loss to themselves, yet under plausible pretexts, such as public interest, &c."[2]

Item: When Richard Nicolls returned to England in 1668 after four years as governor of New York, he found himself almost £9,000 out of pocket because he had been obliged to use his own funds when inhabitants refused to co-operate in paying for badly needed fortifications. Although the Duke of

---

1. Condon, 97-98, 110.
2. O'Callaghan, *Documents*, I, 298.

York promised to repay his erstwhile governor, Nicolls never saw the money during his lifetime.[3]

Item: When New York's tax revenues proved in 1688 to be inadequate, Governor Dongan advanced funds of his own and borrowed on his own credit in order to finance public needs.[4]

Item: When Governor Bellomont addressed the New York Assembly in 1700, a time of frontier insecurity because of the French and Iroquois menace, he pointed out that "the honor and interest of the Crown, and your own private interest are engaged in the right management and preservation of those Indians."[5]

Item: When Mrs. Samuel Provoost, a widow who ran her late husband's importing business in New York City, could not persuade municipal authorities to pave a proper sidewalk for her, she "ordered a quantity of large flat stones to be laid as a sidewalk, not only in front of her place of business but beyond her property and up to the streets on either side of it....The stone 'walking-side' laid down by the private enterprise of a woman was the first pavement in the city of New York. Some of the neighbors followed this praiseworthy example and laid brick walks, which were called 'Strookes,' and by degrees, paving and curbing the streets were undertaken by the municipal authorities, and not left to individual exertions."[6]

Although I have chosen to "itemize" all of my illustrations from the narrative of colonial New York (in order to demonstrate the continuity of this phenomenon in a given locale), I might have done the same with any other colony. The point, quite simply, is that this conflation of the public and private sectors was ubiquitous. Perhaps the best single example, because of its sentimental legacy, concerns William Allen of Philadelphia, a merchant and jurist who advocated construction of a new state house during the 1730s. When labor disputes slowed down the completion of what became Independence Hall, Allen advanced a great deal of money from his private purse, and the colony's debt to him was not fully repaid until 1761.

Having illustrated the historical problem which piqued my interest initially, I shall try to do the following in this paper: define the problem in more generalized terms; determine whether it had European parallels; perceive the phenomenon developing during the colonial period; suggest that contemporaries were quite aware of it; offer some explanations; discuss its relationship to the Age of the American Revolution, both in reality as well as in political theory; and, finally, indicate a few of its legacies for the later course of our history.

3. Ritchie, 271-72; Reich, 6.
4. Leder, "Dongan's New York...," 30.
5. Lincoln, ed., I, 86; Leder, ed., "Dam'me Don't Stir a Man...," 263.
6. Van Rensselaer, 234-36.

When I speak of the public sector, I refer to the state, its institutions and officers, and to the authority they exercise over the common weal. When I speak of the private sector, I refer to the individual, the interest group, and the sect, to personal initiative and the ownership of property. When I juxtapose the public and private sectors for purposes of analysis, I mean to contrast collectivity as against individuality, presumed beneficence as against presumed self-interest, impersonality as against specific identity, public institutions as against private property.[7] These distinctions are overly sharp, of course, and in reality there is always overlap—but recognition of that gets somewhat ahead of our story.

Notions about the public and private sectors played an important part in the conceptual outlook of early modern man, at least in what we call "western civilization." In England the public interest was referred to as "the realm" and as "the common weal." In France we find the phrase "*la chose publique.*" And in Germany Hegel called it "the general estate." In the English colonies men defined the purpose of the public sector as "the Promoting and Florishing of Civil and Sacred Order" by the "exercise of Government" so that "subjects may lead a peaceable and quiet Life in all Godliness and Honesty."[8]

I am prepared to argue that the public and private sectors merged—indeed were sometimes nearly conflated—to an unusual extent in the colonies, and that relations and boundaries between the two shifted elusively in response to critical changes in population growth, modes of public finance, goals of economic development, problems of social control and community welfare.

Above all, the subtle connections between public and private sectors were contingent upon where the necessary initiative came from in order to accomplish projects beneficial to state and society. How and why did "things" get done? Who benefited from the doing of them? What attitudes and legacies were left behind as a result?

I would not argue that private persons did not finance public works in early modern Europe; of course they did. Nor do I wish to deny that individuals there profited from public projects; of course they did. But comparison and contrast with the colonies involves significant differences of degree, distance, and, above all, attitude. We know that England between the twelfth and seventeenth centuries moved gradually from a political consciousness confined by notions of hierarchy, status, localism, and tradition towards a more modern temper characterized by the presumption of a well-defined "public dimension," a commonly shared civic awareness and a belief in secular human

7. Fortes, 194, 207-8, 211; Lowi, vii.
8. Bushman, *From Puritan to Yankee*, 9, quoting John Woodward, *Civil Rulers are God's Ministers* (London, 1712), and Samuel Woodbridge, *Obedience to the Divine Law* (London, 1724).

competence. We also know that English government in the eighteenth century provided institutionalized distinctions between public and private
matters, especially in parliamentary legislation. (One must be careful not to
make too much, too soon, of this distinction. An order of 1751 clearly stated
that "every bill for the particular interest or benefit of any person or persons
...hath been and ought to be, deemed a private bill, within the meaning of the
Table of Fees." Even so, the definitions and procedural differences between
public and private bills remained somewhat unclear and overlapping until
1810 when the Private Bill Office was established.)[9] Although many of the
ethical niceties which we expect today were hopelessly unfulfilled then,
there was nevertheless some sense that certain things ought to be rendered
unto Caesar, while others were not, and that each sort had its place.[10]

Similarly, there existed in France the distinction between *droit publique*
and *droit privée*, a distinction without counterpart in the colonies. And in
the Netherlands, say in 1650, serving on the municipal council of Amsterdam
was nearly a full-time job. Merchants who sat on the council had little leisure
for their own commercial affairs, and subsequently the separation of office-
holding from full participation in private trade began to be more and more
natural.[11] Not so in New Netherland, where men had the time as well as the
inclination for both. There were powerful expectations in the colonies,
especially economic ones; but where politicians and institutions were equally
capricious, expectations had to be fulfilled by the expectors. Self-help mat-
tered, and became in consequence more than just a catch-phrase.

In New Spain, unlike English North America, the public-private relationship was clarified rather than blurred at the critical moment of colonization.
Professor Richard Morse has explained it this way:

The settlement of the Americas came at a time when the revival of Roman
law had established juridical principles of separation between the public and
private orders and, specifically, between land held by persons who were in
feudal relation to the king as a lord and land granted by royal grace or concession by the king as head of the state....In America the Roman tradition
became exclusive, and all lands were conceived to be the property of the king
as monarch, not as a private person. All land titles, then, whether for European settlers or for the Indians themselves, had to flow from royal concessions. Initially the concessions were granted in the name of the king by conquerors, viceroys, governors, or other agents. But as soon as a city was established, this power became an attribute of its town council.

Morse goes on to say that the Spaniards brought with them a fairly clear
distinction between private and communal lands: "Even private lands were

9. For the relationship between public and private bills see Lambert, 29-30, 57-8,
65, 80, 84-5, 192-3.
10. Hanson; Lambert, chs. 5, 9; Williams; Baugh, 254-61, 281-82; Fanning, 47-84.
11. Boxer, 32.

not to be given in perpetuity until four to eight years of effective possession could be shown."[12] How very different from the notorious failures of communalism in early Virginia and Plymouth, where only open concessions to privatism could save those undertakings from withering away with the dried up leaves of autumn.

In the first great age of English colonization, many social functions briefly became part of the public sector's realm of responsibility: transporting, feeding, and sheltering persons. But there soon seemed to be a reaction against this collectivism, a negative response which grew in intensity as the private sector became capable of accomplishing social purposes. By the middle of the seventeenth century, most colonists seemed to believe that people could best be motivated through the stimulus of individual opportunity—personal risks for private gain—and that therein lay the most logical route to economic growth and public improvement. Simultaneously, as colonizing companies and Old World investors began to vanish, there was a marked insufficiency of public funds for commercial expansion and civic betterment. Initiative, therefore, passed to the private sector: and if the private sector didn't do "it," "it" often didn't get done.

The state was relatively weak in colonial America. It consistently lacked funds, it often lacked dignity, and it usually lacked authority. Therefore, to a greater degree than the monarchies and autocracies of Europe, the state had to rely upon the private sector in order to fulfill its social responsibilities. In Europe, for example, the Prince simply hired mercenaries for the duration of a war; whereas in the colonies special blandishments had to be held out to citizen-soldiers of the militia who might otherwise abandon the battlefield at harvest time. Again and again I find the state in early America obliged to make special concessions to private imperatives. Provincial governments relied heavily upon the credit of private individuals as a solution to the recurrent problem of inadequate revenues and increasing demands for expenditures. Wealthy persons, such as Robert Livingston of New York, commonly became the creditors of their colonies; and government officials were normally paid a percentage of the fees they collected, thereby giving them a personal stake in official diligence.[13]

This weakness of the state is noteworthy for many reasons and intersects with a variety of other important phenomena. We tend to assume, for example, some direct and fairly simple relationship between population increase and the growth of governmental apparatus: the more people, the more services and agencies required. The Webbs reach this conclusion in a summarizing chapter of their *History of English Local Government*. But not so in colonial America, where governments often remained rudimentary and inade-

12. Morse, 325-26, 327; Duarte, chs. 2, 3.
13. Leder, *Robert Livingston*, 36, 39-40, 42-44, 48, 78-79.

quate well after demographic growth had become obvious. During the eighteenth century, provincial assemblies were unresponsive to the spread of settlement into new areas. There were rarely enough courts, new units of representation were created only slowly, and people tended to dodge their civic
responsibilities (were quite happy to pay fines rather than serve as fence-
viewers or constables). Jefferson's generation believed that government was
best which governed least; and any cursory glance at the structure of American government, 1789-1828, reveals with stunning force the barebones nature
of public institutions and their personnel.[14]

What all of this suggests, at least to me, is that if government responded
slowly to social needs, then those imperatives would have to be satisfied by
non-governmental means—i.e., the private sector—or else go unsatisfied (and
that happened too). Hence the importance of voluntary associations in eigh-
teenth- and nineteenth-century American life. Settlers were competitive and
litigious; but where the state and its mechanisms of public authority proved
inadequate to mediate disputes, individuals and groups had to resort to their
own devices in order to work out accommodations: personal trade-offs,
church authority, vigilante groups, fraternal organizations, and the charisma
or influence of prominent, powerful persons in the community.

There is, then, a sense in which the early colonists were not only products
of seventeenth-century England, but—owing to their particularism and localism—*also* found themselves thrown back figuratively to the circumstances of
thirteenth-century life as well. Many certainly brought with them and were
quite aware of the growth of civic consciousness in Stuart times. Consequently there must have been, in the minds of educated leaders at least,
some sense of dualism as between their experience of privatism and the discussions then fashionable concerning the public interest.[15] This dualism is
critically important to an understanding of the relationship between political
thought and social behavior in early American life.[16] And it may help to explain the emergence of collective-individualism as a characteristic modality in
the American style.[17]

In any event, there is abundant evidence to suggest their growing self-
consciousness about the conflation of public and private sectors, as well as
their desire to determine a proper relationship between the two in order to
promote public order, social satisfaction, and the pursuit of personal happiness.[18] Let us look at some of the evidence, selecting examples from the
1630s down to the 1750s.

14. L. D. White, *The Federalists*; L. D. White, *The Jeffersonians*.
15. Gunn, chs. 1, 2, 6.
16. Breen, chs. 2, 5, 6; Foster, chs. 3, 4, 6.
17. Kammen, *People of Paradox*, 115-16, 214, 220, 269.
18. For a different emphasis see Bailyn, "Education as a discipline," 133-37, where

In 1638 Philip Vincent published an historical account of the recent, bloody Pequot War, *A True Relation of the Late Battell Fought in New England*. "Whilste men are all for their private profit," he wrote, "the public good is neglected....The New-Englanders, therefore, advanced the public all they could, and so the private is taken care for."[19] In Vincent's didactic message, attention paid to the public sector would, in the nature of things, benefit the private; but not vice versa. His difficulty lay in the fact that his message mirrored English theories common at the time (his tract was published in London), but not the ongoing realities of wilderness life.

One of the major thrusts of provincial thought in the next two centuries, therefore, would be to devise a rationale appropriate to American circumstances. I find it very revealing that Bernard Mandeville's famous *Fable of the Bees; or, Private Vices, Public Benefits* (London, 1714; eight more English editions in the eighteenth century, two Scottish, two French, one German) was never reprinted in an early American edition. Colonial literati were not unaware of its existence; but they knew all too well that private vices in provincial America had not consistently been a source of public benefits. As Royall Tyler has one character exclaim in the first American drama: "It must be so, Montague! And it is not all the tribe of Mandevilles shall convince me, that a nation, to become great, must first become dissipated. Luxury is surely the bane of a nation." (*The Contrast, a Comedy*, Philadelphia, 1790, III, ii. The play was first performed in New York City in 1787.)

Let us return to indications of contemporary sensitivity to the problem. In 1687 the Plymouth colonists were outraged by the "private removal" of their public records to Boston. In 1694 Benjamin Fletcher tried to assure New York's Assembly that funds it had raised would neither be "sunk into any private pocket nor disposed to any private use." The proprietors of Pennsylvania could exempt their own extensive estates from taxation, thereby blurring essential distinctions between public and private sectors, and precipitating a sense of outrage among the colony's citizenry.[20]

Benjamin Franklin may well have been the best barometer of all. "I have not heretofore made much Scruple of giving you Trouble when the Publick Good was to be promoted by it," he wrote to Peter Collinson, the English naturalist, in 1751, "but 'tis with great Reluctance that I think of asking you to interest yourself in my private Concerns." Or in 1755 again to Collinson:

he says "It is anachronistic even to say that private and public functions overlapped and merged before the nineteenth century: the distinctions by which to make such a statement were absent. Contemporaries were aware only of a natural continuum, a subtly colored spectrum at whose barely visible extremities alone could be found what we think of as the two necessary distinctions."

19. Vincent, 42.

20. Lovejoy, *Glorious Revolution*, 197; Lincoln, ed. I, 48; Wm. Smith, Jr., I, 227; Hanna, chs. 3, 5, 11; Hutson, 18-24.

The Quakers have now shown that they can give and dispose of Money for that purpose as freely as any People. If this does not give Satisfaction, the Pique against them must seem to be personal and private, and not founded on Views for the Publick Good. I know the Quakers now think it their Duty, when chosen, to consider themselves as Representatives of the *Whole People*, and not their own Sect only.[21]

In 1750 Sir William Johnson, Superintendent of Indian Affairs, complained that his "daily unavoidable disbursements to the Indians fall very hard upon me," especially because neither Whitehall nor New York was likely to reimburse him for the "pains, Service & Expence I have taken, done & been at." In 1755 he informed a British captain that "in money matters I know the Assemblys on this Continent & particularly ones to the Northward, are not generously disposed & that when the Subjects are not to be conducted by or terminate in the private advantage of some of their own Body or Dependents they are at best prone to such a backwardness & distrust, as often not only retards but Disappoints the public Service."[22]

Although contemporaries perceived aspects of the problem and often complained about it, they could not yet be fully aware of all its dimensions and developments. Therefore we should turn next to a longer look at the phenomenon itself—an examination of it occurring in diverse provincial places and times in order to get some sense of its periodicity and problematic nature in the English settlements.

Unlike Spanish and French colonization in the New World, which were carried out primarily under governmental auspices, the beginnings of English overseas settlement were half under public auspices and half under private ones. Joint stock companies, although comprising private groups of entrepreneurs, were chartered by the Crown. Thus the governance of public affairs in Virginia, Bermuda, and New Netherland began under the supervision of private, profit-seeking corporations. To an even greater degree, moreover, the subsequent proprietary governments involved an anachronistic blending of private possession with public domain. Thus the ambiguous circumstances of politics and society in early Maryland, the Carolinas, Jersies, and Pennsylvania.[23]

The ecclesiology of early New England tended inevitably to complicate the connections between spiritual communities and public order. The notion of a National Covenant insisted that a plethora of private indiscretions would produce public catastrophe. Every springtime between 1634 and 1884, therefore, the sacred and secular were formally joined in Massachusetts by the tradition of the election sermon, a custom practiced in Connecticut as well. A

21. Fleming, ed., 132-33, 146; see also 16, 186, 348.
22. Johnson, I, 278-79, 521-22; VI, 94.
23. Billias, ed., xiii, 11, 79, 92, 93, 96, 107, 122, 165 n. 1, 178-79.

designated minister informed the governor, his advisers, and the newly elected general court that public success required private morality and that public virtue was necessary for private happiness. Understandably, then, there would be a long-standing controversy in Massachusetts over the issue of private tax monies being used for the public support of a particular religious group; and in the 1780 Constitution it was not surprising that sectarian ministers were described as "public Protestant teachers of piety, morality, and religion."[24]

Similarly the Puritan family was simultaneously a public as well as a private entity. The state relied upon the family as an agency of education, socialization, and control. Moreover the Pilgrims regarded marriage, in William Bradford's words, "as being a civil thing," not simply a sacrament but a public contract between two private individuals. "Family and community," writes John Demos, "private and public life, formed part of the same moral equation. The one supported the other, and they became in a sense indistinguishable."[25]

In early modern England, by contrast, the family was much less of a public institution; and, public poor relief there developed earlier than in the colonies. The British moved gradually to supplant what had been certain private functions with public responsibility, thereby delineating a sharper distinction between public and private sectors. The militia, for example, took on greater importance in seventeenth-century America than at "home." Control by a citizen-police force provided a hybrid way of maintaining public order. Even so, problems arose when militia training and muster days interfered with people's private pursuits. Despite the very real security crisis caused by a collapse in French and Indian relations during the 1680s, Governor Dongan received instructions "to take especial care that neither the frequency nor unreasonableness of remote marches, musters & trainings bee an unnecessary Impediment to the Affairs of the Planters."[26]

Most important of all, however, was the ambiguous relationship between private persons and public authority concerning commercial undertakings and economic growth. Colonial merchants in the seventeenth century generally favored government involvement and regulation of the economy; nevertheless they sought and made their fortunes in those marginal areas which were largely unregulated. The careers of John Hull in Massachusetts, William Beekman in New York, and William Byrd I in Virginia are all exemplary in this respect.[27] The town proprietors of New England found themselves engaged in endless conflicts with newcomers over land; and in part those fights arose

24. Sussman, 20-22; Plumstead, ed.; C. Wright, 94-95, 99.
25. Bradford, 86; Demos, 162, 186.
26. O'Callaghan, *Documents*, III, 373, 546.
27. Morison, 159-82; P. White, 15-72; *Dictionary of American Biography*, "Byrd."

because it was very unclear whether land controlled by the proprietors was a public trust or a private reserve. Similarly, members of the Philadelphia Corporation had the administrative responsibility to regulate trade, supervise markets and fairs, etc.; nevertheless they commonly used their position for speculative as well as commercial advantage, but also paid public charges out of their own pockets on occasion.[28]

Let me now conclude this portion of my essay with a few essential institutional illustrations, and then move on to relate the problem of public versus private interests to the revolutionary era.

It is, I think, necessary to note the curiously ambiguous nature of slavery, schools, printers, land banks, and political parties in early America, for all of them were biform in the very sense we have been discussing. Although slaves were private property, their existence was everywhere regulated by public legislation, for the simple reason that their (or their masters') uncontrolled behavior constituted a potential threat to public safety and morals. Harvard's 1650 Charter aimed to establish a private college on the model of Oxford and Cambridge, yet still allow for public control through a Board of Overseers as provided in 1642. For generations thereafter, advanced educational institutions in colonial America were neither public nor private because they were both. Land banks, of course, mobilized private support for the public issuance of currency, thereby opening the messy matter of potential corruption and conflict of interest.

Finally, political factions were deplored throughout the colonies because they seemed to represent the pursuit of private interests rather than the broader public interest. As Governor Bellomont put it to the New York Assembly in 1699, "You all know the mischiefs, both public and private, that feuds and divisions bring on a people or nation."[29] Acceptance of faction would concede the conflation of public and private sectors, thereby heralding a dangerous decline in the quality and character of both. Only slowly, then, would realism replace what had appeared, by dint of constant repetition, as almost a rhetorical posture. A turning point was reached by 1765 when a writer asserted in the *New York Gazette* that "*Self Interest* is the grand Principle of all Human Actions; it is unreasonable and vain to expect Service from a Man who must act contrary to his own Interests to perform it."[30]

What had happened between colonization and the eve of Revolution was complex, but not so very difficult to summarize and explain. There were urgent needs for social services and for economic growth. Provincial and municipal treasuries had neither adequate funds nor power, and therefore insuffi-

28. Akagi, chs. 3, 5; Diamondstone, 183-201.
29. Lincoln, ed., I, 82.
30. I am indebted to Professor Gary Nash of U.C.L.A. for this quotation.

cient initiative to accomplish many of the goals that were generally sought. Public projects and benefits, consequently, were undertaken through private capital and aggressiveness. The State awarded monopolies as public trusts: saying, in effect, here are the exclusive rights to such-and-such a business; now do a good job for the common weal and get what you can for yourself from the opportunity.

Public officials, moreover, were often grossly underpaid; and were thereby forced to supplement their fixed salaries with profiteering of one sort or another. This was especially true of imperial officials, who commonly entered into special deals with local entrepreneurs. The result, as one historian has observed, was that "more often than not these ventures were of public nature operated for private profit by the commissioned agents of the Crown."[31]

There were other factors as well, though perhaps less critically important, underlying the phenomenon we have been examining. One involved the desire by many men to pursue their own interests without restraint, *but also* to exist in an orderly, secure social system. Another entailed the very gradual modification of European assumptions about the proper relationship between church and state in general, the established church and non-conformist sects in particular. Thus the Reverend Francis Makemie would write in his defensive *Narrative* (1707): "We were under a necessity of assembling for Publick Worship in a Private House."[32] Still another invloved the ambiguous role of educational institutions supported by philanthropic individuals. Thus Benjamin Franklin would write in his "Scheme of a Lottery for the Use of the Academy and Charity-School of Philadelphia" (1755) that it "was begun, supported, and now greatly enlarged entirely at the Expence of private Persons, tho' solely calculated for the Benefit of the Publick, and the Honour of the Province."[33]

In 1751, under the pseudonym "Americanus," Franklin published in the *Pennsylvania Gazette* a satirical letter that reveals a new dimension being added to the problem of public and private sectors. Writing in response to Britain's refusal to allow colonial assemblies "to make any Law for preventing or discouraging the Importation of Convicts" (on the grounds "that such Laws are against The Publick Utility, as they tend to prevent the IMPROVEMENT and WELL PEOPLING of the Colonies"), Franklin replied with scorn and sarcasm. "But let not *private Interests* obstruct *publick Utility*," he remarked, "Our Mother knows what is best for us."[34]

At this point, what had been primarily perceived as an indigenous problem became explicitly Anglo-American and therefore politically sensitive as never

31. Judd, 74.
32. H. S. Smith, *et. al.*, eds., I, 260.
33. Franklin, *Papers*, V, 507.
34. Fleming, 130-31. Franklin's italics.

before. Private interests in the colonies had often provided stimuli to growth as well as impediments to the public sector. But once private interests and public policy in England began to conflict with civic consciousness in the colonies, an issue of enormous complexity arose, one that would become increasingly visible in the decades before 1776.[35] A notable illustration occurred when Britain attempted to billet regular troops in private homes. The whole quartering conflict aroused the fiercest resentments imaginable.

Members of the revolutionary generation inherited an ill-defined and inadequate tradition of public administration and finance. Because the War of Independence had to be paid for, available methods of proceeding had to be relied upon; so that, on the surface, little seemed to change. Financial operators like Robert Morris and William Bingham used their influence and inside knowledge for private profit, and pocketed handsome commissions on supplies bought from their business partners for military use. They played a vital role because their personal credit was valid when Congress had virtually none. They financed the Revolution, and it nourished their fortunes, "I need one thousand barrels of flour for the new campaign," wrote Robert Morris in 1781; "I assume your credit as a private gentleman is good for this amount; proceed accordingly, and bill me."[36]

Beneath the surface, however, adaptation and altered perception were beginning to occur, both for intellectual reasons and in response to the realities of revolutionary life. Political theorists began to rationalize and affirm what had been reluctantly or half-recognized for a generation past. Here is Alexander Hamilton in 1775 (citing David Hume):

Political writers...have established it as a maxim, that, in contriving any system of government, and fixing the several checks and controuls of the constitution, *every man* ought to be supposed a *knave*; and to have no other end in all his actions, but *private interest*. By this interest, we must govern him, and by means of it, *make him co-operate to public good*, notwithstanding his insatiable avarice and ambition....

Men are generally more honest in a private than in a public capacity; and will go (to) greater lengths to serve a party, than when their own private interest is alone concerned. Honour is a great check upon mankind. But, where a considerable body of men act together, this check is in a great measure removed; since a man is sure to be approved by his own party, for what promotes the common interest, and he soon learns to despise the clamours of adversaries.

Thus far Hamilton was drinking Hume's draught straight; but then the young pamphleteer added a fillip of his own. "What additional force do

---

35. Wood, *Creation of the American Republic*, 191.
36. Morris to Philip Schuyler, 29 May 1781, in Lynd, *Class Conflict*, 121; See also Ver Steeg, chs. 3-4; Alberts, 103-7, 110; Ferguson.

these observations acquire, when applied to the dominion of one community over another!"[37]

Britain and Hume would be hoist by their own petard, and an altered understanding of public and private interests would emerge, an American version which combined several different strands of experience and ideology. Mandeville's "Fable" of private vices, public benefits had been transformed into a curious new equation: private virtues, public vices controlled.

What were those strands, then, and just what amalgam did emerge? The question is vitally important, and brings me to the very quick of this essay. In the Anglo-American world view of the eighteenth century, there were two prominent conceptions of the relationship between property and personality. One has been called the classical view, or civic humanism, involving the subordination of private needs to public ends, and assuming that the function of property was to make the citizen politically independent and therefore responsible. The other has been called the bourgeois view, or materialism, presuming that the pursuit of personal happiness depends essentially upon the pursuit and accumulation of private property.[38]

My own belief is that the bourgeois view most closely approximated the reality of colonial experiences ever since Jamestown; but that the crisis of conscience that occurred between 1775 and 1788 made the classical view appealing and necessary as well. So it was adapted and hooked up with the bourgeois view in an impure hybrid that might be called "civic materialism." Thus in 1776 we find prominent New York pamphleteers declaring that "*So far as private property will allow*, we must form our government in each province, just as if we had never had any form of government before."[39]

The difficulty, of course, is simply that the two views did not make a neat fit, that the classical theory jarred uneasily against the bourgeois reality, and that once the veneer of republican ideology rubbed thin Americans were left with a characteristic anomaly that has endured to the present: an ethic of civic humanism in tandem with the bourgeois ethos. We refer recurrently to the public interest, but respond most often to the private. Rhetoric thereby becomes dissonant with reality; and the Age of the American Revolution is pivotal in this process because that is when the idea of civic humanism (or Virtue) was first introduced on a broad scale. That, consequently, is when this tension began.[40]

37. Hamilton, I, 94-95; Stourzh, *Alexander Hamilton*, ch. 3. See also James Madison to Thomas Jefferson, March 27, 1780 in Madison, *The Papers*, II, 6.

38. Pocock, *Politics, Language and Time*, 91, 101.

39. Quoted in Champagne, 300. My italics. See also Thomas Smith to Arthur St. Clair, August 22, 1776 in Wood, *Creation of the American Republic*, 227.

40. J. Greene, review of *Papers of George Mason*, 160-61; Howe, ch. 2; Pocock, "Virtue and Commerce", 134; Goldman, 46-62.

I want to conclude with a few observations on the legacies and implications of the phenomenon under discussion. Before doing so, however, I must at least indicate my awareness that a bit of comparative perspective is necessary here. I have not meant to imply that no overlapping of public and private sectors occurred in Europe. Of course it did. I do mean to suggest, though, that there are critical differences both in attitude and in degree. The simple facts remain that Robert Morris fundamentally financed the War of Independence, while George III and Parliament did so for the other side. And if the British Treasury's occasional neglect of "open contracting" elicited criticism in Parliament and the press on account of personal profiteering at the public expense, there was scant colonial counterpart to such commentary.[41]

Whereas the differences between public/private interconnections in early modern England and in her colonies were subtle rather than stark, and whereas there certainly were many similarities as well, contrasts ever since the early nineteenth century have been more clear-cut and self-evident. I am persuaded, therefore, that a very slow process of divergence had occurred between colonization and the end of the revolutionary era; and that at least some of the sources of divergence can be specified: (1) because of abundant land and natural resources, government controls seemed less necessary in the colonies and reliance upon the government for economic development less vital; (2) because of the chronic labor shortage, provincial societies placed higher emphasis upon personal, private motivation—particularly in defining tasks and roles; (3) the young United States did not undergo the long upheaval of Napoleonic war, an experience which demonstrated to the British that their government could play a determinative role in the organization of commerce and industry for military purposes; (4) the young republic did not suffer as England had from intense social dislocation caused by rapid industrialization—a process which made the English elite realize that government must exert a controlling influence or else risk violent insurrection by the oppressed; and (5) the concept of "public interest" developed earlier and with greater clarity in England than in the United States—witness the rise of Benthamite Utilitarianism.

In brief, the colonists began with a blending of public and private sectors evident in Stuart England, and ultimately carried that condition to one possible extreme (given their circumstances), while Britain eventually moved in a different direction—namely, that the private sector should be rather more distinct from and subordinate to the public. What happened in colonial America was not so much intentional or ideological as developmental and

41. Binney; Baker, *Government and Contractors*, chs. 2, 9; Baker, "The Treasury and Open Contracting," 433-54; Syrett, ch. 8.

demographic. Lacking alternatives, Americans accepted and rationalized the inevitable. Exigencies of public finance created new imperatives as well as a peculiar ethos concerning private enterprise in the public sector, and thereby augmented the whole mystique of economic individualism.

Writing just after the turn of the nineteenth century, David Ramsay remarked that "in modern Europe, the revolutions of public affairs seldom disturb the humble obscurity of private life; but the American Revolution involved the interests of every family, and deeply affected the fortunes and happiness of almost every individual in the United States."[42] There is an element of hyperbole here, to be sure, and an excess of comparative exaggeration. It was, however, sincere hyperbole and authentic exaggeration. Ramsay meant what he said and his contemporaries believed it. Insofar as they did, it conveyed for them a psychological truth.

Which brings me, finally, to some perfunctory observations on legacies and implications. Hopefully they are so obvious by this point that they will require little more than invocation. Between, say, 1609 and 1809, between Jamestown's "starving time" and James Madison's inauguration, an extraordinary development occurred. In 1609 private enterprise was supposed to be subordinate to the common weal. By 1809 the public sector—government—sought to be minimal and subordinate: dismantle the military, cut spending, be unobtrusive. In sum, do only those things that no one else can or wants to do. Economic individualism, self-help, and competitiveness had been ideologically unleashed. Insofar as the government could bestow privileges, Jeffersonians believed that there ought to be a democratization of privilege: beneficiaries would be held responsible to the public; and beneficence should be spread as widely as possible. Notice, though, the flow of action: not simply from private virtues (or vices) to the common weal, but from public agencies legitimizing for private individuals the opportunity to do well by doing good.[43]

Ever since the Jeffersonian era, this country has vacillated between the possibilities offered by its colonial experience with public and private sectors. Hence our monopolies have been both public trusts as well as private trysts. Hence we have endured repeated conflicts between private conscience and public law.[44] Political scientists have been ceaselessly disposed to comment upon ambiguities inherent in the American notion of "public interest."[45] I should only like to observe that these conundrums are not simply matters of logical confusion. Rather, their sources are deeply his-

42. Quoted in W. R. Smith, 65; Cobb, 3-30.
43. See also Thomas Jefferson to Joseph Bloomfield, December 5, 1801 quoted in Ellis, 42; Scheiber, 139; Bjork.
44. Buel, *Securing the Revolution*, 12; Whitehead; W. Taylor; Hawley; Regan; Marty.
45. Sorauf, 616-39; Cassinelli, 48-61; Schubert; Friedrich; Held.

torical and have had major, ongoing consequences. As the late David Potter observed:

the American tradition had placed strong taboos upon government activity in any area which could be occupied by private enterprise, and public property had been thrown open, as far as possible, to private use. The great ranchers had been permitted to graze their cattle on the open range of the public domain; the great mining companies had been permitted to stake their bonanza claims on government land at a minimum of expense. Even when the government wanted a transcontinental railroad badly enough to pay the costs of building it, it extended loans and gave gifts of public land to the privately owned Central Pacific and Union Pacific Railroads to enable them to pay the costs of construction.[46]

One of those consequences involves the oppressive sacredness of private property, a cherished shibboleth for which the State is expected to stand as watchdog. A second involves the obsessive tradition of economic individualism which has been responsible for so many of our enduring social problems.[47] And third is the genuine confusion about public policy that prompted Charles E. Wilson to remark that "what was good for our country was good for General Motors, and vice versa."[48]

American ambiguity about the proper relationship between public and private sectors may well be one of our most pervasive dilemmas, and we would do well, perhaps, to recall the words of James Madison in *Federalist* Number 10: "To secure the public good, and private rights,...and at the same time to preserve the spirit and form of popular government, is then the great object to which our inquiries are directed."

46. D. Potter, 57.
47. Lemon, xv, 227-28; Warner, x-xi, chs. 1-2.
48. Dyckman, 23-42.

A Three-fold American Revolution

ELISHA P. DOUGLASS

My initial concern in preparing this essay was the impact of the Revolution on the frontier, which during the Revolution might be thought of as a line drawn from the Adirondack Mountains in northern New York southwesterly to the crest of the Allegheny Mountains in western Pennsylvania and thence southward along the crest of the Appalachians to northern Georgia. From there the line bent southeasterly to approximately the mouth of the St. Mary's River in northern Florida. On studying the course of the war in this region I was struck by the fact that the struggle here was something quite different from that which took place in the more settled backcountry, and that both differed sharply from the course of the Revolution in the seaboard regions. It appeared to me that there were actually three separate and distinct revolutions taking place between 1765 and 1785. The first of these is the most familiar and supplies the relevant characteristics for most current interpretations. We might call it the "statehouse revolution" because it was carried on in the colonial capitols and their environs by the ruling groups who dominated the assemblies, provincial congresses, and committees which constituted the infrastructure of revolutionary organization. From 1765 to 1776 the issues of the statehouse revolution became almost exclusively political. What started out as a squabble over taxes eventuated in the formulation of basic principles and institutions of free government. The story of this process is by now a familiar one. Suffice it to say here that the concepts of constitutionalism, republicanism, reserved rights, and federalism which were to have worldwide influence were the heritage of the statehouse revolution.

The Revolution on the frontier took place in a quite different world. Here all of the political issues of such vital importance to the statehouse leaders were entirely irrelevant. The conflict was simply a naked struggle for the control of territory. The participants were settlers surging westward over the Appalachians in increasing numbers after the collapse of British authority in the colonies, Indians desperately defending their way of life, loyalist fur traders often acting as the military leaders of Indian war parties, and land speculators Tory and Whig who through large companies were making grandiose and conflicting claims to huge areas of the West.[1]

The settlers usually undertook their migrations in family groups. Sometimes they leased land from land companies or from speculators who had acquired hazy titles from Indian tribes; more often they merely squatted on promising tracts beside water transportation. Until 1775 they usually encountered no organized opposition because tribesmen had ceded millions of acres to the British government under the treaties of Fort Stanwix, Hard Labor, and Lochaber, all negotiated in the late 1760s.[2] In 1774 the First Continental Congress and the two British Indian superintendents—Guy Johnson for the northern tribes and John Stuart for the southern—attempted to keep the Indians neutral in the event of further hostilities breaking out in the East. Both sides were aware of the devastating consequences of a general uprising like Pontiac's Rebellion of the previous decade. But after Stuart fled to Florida and Johnson to Canada, the superintendents and Indian commissioners appointed by Congress in 1775 became increasingly convinced that their opponents were secretly forming military alliances with the Indians. The tribesmen themselves, alarmed at the inrush of settlers, doubtless regretted the concessions they had made in the land cession treaties. As a primitive people locked into a circle of economic relationships with Britain by the fur trade, they needed immense areas of unbroken forest merely to survive. The white settlers, who drove the fur-bearing animals and other game further westward, were therefore virtually threatening the Indians with extinction. Hence the uneasy peace of 1774 degenerated into particularly vicious guerilla warfare.

Fur traders, by virtue of their close economic connection with the Indians, became their natural allies. Even though the traders exploited the red men in notorious fashion, they provided the only market for the Indians' single product and were the only source of supply for the arms and ammunition, blankets, tools and hardware which by the time of the Revolution were indispensable for the Indian way of life. After 1776 nearly all of the important fur traders in western New York and western Pennsylvania made their way to Niagara or Detroit to join Tories and Indians preparing marauding expeditions against the agricultural frontier. All settlers there now

1. Various aspects of frontier history are treated by the following authors: Philbrick, Sosin, *Revolutionary Frontier*, Shy, Van Every, Abernethy and Volwiler.
2. Philbrick, 24, 32; Van Every, 9.

were fair game since they now presumably did not acknowledge the geographical limitations of settlement established by the British-appointed Indian superintendents in the treaties of Fort Stanwix, Hard Labor and Lochaber. So extensive were the defections of frontier leaders from the American cause that many of impeccable credentials came under suspicion of Toryism. George Croghan, the great land speculator and fur trader, was ordered to present himself for trial and Daniel Boone was court martialed on charges that he had attempted to deliver Boonesborough to the enemy. Croghan was released and Boone acquitted,[3] but the fact that their loyalty to the United States was questioned illustrates the pervasive nature of frontier Toryism.

In addition to settlers, Indians, and Indian traders, the large speculative land companies formed after 1763 played an important role in the frontier revolution. Although the Proclamation of 1763 temporarily forbad further settlement beyond the crest of the Appalachian chain, companies were formed in great profusion which proposed to build empires in the West. The companies were made up of two sets of partners, one located in frontier posts such as Fort Pitt and the other in colonial capitols and in London. The former located the areas to be exploited and purchased them from Indians. The latter then lobbied vigorously with the Board of Trade and the ministry to have the titles validated. The attitude of British officials toward the companies was ambivalent. Since the lobbyists were important men of affairs their importunities had to be taken seriously. Moreover, there was ample precedent for making large land grants if these could be justified by current mercantilist principles. From the very beginning of the colonies huge areas had been granted contingent upon the grantees establishing stipulated numbers of settlers on the land. But under the existing circumstances if settlers were funneled into the West in large enough numbers to justify grants of an extensive nature, trouble with the Indians like Pontiac's Rebellion would almost certainly follow and the fur trade would suffer proportionally. Moreover, the self-sufficient farmers who produced no staple crops and bought no British manufactures would in no way further the mercantilist purposes of the empire, and since they were far from any seat of authority they might intensify the already intractible behavior of the colonies. Therefore, the imposing imperial plans of such organizations as the Indiana Company, the Illinois Company, the Grand Ohio Company, and the Vandalia Company never reached fruition. The Vandalia project, which contemplated the creation of a fourteenth colony, came near to acceptance in 1773, but thereafter was quietly dropped because of the mounting controversy between Britain and the colonies.[4]

3. Volwiler, 326; Van Every, 172.
4. Abernethy, 45-56; Sosin, *Revolutionary Frontier*, 35; Philbrick, 43.

The plans of the land companies received a severe blow in 1774 when the government inaugurated a new land system whereby unsettled areas in the West were to be surveyed into tracts of from 100 to 1,000 acres and sold at auction to the highest bidder.[5] But because of the dissolution of British authority in the colonies during the following two years the plan was never put into effect. Actually the operations of the land companies entered a new phase when Richard Henderson, of Hillsborough, North Carolina, in 1775 bought a large tract of land in what is now east Tennessee and east Kentucky from Indians and proceeded to establish settlers on it without any sanction from London at all.[6]

With the coming of independence the land companies hedged their bets on the outcome of the Revolution by extending their lobbying activities to state legislatures and the Continental Congress as well as to British officialdom. By now, of course, the claims of the companies were hopelessly overlapped and the Indian "titles" almost worthless. It is understandable, therefore, that outside of the conduct of the war no question occasioned more bitter debate in Congress and state legislatures than the disposition of western land claims. George Rogers Clark's expedition into the Illinois country was in large measure a maneuver of Virginia land speculators, prominent among whom was Patrick Henry. The adoption of the Articles of Confederation was delayed four years from 1777 to 1781 by controversies between rival groups of land speculators.

The war in the West was carried on with a ferocity unequaled in any conflict in which Americans have participated. As in the recent Viet Nam war, the results of the savage fighting fell most heavily on non-combattants—often women and children. Tory partisans, leading their Indian bands, burned, pillaged, and massacred deep into the transappalachian West. Local rangers and militia retaliated in kind where they could. In an atmosphere in which both sides paid bounties for scalps the atrocity was the rule rather than the exception. For example, in 1782 Pennsylvania militia massacred and scalped 90 unarmed, peaceable Christian Indians in the frontier village of Gnadenhutten.[7] At first sight the wonder is that the American settlers stuck it out. During Pontiac's Rebellion most frontier families had fled eastward and the frontier bent back to the eastern slopes of the Appalachians, but during the Revolution, despite the terror, the westward flow of settlers actually increased. Probably the reason why the settlers stood their ground was that they were better armed than in 1763 and the neighborhood stockades in every settled locality usually proved able to withstand Indian attacks. None-

5. Abernethy, 100; Volwiler, 295.
6. Sosin, *Revolutionary Frontier*, 37-38, 163-64; Abernethy, 131; Philbrick, 89-90.
7. Van Every, 285-86.

theless, it was a hardy generation which year after year could live with the omnipresent possibility of sudden death in an Indian attack on the isolated frontier farms or famine and disease in insufferably crowded stockades.

The characteristics of the Revolution in the backcountry differed sharply from those of the statehouses and the region I have been describing. Like the frontier settlers, most of the farmers living between the Appalachians and the fall lines of the eastern rivers flowing into the Atlantic were simply not touched by the great issues of principle which dominated the struggle in eastern urban centers. One reason was that many of these farmers were recent German or Scottish immigrants who had arrived under the patronage of the British government and as yet lived in a kind of cultural isolation from the Anglo-American stock. But more important, the farmers who by long residence had lost any feeling of affinity for the old country had certain local grievances against the provincial ruling groups. In several colonies there were violent uprisings against established colonial authority between 1765 and 1772. These were all suppressed with considerable severity and produced varying degrees of resentment against the gentlemen who dominated the provincial assemblies. From 1774 onward Tory sentiment flourished in these backcountry areas to such an extent that the Revolution came to resemble a civil war.

Central New York provides a leading example of the backcountry disenchantment with the revolutionary impulse. In this area most of the land had been engrossed by leading families and was worked by tenant farmers. Smoldering resentment against landlords during the early 1760s finally resulted in the "Great Rebellion of 1766."[8] The immediate cause was the decision on the part of farmers on the great Philipse estate in Westchester County to accept from Indians, who claimed the land under treaty with the crown, leases with much more favorable terms than offered by the Philipse family. When the family responded with ejectment suits, the farmers took their case to the courts, which found against them. Now certain that they could get no justice by recourse to law, the farmers turned to violence. They were soon joined by tenants on other great manors, among them Livingston and Van Rensselaer. All demanded more liberal leases, and refused to pay further rent until they got them. Pitched battles took place with the sheriffs' deputies sent by the landlords to eject the clamorous tenant farmers.

The latter confidently expected support from the Whig leaders of New York City, who only a few months before had with great enthusiasm nullified the Stamp Act. But these leaders, some of whom were large landholders in upstate New York, did not view violence against vested property in the same light as the flouting of British imperial legislation. Dubbing the farmers

8. Mark, 131-164.

"levellers," the Liberty Boys joined forces with the great landowners and called loudly for royal troops to put down the insurrection. One observer commented caustically that the substantial Whigs of the city "are of the opinion that no one is entitled to riot but themselves."[9] The disturbances were eventually suppressed and a New York court, numbering among its judges the Whig leaders John Morin Scott and Robert R. Livingston, meted out severe sentences to ringleaders.

It is certainly more than coincidence that the Revolutionary cause found relatively few enthusiastic supporters in upstate New York. One observer wrote in 1775 that in Dutchess county, center of the "Rebellion of 1766," "are all Tories, only a few excepted." Only nine of the fourteen counties elected delegates to the Second Provincial Congress, and in these nine the delegates were chosen by gatherings so small that they could scarcely be called representative.[10] For example, it was charged that the delegates from Orange County, about 75 miles northwest of New York City, were chosen by only twenty of the county's some 1,000 qualified voters. Evidence of this sort leads the historian of New York, Alexander C. Flick, to conclude that "the rural districts of New York were indifferent or hostile" to the Revolutionary effort.[11] The reason for the farmers' attitude was not a continuing loyalty to Great Britain—after all, many of their landlords were Tories—but a conviction that the Whig gentlemen who had seized power in New York City would provide a government which might be even less equitable than government under the crown regardless of the vocabulary of freedom used so generously by the Whig leaders.

In North Carolina as well as New York occurred a violent pre-Revolutionary outbreak against established authority in the backcountry—the Regulator movement—and here also we find that the people of the area in which the rising took place were mostly apathetic or hostile to the Revolution. Widespread complaints were heard from farmers of backcountry Orange and Granville counties from 1766 to 1770 that courthouse officials were charging exorbitant fees and were engaged in a wide variety of other fraudulent practices that laid heavy financial burdens on the poor people of the neighborhood. When the governor and assembly took no remedial action, the farmers formed vigilante groups "to regulate abuses of power." Refusing to pay taxes until sheriffs gave an accounting of their tax collections, which the sheriffs could not do because they were deep in embezzlement, the "Regulators"—as the vigilantes called themselves—broke up the Orange County

9. Mark, 138.
10. Becker, *The History of Political Parties*, 229; B. Mason, 113-117, also, 64, 42-44, 86-88; Lynd, "Who should Rule at Home...," 336-337.
11. Flick, 24.

Court at Hillsborough in 1770 and tried the cases on the docket themselves. This action so alarmed Governor William Tryon that he called up militia from eastern counties and marched toward Hillsborough. Nearly all of the top brass in the governor's force became officers who fought with distinction in the Continental Line during the Revolution. The Regulators assembled a ragtag force and a battle of sorts took place at Alamance, Orange County, in 1771. Tryon had little trouble dispersing the insurgents. The leaders who did not escape were punished, six being hanged for treason. It now appeared that the Regulator Movement was dead.[12]

But by 1776 the Revolutionary leaders of North Carolina began to fear that they might have to face the Regulators on another field. At the urging of leading Whigs, Presbyterian ministers in Philadelphia sent letters to flocks in backcountry North Carolina explaining that in supporting the Provincial Congress they were doing the Lord's work. But these epistles apparently had little effect. Governor Josiah Martin, who had replaced Tryon, found resentment still seething in the backcountry, and wrote to Lord Hillsborough that the people of that region had been the victims of cruel provocation. In the spring of 1775 addresses of loyalty to the Crown carrying about 500 signatures were sent to the governor from Guilford, Rowan, Surry, and Anson counties. Nineteen inhabitants of Dobbs begged the governor "to open our eyes aright so that we may not be deceived by every voice of cunning, crafty men." In 1776 the governor claimed that he could raise a Tory force of 4,000 in the colony.[13]

During the war the backcountry was in a state of anarchy much of the time. Although Toryism was strong, indifference was the attitude exhibited by most farmers. Again, though more former Regulator leaders joined the Whigs than the Tories, still Cornwallis considered the disposition of backcountry North Carolina so favorable to his cause that he set up his standard at Charlotte in 1780 and invited the local inhabitants to join him. But the Tory leaders were no match for their Whig counterparts. A sizable Tory force was dispersed on its way to join Cornwallis and he himself retired into South Carolina when news of the Battle of King's Mountain arrived. In the next year a roving Tory band captured Governor Thomas Burke at Hillsborough, and the backcountry lapsed again into an anarchy which outlasted the war by years.[14]

In the backcountry of South Carolina sentiment was even more suspicious of the Whig leadership than in North Carolina, not because of oppression, but because of a pervasive feeling of alienation from a center of power indifferent to any except tidewater interests. Although immigrants flooded into

12. Douglass, *Rebels and Democrats*, 71-101.
13. Douglass, *Rebels and Democrats*, 103-107, 108-110.
14. Lefler and Newsome, 178, 215-216, 232-235; DeMond.

the backcountry from the North during the 1760s, by 1770 it contained only three of the colony's twenty-two parishes, on which representation was based, and had no county courts.[15] Bandits had roamed the country at will from 1765 to 1768, and these were finally put down not by militia from the eastern parishes but by local vigilante groups which took the same name as the North Carolina groups formed for an entirely different purpose—Regulators.[16] The indifference of the Charleston government to the plight of the backcountry promoted the drafting of a petition to the Commons House written in 1767 by the eloquent and contentious missionary from the Society for the Propagation of the Gospel, Charles Woodmason, demanding a series of reforms, the most important of which were the establishment of county courts and schools, and the granting of representation.[17] Serious consideration was given to a march on Charleston to dramatize the settlers' plight. Woodmason in a newspaper article also called attention to the inconsistency of the Commons House in protesting against British taxation of the colonies without representation at the same time that the members denied representation to the backcountry farmers.[18]

Although the Commons House did take note of the crime wave by commissioning the Regulators into companies of Rangers and passed an act creating a circuit court in 1768, it paid little further attention to the backcountry. Probably many members agreed with the planter who wrote of the farmers, "They are strangers to our interests, our customs, and our concerns."[19]

This statement reflected a sharp contrast between the economic conditions of tidewater and backcountry South Carolina. Charleston at this time was the leading center of wealth in the colonies, primarily because of its production of rice. But since rice could be grown only in a relatively small area watered by tidal estuaries and required large infusions of capital for the building of dikes and water gates and the purchase of slaves, rice culture was centripetal in nature and for expansion absorbed most of the surplus funds of the planters. Therefore, from the economic point of view, the backcountry was for the planters a useless land which offered them no economic advantage. This fact alone could in large measure account for the indifference of the planters to the welfare of the region.

Since such an attitude could be expected to promote reciprocal feelings, it is understandable that there was little enthusiasm in the backcountry for the Revolutionary agitation of the Charleston Whigs in 1774 and 1775. But

15. Barnwell, 3.
16. R. M. Brown, *The South Carolina Regulators*.
17. R. M. Brown, *The South Carolina Regulators*, 42-43.
18. Woodmason, 260-264.
19. P. Davidson, 2.

the Charleston Council of Safety, belatedly concerned in 1775 because of a potential threat in the rear, sent William Henry Drayton and the Presbyterian minister William Tennent on a trip through the backcountry to explain and justify the Whig cause. Although the two made some converts, they found that between the Broad and Saluda rivers the farmers and planters had pronounced Tory leanings and that throughout the backcountry most people believed that "no man from Charleston can speak the truth, and that all the papers are full of lies."[20] Indeed, in the opinion of Edward McCrady, the historian of South Carolina and a former Confederate general, until 1781 "a majority of the people of the state" were opposed to independence.[21]

The fall of Charleston to the British in 1780 inaugurated a bloody period of civil war far worse than that in North Carolina. Although the British re-established royal government in Charleston and controlled the country as far northwest as Ninety-Six, after the Battle of King's Mountain their forces slowly retired to Charleston and the backcountry reverted to anarchy. Bands of Tory partisans and patriot contingents under such leaders as Sumter and Pickens supported themselves by plunder, and atrocities against prisoners and non-combatants were as common as on the frontier. As in North Carolina, order was not restored until years after the signing of the Treaty of Paris.

If economic considerations can account for the sectional hostility between tidewater and backcountry South Carolina, the same can explain in large measure the strong unity of purpose and interest which characterized the tidewater planters of Virginia and the farmers and leading men of the Valley of Virginia, which was locked behind the first range of the Blue Ridge Mountains. While the rice economy of South Carolina was burgeoning between 1765 and 1775, the tobacco economy of Virginia experienced a deepening depression because of low prices, declining yields, and soil exhaustion. Hence the leading tidewater planters during these years became vitally interested in western expansion and diversification.[22] Virginians were in the forefront of all the great western land speculation schemes of the period and younger sons of leading families carved out plantations for themselves in the most promising of the western regions, the Valley of Virginia. Since the settlers there needed the constant support of the provincial government against Indians, ties of interest as well as family united the leading men of the region with the tidewater leaders. By 1778 seven counties had been established in the Valley,[23] in contrast to the three parishes for the whole of backcountry South Carolina. Under the circumstances the statement by Freeman H. Hart,

20. Hooker, ed., 189; see also David Ramsay, *History of the Revolution of South Carolina*, I, 68; Barnwell, 135-136.
21. McCrady, 479.
22. Douglass, *Coming of Age*, 17-18.
23. Hart, 6.

historian of the Valley, is quite understandable: "No frontier area of colonial America surpassed the Valley in its zeal for the Revolutionary movement."[24]

In Vermont we see still another variation of the backcountry revolution, and one which had no reflection in the course of events in the thirteen states. Here the settlers' main purpose in the war was to validate land titles and the leaders' objective was to bring speculative land schemes to a successful conclusion. During the eighteenth century, because of an inconsistency in charter terms, the land lying west of the Connecticut River and east of Lake Champlain was in dispute between New Hampshire and New York. Nevertheless, from 1749 to 1764 the New Hampshire governor, Benning Wentworth, granted some three million acres in the region, some to bona fide settlers and some to speculative partnerships.[25] Of course the governor and council of New York denied the validity of these titles and made other grants in the same area to New York settlers and speculators. Occasional conflict broke out between Yankees and Yorkers with overlapping claims, but by the outbreak of the Revolution the New Hampshire grantees were in a majority and had a strong and militant leadership in two of the Allen brothers, Ethan and Ira, and a group of their associates in land speculation. The great majority of Vermonters, as they now called themselves, took the Whig side, apparently because they were afraid that the crown would confirm the Yorkers' land claims and invalidate their own. The ministry had given some indication of leaning in this direction, and certainly Lt. Gov. Cadwallader Colden and the New York landed families had much more influence at Whitehall than the farmers and speculators in possession of the New Hampshire grants.

In 1777 the Vermont leaders called a convention which declared independence from Britain and wrote a strongly democratic constitution modeled on that of Pennsylvania. At the same time they brought pressure to bear on Congress to recognize Vermont as a state and thereby, of course, allow the Vermont legislature to validate the New Hampshire titles and invalidate those granted by New York. Congress refused recognition, not wishing to offend the powerful state of New York now in such a parlous condition because of the strong Tory movement there. No doubt Congress also hesitated to take an action which might be used as a precedent for justifying the secession of dissident elements from other states.

Sir Henry Clinton, commanding British troops in New York, saw an opportunity to utilize the conflict between Vermont and New York to British advantage. Through intermediaries he made an offer to Ethan Allen that if Vermont would consent to be annexed to Canada, the crown would grant the state provincial status like that formerly held by Connecticut, saving only

24. Hart, 83.
25. Williamson, *Vermont in a Quandary,* 7; Jellison, 19-20.

that the crown would appoint a royal governor.[26] The fire-breathing conqueror of Ticonderoga "in the name of the almighty God and the Continental Congress" was immediately interested. He, his brothers, and associates powerful in the Vermont government had extensive landholdings in the northern part of the region. Acceptance of Clinton's offer would secure the holdings there from the threatening grasp of New York and assure the clique positions of great influence in a new provincial government as well.

Beginning in 1778 secret negotiations for the surrender of Vermont went forward, often under the guise of conferences for the exchange of military prisoners. The result was the formation at Montreal of a British expedition in 1781 designed to liberate Vermont from the United States. According to the plan, while the troops were en route southward, the Allens, by means never made specific, would somehow swing the state assembly to the support of the British proposal. But the scheme misfired. Although the expedition got off to an auspicious start, unexpected opposition developed in Vermont as details of the plan leaked out. News of Cornwallis's surrender at Yorktown sent the British scurrying back to Montreal. Yet Ethan Allen would not accept defeat, and a year later wrote to General Frederick Haldimand, commander of the British forces in Canada, "I shall do anything in my power to render this state a British province."[27] The conspiracy died in 1783, of course, when by the terms of the Treaty of Paris Vermont was included within the boundaries of the United States.

One further example of the backcountry revolution deserves mention, because it revolved about still others of the variegated issues which troubled the farmers of that vast area.

In the years leading up to the separation from Britain, backcountry farmers in Massachusetts had many of the same grievances against the provincial government as did the piedmont farmers of North and South Carolina against the regimes of these colonies. Probably the most notable of these shared complaints were against the inefficient, expensive, and sometimes arbitrary action of the court system.[28] But the backcountry people of Massachusetts had a higher degree of political maturity than those of the south, stemming in part from a tradition of local self-government and reserved rights granted under the charters of 1628 and 1691. During the years 1765 to 1774 the backcountry towns of Berkshire and Hampshire Counties tended to stay aloof from the mounting agitation churned up by the Boston Committee of Correspondence, usually ignoring its voluminous communications and sometimes tartly contesting them. But the closing of the port of Boston and the

26. Jellison, 280.
27. Jellison, 285.
28. R. Taylor, 27-33; see also R. D. Brown, *Revolutionary Politics in Massachusetts*, 8.

other Intolerable Acts brought these towns into a strong and unified front with Boston and the eastern towns. The theoretical core of the Massachusetts case was the conviction that the Charter of 1691 was a compact above and beyond the power of Parliament to alter or abrogate. Berkshire and Hampshire towns joined in suppressing British authority in 1774, but in the next year, when the Provincial Congress "resumed" the Charter of 1691 and nominated a council to perform the executive duties of a governor, a sharp rift developed between the General Court and the backcountry towns. The immediate issue was the attempt of the legislature to re-establish the much disliked court system. Throughout Berkshire County the courts were prevented from sitting during the period of government under the resumed charter.[29]

In justifying their action the towns turned against the General Court the same constitutional theory the Court had used against Parliament. If legitimate government could operate only under compact freely agreed to by the rulers and the ruled, then the Court had no more authority in Massachusetts than Parliament. To some extent, this argument was a pretext to give color of legality to a refusal to allow the collection of debts, but nevertheless the deductions from compact theory were sound and indicate a considerable degree of political sophistication entirely lacking in the southern backcountry. Furthermore, the position of the Berkshire towns contributed to the development of constitutional theory and to the state Constitution adopted in 1780. Although originally agreeable to allowing the General Court to draft a constitution for submission to the towns for ratification, by 1779 most of the towns in Berkshire County insisted that a legally binding constitution could only be drafted by a convention chosen for the purpose. The Constitutional Convention which met in that year was the embodiment of this logic and established the precedent for the drafting of fundamental law which is basic to American practice today.[30]

But if the General Court bowed to the logic of the Berkshire towns in constitutional matters, it and its successor legislatures did nothing to rectify specific backcountry grievances. Quite the contrary, it exacerbated them in the years leading up to 1786, and Shay's Rebellion was the result.[31]

The pattern of backcountry revolution in Massachusetts varied considerably from the pattern in the middle and southern colonies. While the farmers in these latter areas tended toward indifference or support of the Tories, the backcountry farmers of Massachusetts supported the war effort as strongly as those in the East. But then, somewhat paradoxically, backcountry protest against grievances took a much stronger form than elsewhere and finally

29. R. Taylor, 76.
30. R. Taylor, 75-103; Douglass, *Rebels and Democrats*, 187-188, 211.
31. R. Taylor, 128-132.

resulted in violent rebellion against the very constitutional regime which the Berkshire farmers had played such an important part in establishing. But the paradox is more apparent than real. The movement for a constitution drafted by a convention stemmed from a desire to limit the political power of Boston and other large eastern towns, and when it signally failed to achieve this result, rebellion appeared the desperate measure of last resort as protection against courts and taxes.

In their outcome the statehouse, frontier, and backcountry revolutions differed as sharply with each other as in their inherent characteristics. The statehouse revolution was of course decisive, and the principles which it vindicated have become the cornerstone of our political institutions. But the outcome of the other two revolutions came long after the peace treaty was signed in 1783. The frontier war reached its peak of intensity after Yorktown and the bloody raids and atrocities only gradually petered out in 1784. A lasting peace did not come until the vindication of the national domain by the Jay Treaty and the Battle of Fallen Timbers in 1794 and the Pinckney Treaty of 1795. Until the mid-eighties the land companies continued their efforts to get recognition of their claims by Congress even though most of these lay in the area north of the Ohio River ceded by Virginia to Congress in 1781 with the express condition that all titles derived from Indians be canceled. None of the companies formed before the Revolution succeeded in validating its claims, but not because public authority anywhere condemned land monopoly. The companies were simply shoved aside by newer organizations with more political muscle. The Ohio Company of Associates and the Scioto Company, formed in 1786, fell heir to much of the territory claimed by the older companies, and the imperial dreams of privileged land speculation reached fulfillment in the notorious Yazoo scandal of 1789-1810.[32] After 1800 the form of land speculation changed, but not the substance. In that year Congress paid the British ministry the compliment of adopting the auction system for the disposal of public lands which the ministry had attempted to inaugurate in 1774. Henceforth no direct grants were made by legislatures to individuals or companies, and the little man was able to get into the game of speculation along with the moneyed corporations. Seen in perspective, the careers of the land companies were usually unprofitable and they did little if anything to speed the pace of settlement.

The effects of the backcountry war lingered even longer than that of frontier war. The claims of New York to Vermont territory were not extinguished until the latter state was received into the union in 1791. In North and South Carolina the state constitutions to some degree satisfied backcountry complaints, but the constitution of South Carolina, because of a

32. Douglass, *Coming of Age*, 64-70.

steep scale of property qualifications for voting and officeholding, limited participation in government only to the well-to-do and the wealthy.[33] In this state also the almost unparalleled savagery of the war left a heritage of violence which can be detected up until the Civil War. In both states unfulfilled efforts of the backcountry to obtain its fair share of representation in the legislature contributed to an east-west sectionalism which survived into the twentieth century.

Only in the special case of Pennsylvania do we find an instance of backcountry war which was decisively won. In this case the grievance antagonizing western farmers prior to the Revolution was the failure of the Quaker-dominated assembly to provide adequate protection for the Allegheny frontier during the French and Indian War and Pontiac's Rebellion. Resentment rose to such a point that in 1763 a group of farmers in backcountry Paxton township murdered an entire settlement of Christianized Indians and then marched on Philadelphia to place demands for certain reforms before the assembly, chief among which was the apportionment of more representatives to the western counties. Upon reaching the outskirts of Philadelphia the march broke up without violence, partially because of the intervention of Benjamin Franklin, and the assembly grudgingly, and only partially, yielded to the Paxton Boys' demands. In the succeeding years resentment seemed to simmer down, and leadership in the agitation against Britain beginning in 1774 was taken by men from the same merchant and professional groups which provided leaders in other colonies. But in 1776 the men of affairs in Philadelphia and its environs lost control of the Revolutionary movement, a situation which happened in no other state. A provincial conference made up of radicals with heavy western representation called a constitutional convention in which the eastern counties were relatively as underrepresented as the western counties had been before the war. The Convention wrote a truly democratic constitution—along with that of Vermont one of the two of the Revolutionary period, carried on the administration of government, and solidified a whole new group of leaders in power. It is understandable then that the people of western Pennsylvania reacted entirely differently to the Revolution than the people of western North and South Carolina. The western Pennsylvanians, confident of support from a state government which was perhaps more responsive to their needs than to the needs of the eastern counties, rallied enthusiastically to the Revolutionary cause.[34]

Revolutions, when viewed in the terms presented by their leaders, have a deceptive simplicity and unity. It is only as they progress that it becomes

33. Thorpe, VII, 3248-3257.
34. Douglass, *Rebels and Democrats*, 240-263.

apparent that what are ends for one group are only means for others, and that internal conflicts are only temporarily shelved in pursuit of a common objective. As time goes on, these internal conflicts become more clearly revealed, and revolutions acquire the complexity inherent in the normal course of politics. This course can be clearly seen in the French and Russian Revolutions but is not so apparent in our own because historians, probably rightly, have given most of their attention to the statehouse revolution and the warfare carried on by armies in the eastern states. In terms of consequences this aspect of the Revolution is the most important, but a more complete understanding of the Revolution requires attention to its many complexities and paradoxes in the backcountry and on the frontier.

Attitudes Toward Violence in the Pre-war Period

JOHN HOWE

The decade of the 1960s is gone, but it has left its mark on American historical studies. A growing interest in techniques of quantification, exhortations to tie historical inquiry directly to social science theory, attempts to portray the historical experience of the inarticulate—these will certainly be among the decade's lasting contributions. Renewed interest in the study of violence as part of the American past might well be added to the list.

In some ways this interest in patterns of historical violence represents a return to earlier themes of historical explanation. For after all, conflict formed the central motif of Progressive historiography.[1] And yet the violence studies of the 1960s differed notably from their predecessors. For the Progressives, struggles between opposing socio-economic interests, whether or not leading to violent encounter, provided the focus for historical study. For scholars of the 1960s, however, episodes of violence became themselves the object of analysis. Moreover, acts of physical violence came usually to be described not in terms of class struggle, but as expressions of broad cultural values. "Violence," declared Rap Brown in one of the decade's more memorable aphorisms, "is as American as cherry pie." Brown's historian contemporaries, in less clever though more elaborate terms, concluded much the same thing.

A wide range of explanations has been offered for America's violent modes of behavior. Some have cited the harsh effects of frontier life, with its emphasis on gun-toting, rugged individualism. Others have pointed to the absence of stabilizing social institutions such as an established church or aristocratic

1. See, for example, Beard, *An Economic Interpretation of the Constitution*; Becker, *The History of Political Parties in the Province of New York.*

upper class, or have seen in the stresses generated by rapid social change, particularly in the nineteenth century, triggers of violent behavior. Still others have, ironically, discovered explanations in America's democratic faith with its nervous emphasis on internal conformity and its "paranoid" stance toward suspected enemies both within and without. And finally, we have been told that much of America's violent past can best be explained in terms of "vigilance" movements, attempts by private citizens to establish conditions of "law and order" where governmental agencies were incapable of meeting the need.[2]

Each of these propositions has a certain explanatory force, and each has been applied in general terms to eighteenth century America, often to considerable profit. Professor Pauline Maier, for example, has told us a great deal about patterns of eighteenth century violence by arguing that the limited problem-solving powers of colonial governments prompted individuals to act on their own, and that dominant ideological assumptions about the dangers of governmental power and the importance of citizen vigilance in defending their liberties gave legitimacy to the notion of the people taking the law into their own hands.[3] Gordon Wood and Bernard Bailyn, by playing off the American experience against patterns of European crowd violence as described by George Rudé, have added further dimensions to our understanding of America's eighteenth century situation.[4] And Jesse Lemisch, in a more direct attempt to examine the often aggressive behavior of the inarticulate, has explained how colonial seamen rioted to protect themselves against the arbitrary acts of British press gangs.[5]

Inevitably, of course, there is more to be said about the matter. (Indeed upon the general truth of that statement rests the logic of this conference and the entire future of the historical profession!) I should like then to suggest a few of my own thoughts about the problem, especially as it relates to the several decades immediately preceding American independence.

To begin with, I should like to propose that the experience of crowd violence was in many ways less traumatic for eighteenth century Americans than it would later be for their descendants. Certainly the colonists theorized less about it than do we. I have, for example, been able to discover no colonists extolling the moral virtues of violent confrontation or philosophizing about the purifying effects of confrontation. One does find members of the Revolutionary generation talking about being molded in "the furnace of af-

---

2. Frantz; Elkins; Richards; Davis; R. M. Brown, "The American Vigilante Tradition."
3. Maier, "Popular Uprisings and Civil Authority..."
4. Wood, "A Note on Mobs in the American Revolution"; Bailyn, *Pamphlets*, 581-584.
5. Lemisch.

fliction." And certainly the Adamses, the Jeffersons, and the Washingtons believed that they carried out of their revolutionary trials a special understanding of America's republican faith. But these things were typically said
in reference to the overall struggles of independence and nation-building, not
to episodes of violence per se. They represented more a Calvinist appreciation
of trial and purification than a Maoist glorification of force.

During the troubles with England, acts of crowd violence were discussed
almost entirely in tactical terms; for example, as they might stiffen British
determination or threaten the unity of colonial forces. When violence did
occur, of course, it proved powerfully upsetting to the people who were its
objects. Even a cursory reading of Loyalist writings makes this clear. And
one can find individuals such as John Adams angrily denouncing the appearance of what he called "private mobs," outbursts in which people took advantage of the general turmoil to settle personal scores. But even Adams gave
enthusiastic endorsement to the use of force for achieving necessary public
ends. The initial Stamp Act protests of 1765, he declared "an honorable
and glorious action, not a riot." Crown officials had "everywhere trembled,
and all their little Tools and Creatures, been afraid to speak and ashamed to
be seen." And the destruction of the tea in Boston harbor nearly a decade
later he thought "the grandest event" since the controversy with England
had begun.[6]

There are, I think, a number of reasons why the experience of crowd violence carried less emotive impact then than it would later on. Perhaps most
importantly, colonial Americans were not inclined to extract from individual
acts, violent though their consequences might be, general statements about
the health and stability of society as a whole. If one examines the Regulator
movement in the Carolina backcountry around 1770, for example, one looks
in vain either for the rhetoric of social revolution or for expressions of
anxiety that this might be threatened. To be sure, the Regulators did question the monopolization of political power by the eastern, coastal, planter-
dominated counties. And yet Regulator writings consist of little more than
specific complaints about problems that were not being met—the high cost of
legal fees, the lack of adequate protection against Indian raids, the need for
roads and new county governments.[7] In similar fashion, the Massachusetts
and New York farmers pressing their claims against the large Hudson valley
landed proprietors during the 1760s, encased their arguments in very little
theoretical trapping. Their demands were quite tangible: access to land that
they felt the Livingstons and other powerful families were monopolizing.
Nor did the proprietors perceive in these challenges, some of them involving

6. John Adams, *Works*, IV, 74-75; IX, 333.
7. Powell; Woodmason; R. M. Brown, *The South Carolina Regulators*.

armed skirmishing, generalized threats to their privileged way of life. Their concern was also immediate and direct: the prospect of having taken from them land that they claimed as rightfully their own.[8]

In short, eighteenth century Americans, whether at the top or the bottom of the social hierarchy, did not operate out of clear ideological systems capable of giving general significance to specific episodes of social or economic conflict. Lacking was any broadly held theoretical alternative to the dominant model of a deferential and modestly hierarchical social order. The prevailing ethos emphasized social harmony, corporateness, and continuity over time; not differentiation, conflict or change. Individuals might be fair or unfair, ruly or unruly, domineering or responsive; but the social system as a whole was not seen as open to serious challenge.[9] Within the next hundred years much of this would change—in response to the American and even more to the French Revolution, and to the great transformations wrought by industrialization. But all of this lay in the future. In pre-Revolutionary America, individual episodes of crowd violence most often seemed locally troublesome but without broader import.

Secondly, I should like to propose that episodes of crowd violence occurred as frequently as they did because colonial Americans often found it necessary to go beyond established legal and constitutional procedures—what I would designate as "indirect" modes of action—to more immediate, forceful, "direct" strategies of political behavior, strategies which often generated violent results. This may appear simply a truism; that physical violence is more likely to occur when people strike out directly to achieve their ends than when they operate through indirect legislative or administrative channels. And yet the compelling historical fact is that eighteenth century Americans resorted to direct, often violent forms of action with considerable frequency. The New York land riots and the Regulator movement were but the most dramatic of countless episodes that dotted the mid-century decades.[10] The question is why so many of them occurred?

Professor Maier has suggested elsewhere that this pattern of behavior represented attempts to extend the authority of the colonial regimes, for purposes of meeting some pressing public need, into situations where it ordinarily did not reach. Thus she cites the appearance of mobs bent upon the destruction of houses of prostitution, or the levelling of a barn that stood in the path of a proposed road, or the protection of a town from contamina-

8. See Bonomi; Mark; related documents may be found in O'Callaghan, *Documentary History of New York.*

9. For helpful analysis of eighteenth century social and political thought see Buel, "Democracy and the American Revolution..."; Kirby; Sydnor; Zuckerman, *Peaceable Kingdoms.*

10. W. A. Smith.

tion by a nearby smallpox asylum, as occurred in Marblehead, Massachusetts. Where government proved unwilling or unable to act, the people took the situation into their own hands.[11] Many of these incidents make good sense in precisely these terms.

Yet the question remains: why did the provincial regimes so frequently fail to function and why did these kinds of direct action become necessary? In part, the explanation lies in the limits placed upon the provincial assemblies by the imperial tie. Colonial laws were subject to royal disallowance and always had to mesh with the broader demands of imperial policy. In important ways this reality put restraints on what the colonial legislatures could and did attempt to do.

A fuller explanation, however, is I think to be found in the less than satisfactory ways in which the colonial *political systems* performed the essential task of translating social demands into official, governmental action. This, of course, is primarily what political systems are expected to do. In pre-Revolutionary America, they seem not to have done this job very well.

This is no place to launch an extended discussion of late colonial politics— a large and growing literature, increased by several papers presented at this conference, has grown up around the topic. But I should like to say just a few things about the colonial political systems that may help to understand why Anglo-Americans so often found it necessary to operate outside of them. For one thing, in colonial America there were no political parties in the modern sense of the term, no institutional structures capable of aggregating interest pressures, focusing public attention upon elections, organizing legislative majorities, and in other ways mediating between social needs and the governing process. Some of the colonial assemblies had, by mid-century, developed sophisticated legislative machinery—committee structures, leadership positions, and so forth. But in the absence of political parties, there were only informal and highly imperfect mechanisms for initiating legislative action from the outside, or focusing public attention on and involving people actively and consistently in the political/governmental process. For most colonials most of the time, provincial politics seemed at a distance and not terribly relevant.[12] Nor was there as yet any informed structure of special interest groups that might have served some of the same functions by generating lobbying pressures on the assemblies. Economic development and social differentiation had simply not yet carried far enough to generate the kinds of sharp interest alignments that we, or even 19th century Americans would come to know.

11. Maier, "Popular Uprisings and Civil Authority...", 4 ff.
12. See, for example, Bailyn, *The Origins of American Politics*; Katz; J. Greene, *Quest for Power*; Zemsky.

In addition, neither in its value system nor its leadership arrangement did colonial politics provide for the intimate flow of information and responsibility between constituents and representatives. This was not the politics of democracy but the politics of deference, in which the better sort of people did and were expected to occupy positions of leadership in the assemblies, and the broader society, except in unusual situations, concurred. The working assumption was one of distance rather than intimacy in the relationship between representative and constituents, and the flow of influence moved characteristically from the leadership elite down, rather than vice versa.[13]

Finally, there is evidence that in the decades leading through mid-century, the community of notables that dominated leadership positions was becoming more exclusive, more continuous in its makeup, and thus less sensitive to the changing circumstances of colonial society. Certainly this is suggested by the membership patterns of the colonial assemblies, where right up to the turmoil of 1775 and 1776 a steady decrease in the appearance of new men took place. To be sure, assembly men remained dependent upon election for their seats, and there are more than a few instances of people being turned out of office against their wishes. But in the normal course of things, their tenure was becoming more rather than less secure, adding further to the separation between large segments of the society and their political leaders.[14]

The consequence of all this was that colonial politics was not arranged in ways designed to tie society and government closely together. As representatives of local towns and counties, assemblymen had to take the needs of their constituents into account. Yet the evidence suggests that legislative behavior reflected the wishes of the leadership notables more than the needs of the broader society.

The importance of this point is given emphasis when one realizes that these years witnessed an increasing tempo of social and economic change—note the religious and social upheavals of the Great Awakening, the rapid growth of population and its pressure on available land in older, settled areas, the economic instabilities generated by the continuing Anglo-French wars, and the impact of rapid commercial development within the British empire.[15] All of these developments generated an increasingly complex

13. In addition to items cited in note 9 above, see also Pole.
14. Main, "Government by the People." My own as yet unpublished research on legislative officeholding in Massachusetts during the last half of the eighteenth century indicates much the same thing. For instance, during the 1750s the appearance of "new men" in the General Court (that is, men who had never sat before) averaged out at about 22%. During the 1760s, the average annual rate had dropped to 17%.
15. For basic studies of these very broad problems see Bushman, *From Puritan to Yankee*; Egnal and Ernst; Lemon; Greven; J. Potter; Gaustad.

array of social needs, many of which the political system failed to handle. Thus the practice developed of going outside established political and governmental procedures to more immediate, forceful methods of problem-solving.

Direct action, thus, was a constant in colonial political life. It came quickly to be a basic part of the colonial protest movement against England as well. And, I would suggest, for a similar reason—because existing imperial institutions proved incapable of meeting important colonial needs. Feeling that their interests could not be protected by the formal political and constitutional arrangements of the empire, the American colonists resorted to such extralegal and ultimately illegal strategies as non-importation, crowd action, and finally military force and revolution. And once again it was in connection with these strategies that episodes of physical violence occurred.

Recent analyses of the late colonial and Revolutionary eras have emphasized the ways in which England's North American colonies, whether in their economic, cultural, or political affairs, were around mid-century becoming more intimately connected with England and more clearly subject to imperial developments and influences.[16] In part this reflected colonial initiative, provincial emulation of metropolitan ways of life. One finds, for example, attempts by the colonial merchant and planter elite to become more like London barristers or English landed gentry. Thus they imported English apparel and furnishings, read English books, and where possible sent their sons to the mother country for polish and training. In the process, they were asserting their own importance before their fellow colonists and were finding ways of solidifying their local leadership positions.

But the process of colonial absorption in webs of imperial connection also involved changes within England and the broader empire. Throughout much of the 18th century, English officials had talked about the need to establish their control more firmly over the colonies. The continuing series of imperial struggles with France pointed up this necessity and the massively expanded debt and vastly increased empire left by the Seven Years' War in 1763 made the need for imperial reorganization more pressing than ever before. It was, of course, the attempts at imperial reorganization, beginning about 1765, that precipitated the revolutionary crisis. In addition, the rapid expansion of England's commercial economy during these same 18th century years created increased demands for colonial raw materials and pressures for the colonial absorption of English manufactured goods—in the process making the colonial economy unusually vulnerable to needs felt and decisions taken in England.[17]

16. Murrin, "Anglicization of an American Colony"; J. Greene, "Search for Identity"; J. Greene, "Political Mimesis"; Kammen, *People of Paradox.*
17. See Kammen, *Empire and Interest*; Egnal and Ernst; also Lynd's essay in the present volume.

Beyond this, historians, among them Professor Michael Kammen, have recently begun to use the term "Anglo-American" politics to argue that colonial political behavior in the 18th century can be understood only in the context of a wider political system stretching from Boston and Philadelphia and Williamsburg directly to London.[18] Ultimate authority, we are reminded, lay not with the colonial assemblies or even the royal governors, but with Parliament, the King, and his ministers in London. Thus colonial laws were subject to royal veto if they conflicted with imperial policy, and Parliamentary statutes were applied to Englishmen living in North America as well as at home.

All of this meant, of course, that colonial politics was deeply affected by who was in power and what was decided in England. And Anglo-American politicians in the colonies had to take this carefully into account as they plotted their own local strategies of action and determined how they could effectively protect colonial interests in Whitehall and Westminster, where the most important decisions were made.

By mid-century, then, the American colonists had come to feel, and with good reason, that they were being absorbed into broad patterns of economic, political, and cultural life over which they had little control; that they were losing initiative in their own affairs. Many of them confronted this prospect with genuine uneasiness, especially the colonial elites with their expanding sense of self-importance. Connections with England they valued highly, but only when they could define them on their own terms.

In many ways, the sense of uneasiness remained vague and unspecified; for example, colonists were attracted by the sophistication and splendor of metropolitan England, yet harbored a provincial suspicion of its refinements and a fear of colonial "corruption" from too intimate a connection.[19] The consequences of close colonial involvement in the empire, however, were more tangible than this. There was the concern of Virginia planters at the growing control of Scots middlemen over the colonial tobacco trade; the general mutterings about British troops inserted into the colonies during the Seven Years' War with France and left to stay after the war was over; and what the colonists perceived as continuing English pressure to establish an Anglican bishopric in North America. In addition, there was the series of Parliamentary statutes and administrative decisions beginning about 1760 that touched directly upon colonial rights and practices: the issuance of general writs of assistance in 1761 that opened colonial domiciles to easy and unregulated search by royal officials, the Proclamation Line of 1763 forbidding

18. Kammen, *Rope of Sand*; see also essays in Olson and Brown, eds.
19. This kind of ambivalence is illustrated in Colbourn, ed., "A Pennsylvania Farmer at the Court of King George."

white settlement west of the Appalachian crest, the Stamp Act of 1765 designed to raise revenue rather than regulate trade of the empire, and so forth.

All of these circumstances posed difficulties for the colonists when, around 1765, they were confronted with the task of trying to defend their interests within the imperial system. Throughout the deepening imperial crisis they used the familiar machinery that was available to them: lobbying through their colonial agents and other connections in England for the repeal of undesirable measures and petitioning the Parliament, the King and even the English people for greater sensitivity to colonial liberties. In certain instances these measures had effect. But several hard lessons were brought home very quickly: that colonial interests often did not jibe with those of England, that the colonies were subordinate parts of the empire and must give way where conflicts of interest arose, and ultimately that they were subject to official decisions over which they had virtually no control.[20] As a result, the colonists were persuaded to seek out other, more direct means of protecting themselves against the tightening embrace of the empire, means that might be more effective and that in any case offered the colonists a greater sense of control over their own affairs.

The usefulness of colonial direct action was born out quickly in the Stamp Act crisis of 1765. Both formally and informally, by direct petition to the King and Parliament as well as by personal contacts, the colonial assemblies had made known their opposition to the proposed measure, but to no avail for it became law in March of 1765.

The American reply was immediate, all of the colonies reacting with anger and determination. One strategy was to continue petitioning through established, indirect channels. Thus both individual assemblies and the Stamp Act Congress forwarded memorials of protest and appeal. At the same time, however, more forceful, direct plans were devised. One of the most important of these involved the use of non-importation agreements, according to which colonial merchants ceased importing English goods until the Stamp Act was repealed. By threatening to cut off one major segment of England's imperial trade, the colonists hoped to create pressures for a change in British policy.

Non-importation, however, had as its object the long term goal of repeal. Something was needed in the meantime to prevent implementation of the tax. The solution was another kind of direct action, crowd confrontation of stamp agents and distributors to persuade them to resign their positions. It was primarily around these episodes that patterns of violence developed, patterns that depended for their precise shape upon a number of variables, most of which were not subject to close control: the stubbornness of stamp

20. See Kammen, *Rope of Sand*; Sosin, *Agents and Merchants*; Ritcheson.

agents, the extent to which preexisting personal and political animosities lent emotion to the scene, the abilities of protest leaders to control the crowd's behavior, and the presence or absence of British troops. Crowd actions erupted up and down the coast: in Boston where mobs forced the resignation of the local stamp agent and then regrouped to sack the house of Lieutenant Governor Hutchinson; in New York where an angry crowd of perhaps 3000 surrounded the small British garrison holed up in Fort George and dispersed only after a frightening, though ultimately futile attempt to batter down the front gate; and in Charleston where two stamp agents fled for their lives and agreed to suspend their official duties, explaining nervously to their superiors in England that they had done so only "to prevent Murther and the destruction of the town which we were well informed by our friends would certainly have happened the Inspectors house having already been rendered uninhabitable himself burnt in Effigie and the Mobs further resolution of...putting us to death unless we agreed to suspend...."[21] This strategy seemed to work, for in most colonies the act never did go into effect and in February of 1766, Parliament moved its repeal.

As early as 1765, then, the strategy of direct action became central to the colonial stance toward England. And because this was true, the prospect and the reality of physical violence by colonial mobs and English troops remained ever present, lending its own complication to the deepening imperial crisis.

As one examines the course of events between 1765 and the outbreak of fighting a decade later, however, one is struck not so much by the extent of violent confrontation, as by its relative absence. In comparison with other and more recent independence struggles, the American experience, again prior to the outbreak of war, seems notably lacking in open strife. Not until 1775 at the earliest did the prospect of large-scale violence such as had taken place a decade before recur, and then it was in the quite different context of military conflict. Can we discover why this was so?

Part of the answer certainly involves the relative weakness of British authority in local situations—there were seldom enough British troops to stand firmly against colonial mobs and precipitate bloody encounters. Some English officials such as General Gage, sensing that the presence of redcoats was often inflammatory, took steps to avoid conflict—for example, by withdrawing troops from Boston following the "Massacre" of 1770. For these reasons and because it was so difficult for England to extend its authority forcefully across several thousand miles of ocean, strategies of limited direct action seemed effective, if not in turning England aside from her plans of imperial consolidation, at least in blunting the impact of specific British mea-

21. Morgan and Morgan, 202.

sures. More violent tactics, as a consequence, seemed unnecessary. With the dramatic reassertion of British power, beginning in 1774 with the Intolerable Acts closing the port of Boston, removing the provincial government from Boston and limiting town meetings, the likelihood of violent confrontation rose dramatically.

In addition, until quite late in the imperial crisis most Anglo-Americans remained hopeful that an accommodation could be worked out between themselves and England, and that the empire could go back to functioning as it had, or at least as the colonists now imagined that it had before all the recent troubles had begun. The colonial stance, as historians have frequently pointed out, was one of opposition to arbitrary English acts rather than rebellion against all British authority. The decision for independence was an extraordinarily difficult one, and for most Americans it didn't come until fighting had actually begun.[22]

Professor Robert Palmer has defined a "revolutionary situation" in the following terms:

By a revolutionary situation is here meant one in which confidence in the justice of reasonableness of existing authority is undermined; where old loyalties fade, obligations are felt as impositions, law seems arbitrary, and respect for superiors is felt as a form of humiliation; where existing sources of prestige seem undeserved, hitherto accepted forms of wealth and income seem ill-gained, and government is sensed as distant, apart from the governed and not really "representing" them. In such a situation the sense of community is lost....No community can flourish if such negative attitudes are widespread or long-lasting. The crisis is a crisis of community itself, political, economic, sociological, personal, psychological, and moral at the same time. Actual revolution need not follow, but it is in such situations that actual revolution does arise.[23]

Not until the American colonists had reached such a point, not until they had become persuaded that England was bent upon their "enslavement," that is not until the spring and summer of 1775 could they bring themselves to contemplate the violent and treasonous act of independence. Nor until that point did they develop a sense of anger and frustration intense enough to produce acts of physical violence.

Finally, the tactic devised by colonial protest leaders of building as broad a base of support as they could, dampened inclinations toward violent confrontation. Certainly one of the notable achievements of the protest movement was the network of Committees of Correspondence, Safety, and Inspection, Sons of Liberty, ad hoc conventions, Provincial Congresses, and intercolonial assemblies that was constructed during the decade between the

22. See Maier, *From Resistance to Revolution.*
23. Palmer, 21.

Stamp Act and independence.[24] The accomplishments of these bodies were substantial: awakening the American people to their rights, mobilizing them on behalf of these rights, and, not incidentally, providing protest leaders with the security of large numbers of supporters.

One result of this decision to broaden the protest base rather than depend upon small cadres of activists, however, was to insure that debate would absorb at least as much protest energy as would action. Every resistance movement faces the same basic decision: whether to count primarily upon a core of true believers or to seek allies among other, only partially committed groups. Clearly the latter course involves compromise and accommodation, for there is no other way to form effective alliances among people who do not fully agree either upon tactics or the goals to be achieved. Time must be given to discussions that hopefully will lead toward the clarification of common purposes. And this in turn creates pressures for the postponement of action, especially of an extreme character that might precipitate a crisis before the movement was ready.

Words are obviously capable of inciting men to violent acts; this appears to have been precisely what Thomas Paine's *Common Sense* accomplished in 1776. But where a sense of immediate and overwhelming crisis has not developed or common purposes have not been clearly defined, words are more likely to prove soporific, deadening to action. Such was the process at work during most of the colonial protest movement against England.

There were, to be sure, protest activists who argued that loyalty to the colonial cause would come only with some visible and irreversible act of personal commitment, and that confrontations were most likely to force such acts of decision. And yet in general the process of broadening the base of colonial support worked in just the opposite way.

The most remarkable thing about the independence movement, John Adams observed in retrospect, was that thirteen clocks were made to strike as one. Clearly the strategy of holding together against England's superior strength was endorsed by most colonial activists. This may well have been what enabled the movement toward independence finally to succeed. It was largely responsible as well for guiding the movement along more cautious, less violent courses of political action.

24. See, for example, R. D. Brown, *Revolutionary Politics in Massachusetts*; Maier, *From Resistance to Revolution*.

Mobilizing Armed Force in
the American Revolution

JOHN SHY

Armed force, and nothing else, decided the outcome of the American Revolution. Without armed force mobilized on a decisive scale, there would not today be a subject for discussion; shorn even of its name, the Revolution would shrink to a mere rebellion—an interesting episode perhaps, but like dozens of others in the modern history of Western societies. Crude, obvious, and unappealing as this truism may be, it is still true. And its truth needs to be probed and understood if we are to understand the Revolution, because that revolution overcame the armed resistance of one of the two militarily strongest powers in the eighteenth-century world.

If the subject of mobilizing armed force in the American Revolution is important, it is also an exceptionally difficult one. Violence, with all its ramifications, remains a great mystery for students of human life, while the deeper motivational sources of human behavior—particularly behavior under conditions of stress—are almost equally mysterious. When these two mysteries come together, as they do in wars and revolutions, then the historian faces a problem full of traps and snares for the unwary, a problem that challenges his ability to know *anything* about the past. A certain humility is obviously in order. Any of us who are tempted not to be humble might recall how recently intelligent, well-informed American leaders spoke glibly about winning the "hearts and minds" of another few million people caught up by war and revolution. That is our subject: the hearts and minds of Americans whose willingness to engage in violence, two centuries ago, fundamentally changed the course of history.

Ideas on our subject, as opposed to analysis based solidly on evidence, come cheap. Writing about an earlier revolutionary war, Thomas Hobbes expressed a cynical view of the relationship between armed force and mere public opinion—like that in the Declaration of Independence—when he said that "covenants without swords are but words." But a century later David Hume tempered Hobbes' cynicism with realism: "As Force is always on the side of the governed," Hume wrote, "the governors have nothing to support them but opinion." Perhaps Hume's view has lost some of its validity in our own time, when technology vastly multiplies the amount of force that a few people can wield, but it certainly held good for the eighteenth century, when even the best weapons were still relatively primitive and widely available. If Hobbes—like all his fellow cynics down through history—is right in believing that public opinion is a fairly fragile flower which can seldom survive the hot wind of violence, Hume reminds us that no one uses force without being moved to do so. John Adams put his finger on this matter of motivation when he said that the real American Revolution, the revolution that estranged American hearts from old British loyalties and readied American minds to use (and to withstand) massive violence, was over before the war began. Adams also opined that a third of the American people supported the revolutionary cause, another third remained more or less loyal to Britain, and that the rest were neutral or apathetic.[1] Clearly, even Adams conceded that not all hearts and minds had been affected in the same way. Many British observers thought that the real American revolutionaries were the religious dissenters, Congregationalists and Presbyterians who had always been secretly disloyal to the Crown because they rejected the whole Anglican Establishment, whose head was the king; and that these revolutionaries persuaded poor Irishmen, who had poured into the American colonies in great numbers during the middle third of the eighteenth century, to do most of the dirty business of actual fighting. American observers, on the other hand, generally assumed that all decent, sane people supported the Revolution, and that those who did not could be categorized as timid, vicious, corrupt, or deluded. Each of these ideas on our subject contains a measure of truth; but they seem to contradict one another, and they do not carry us very far toward understanding.

Like these stock ideas, we have two standard images of the popular response to revolutionary war. One is of whole towns springing to arms as Paul Revere carries his warning to them in the spring of 1775. The other is of a tiny, frozen, naked band of men at Valley Forge, all that are left when everyone else went home in the winter of 1778. Which is the true picture? Both, evidently. But that answer is of no use at all when we ask whether the Revolution succeeded only by the persistence of a very small group of people, the intervention of France, and great good luck; or whether the Revolution was—

1. Rossiter; Nelson, *The American Tory*, 92; Palmer, I, 200; Alden, 87; John Adams, *Works*, X, 63, 87.

or became—unbeatable because the mass of the population simply would not give up the struggle, and the British simply could not muster the force and the resolution to kill them all or break their will or sit on all, or even any large proportion, of them. Who actually took up arms and why? How strong was the motivation to serve, and to keep serving in spite of defeat and other adversities? What was the intricate interplay and feedback between attitude and behavior, events and attitude? Did people get war-weary and discouraged, or did they become adamant toward British efforts to coerce them? If we could answer these questions with confidence, not only would we know why the rebels won and the government lost, but we would also know important things about the American society that emerged from seven years of armed conflict.

A suitably humble approach to these staggering questions lies readily to hand in a book written by Peter Oliver, who watched the Revolution explode in Boston. Oliver descended from some of the oldest families of Massachusetts Bay, he was a distinguished merchant and public official, and he became a bitter Tory. His book, *The Origin and Progress of the American Rebellion*, not published until 1961 and recently out in paperback, is a fascinatingly unsympathetic version of the Revolution, and in it Oliver makes an attempt to answer some of our questions. Using the technique, perfected by S. L. A. Marshall during the Second World War, of the after-action interview, Oliver asked a wounded American lieutenant, who had been captured at Bunker Hill, how he had come to be a rebel. The American officer allegedly replied as follows:

The case was this Sir! I lived in a Country Town; I was a Shoemaker, & got my Living by my Labor. When this Rebellion came on, I saw some of my Neighbors get into Commission, who were no better than myself. I was very ambitious, & did not like to see those Men above me. I was asked to enlist, as a private Soldier. My Ambition was too great for so low a Rank; I offered to enlist upon having a Lieutenants Commission; which was granted. I imagined myself now in a way of Promotion: if I was killed in Battle, there would be an end of me, but if my Captain was killed, I should rise in Rank, & should still have a Chance to rise higher. These Sir! were the only Motives of my entering into the Service; for as to the Dispute between great Britain & the Colonies, I know nothing of it; neither am I capable of judging whether it is right or wrong.[2]

Those who have read U. S. Government publications over the last decade will find this POW interrogation familiar; during the Vietnam war, the State and Defense Department published many like it, and more than one Vietcong prisoner is said to have spoken in the vein of the wounded American lieutenant so long ago.

2. Oliver, 129-30.

Now the lieutenant was not a figment of Oliver's embittered imagination. His name is given by Oliver as Scott, and American records show that a Lieutenant William Scott, of Colonel Paul Sargent's regiment, was indeed wounded and captured at the Battle of Bunker Hill.[3] Scott turns out, upon investigation, to have been an interesting character. Perhaps the first thing to be said about him is that nothing in the record of his life down to 1775 contradicts anything in Oliver's account of the interview. Scott came from Peterborough, New Hampshire, a town settled in the 1730s by Irish Presbyterians.[4] Scott's father had served in the famous Rogers' Rangers during the French and Indian War. At the news of the outbreak of fighting in 1775, a cousin who kept the store in Peterborough recruited a company of local men to fight the British. Apparently the cousin tried to enlist our William Scott—known to his neighbors as "Long Bill," thus distinguishing him from the cousin, "Short Bill." But "Long Bill"—our Bill—seems to have declined serving as a private, and insisted on being a lieutenant if cousin "Short Bill" was going to be a captain. "Short Bill" agreed. So far the stories as told by Oliver and as revealed in the New Hampshire records check perfectly. Nor is there any reason to think that "Long Bill" had a deeper understanding of the causes of the Revolution than appear in Oliver's version of the interview.

What Peter Oliver never knew was the subsequent life history of this battered yokel, whose view of the American rebellion seemed so pitifully naive. When the British evacuated Boston, they took Scott and other American prisoners to Halifax, Nova Scotia. There, after more than a year in captivity, Scott somehow managed to escape, to find a boat, and to make his way back to the American army just in time for the fighting around New York City in 1776. Captured again in November, when Fort Washington and its garrison fell to a surprise British assault, Scott escaped almost immediately, this time by swimming the Hudson River at night—according to a newspaper account—with his sword tied around his neck and his watch pinned to his hat. He returned to New Hampshire during the winter of 1777 to recruit a company of his own; there, he enlisted his two oldest sons for three years or the duration of the war. Stationed in the Boston area, he marched against Burgoyne's invading army from Canada, and led a detachment that cut off the last retreat just before the surrender near Saratoga. Scott later took part in the fighting around Newport, Rhode Island. But when his light infantry company was ordered to Virginia under Lafayette in early 1781, to counter the raiding expedition led by Benedict Arnold, Scott's health broke down; long marches and hot weather made the old Bunker Hill wounds ache, and he

3. Heitman, 485-86. Heitman has actually confused two William Scotts, who were cousins, but there is no doubt that the officer wounded and captured at Bunker Hill was a William Scott.

4. *Massachusetts soldiers...*, XIII, 929-30; Smith, 10-11, 326-33.

was permitted to resign from the army. After only a few months of recupera-
tion, however, he seems to have grown restless, for we find him during the
last year of the war serving as a volunteer on a navy frigate.

What would Scott have said if Oliver had been able to interview him again,
after the war? We can only guess. Probably he would have told Oliver that his
oldest son had died in the army, not gloriously, but of camp fever, after six
years of service. Scott might have said that in 1777 he had sold his Peterborough farm in order to meet expenses, but that the note which he took in
exchange turned into a scrap of paper when the dollar of 1777 became
worth less than two cents by 1780. He might also have said that another
farm, in Groton, Massachusetts, slipped away from him, along with a down
payment that he had made on it, when his military pay depreciated rapidly
to a fraction of its nominal value. He might not have been willing to admit
that when his wife died he simply turned their younger children over to his
surviving elder son, and then set off to beg a pension or a job from the
government. Almost certainly he would not have told Oliver that when the
son—himself sick, his corn crop killed by a late frost, and saddled with three
little brothers and sisters—begged his father for help, our hero told him that,
if all else failed, he might hand the children over to the selectmen of Peterborough.

In 1792, "Long Bill" Scott once more made the newspapers: he rescued
eight people from drowning when their small boat capsized in New York harbor. But heroism did not pay very well. At last, in 1794, Secretary of War
Henry Knox made Scott deputy storekeeper at West Point; and a year later
General Benjamin Lincoln took Scott with him to the Ohio country, where
they were to negotiate with the Indians and survey the land opened up by
Anthony Wayne's victory at Fallen Timbers. At last he had a respectable
job, and even a small pension for his nine wounds; but Lincoln's group caught
something called "lake fever" while surveying on the Black River, near San-
dusky. Scott, ill himself, guided part of the group back to Fort Stanwix,
New York, then returned for the others. It was his last heroic act. A few
days after his second trip, he died, on September 16, 1796.

Anecdotes, even good ones like the touching saga of "Long Bill" Scott,
do not make history. But neither can a subject like ours be treated in terms
of what Professor Jesse Lemisch has referred to as the lives of Great White
Men—Washington, Adams, Jefferson, Hamilton, and the handful like them.
Scott's life, in itself, may tell us little about how armed force and public opinion were mobilized in the Revolution; yet the story of his life leads us directly—and at the level of ordinary people—toward crucial features of the
process.

Peterborough, New Hampshire, in 1775 had a population of 549.[5] Town, State and Federal records show that about 170 men were credited to Peterborough as performing some military service during the Revolution. In other words, almost every adult male, at one time or another, carried a gun in the war. Of these 170 participants, less than a third performed really extensive service; that is, service ranging from over a year up to the whole eight years of the war. Only a fraction of these—less than two dozen—served as long as Bill Scott. In Scott we are not seeing a typical participant, but one of a small "hard core" of revolutionary fighters—men who stayed in the army for more than a few months or a single campaign. As we look down the list of long-service soldiers from Peterborough, they seem indeed to be untypical people. A few, like Scott and his cousin "Short Bill" and James Taggert and Josiah Munroe, became officers or at least sergeants, and thereby acquired status and perhaps some personal satisfaction from their prolonged military service. But most of the hard core remained privates, and they were an unusually poor, obscure group of men, even by the rustic standards of Peterborough. Many —like John Alexander, Robert Cunningham, William Ducannon, Joseph Henderson, Richard Richardson, John Wallace, and Thomas Williamson—were recruited from outside the town, from among men who never really lived in Peterborough. Whether they lived *anywhere*—in the strict legal sense—is a question. Two men—Zaccheus Brooks and John Miller—are simply noted as "transients." At least two—James Hackley and Randall McAllister—were deserters from the British army. At least two others—Samuel Weir and Titus Wilson—were black men, Wilson dying as a prisoner of war. A few, like Michael Silk, simply appear to join the army, then vanish without a documentary trace. Many more reveal themselves as near the bottom of the socioeconomic ladder: Hackley, Benjamin Allds, Isaac Mitchell, Ebenezer Perkins, Amos Spofford, Jonathan Wheelock, and Charles White were legal paupers after the Revolution; Joseph Henderson was a landless day-laborer; Samuel Spear was jailed for debt; and John Millet was mentally deranged.

We can look at the whole Peterborough contingent in another way, in terms of those in it who were, or later became, prominent or at least solid citizens of the town. With a few exceptions like "Short Bill" Scott and "Long Bill's" son John, who survived frost-killed corn and a parcel of unwanted siblings to become a selectman and a leader of the town, these prominent men and solid citizens had served in the war for only short periods—a few months in 1775, a month or two in the Burgoyne emergency of 1777, maybe a month in Rhode Island or a month late in the war to bolster the key garrison of West Point. The pattern is clear, and it is a pattern that reappears wherever the surviving evidence has permitted a similar kind of

5. Smith, 165-394.

inquiry. Lynn, Massachusetts; Berks County, Pennsylvania; Colonel Small-wood's recruits from Maryland in 1782; several regiments of the Massachusetts Line; a sampling of pension applicants from Virginia—all show that the hard core of Continental soldiers, the Bill Scotts who could not wangle commissions, the soldiers at Valley Forge, the men who shouldered the heaviest military burden, were something less than average colonial Americans.[6] As a group, they were poorer, more marginal, less well anchored in the society. Perhaps we should not be surprised; it is easy to imagine men like these actually being attracted by the relative affluence, comfort, security, prestige, and even the chance for satisfying human relationships offered by the Continental army. Revolutionary America may have been a middle-class society, happier and more prosperous than any other in its time, but it contained a large and growing number of fairly poor people, and many of them did much of the actual fighting and suffering between 1775 and 1783: A very old story.[7]

The large proportion of men, from Peterborough and other communities, who served only briefly might thus seem far less important to our subject than the disadvantaged minority who did such a large part of the heavy work of revolution. This militarily less active majority were of course the militiamen. One could compile a large volume of pithy observations, beginning with a few dozen from Washington himself, in which the value of the militia was called into question. The nub of the critique was that these part-time soldiers were untrained, undisciplined, undependable, and very expensive, consuming pay, rations, clothing, and weapons at a great rate in return for short periods of active service. By the end of the war, the tendency of many Continental officers, like Colonel Alexander Hamilton, to disparage openly the military performance of the militia was exacerbating already strained relations between State and Continental authorities. And indeed there were a number of cases in which the failure of militia to arrive in time, to stand under fire, or to remain when they were needed, either contributed to American difficulties or prevented the exploitation of American success. But the revolutionary role of the men from Peterborough and elsewhere who did *not* serve as did Bill Scott, but whose active military service was rather a sometime thing, is easily misunderstood and underestimated if we look at it only in terms of traditional military strategy and set-piece battles.

To understand the revolutionary militia and its role, we must go back to the year before the outbreak of fighting at Lexington and Concord. Each colony, except Pennsylvania, had traditionally required every free white

6. H. Sanderson; Montgomery; *Pennsylvania Archives*, 3d ser., vol. 18; 5 ser., vols. 1-5; Papenfuse and Stiverson; Sellers; Dorman.

7. Lemon and Nash; Grant, 83-103, 171-172, 214.

adult male, with a few minor occupational exceptions, to be inscribed in a militia unit, and to take part in training several times a year. These militia units seldom achieved any degree of military proficiency, nor were they expected to serve as actual fighting formations. Their real function might be described as a hybrid of draft board and modern reserve unit—a modicum of military training combined with a mechanism to find and enlist individuals when they were needed. But the colonial militia did not simply slide smoothly into the Revolution. Militia officers, even where they were elected, held royal commissions, and a significant number of them were not enthusiastic about rebellion. Purging and restructuring the militia was an important step toward revolution, one that deserves more attention than it has had.

When in early 1774, the news reached America that Parliament would take a very hard line in response to the Boston Tea Party, and in particular had passed a law that could destroy economically and politically the town of Boston, the reaction in the colonies was stronger and more nearly unanimous than at any time since the Stamp Act. No one could defend the Boston Port Act; it was an unprecedented, draconian law the possible consequences of which seemed staggering. Radicals, like Sam Adams, demanded an immediate and complete break in commercial relations with the rest of the empire. Boycotts had worked effectively in the past, and they were an obvious response to the British hard line. More moderate leaders, however, dreaded a hasty confrontation that might quickly escalate beyond their control, and they used democratic theory to argue that nothing ought to be done without a full and proper consultation of the popular will.[8] Like the boycott, the consultative congress had a respectable pedigree, and the moderates won the argument. When the Continental Congress met in September, 1774, there were general expectations in both Britain and America that it would cool and seek to compromise the situation.

Exactly what happened to disappoint those expectations is even now not wholly clear; our own sense that Congress was heading straight toward revolution and independence distorts a complex moment in history, when uncertainty about both ends and means deeply troubled the minds of most decision-makers. Congress had hardly convened when it heard that the British had bombarded Boston. For a few days men from different colonies, normally suspicious of one another, were swept together by a wave of common fear and apprehension. Though the report was quickly proved false, these hours of mutual panic seem to have altered the emotional economy of the Congress.[9] Soon afterward it passed without any serious dissent a resolution in favor of the long-advocated boycott, to be known as the Association. Local

8. Force, 4th series, I, 406-7, 434, 441, 531-34.
9. Burnett, ed., I, 18-19, 34, 36.

committees were to gather signatures for the Association, and were to take necessary steps to enforce its provisions. The Association was the vital link in transforming the colonial militia into a revolutionary organization.

For more than a year, a tenuous line of authority ran directly from the Continental Congress to the grass roots of American society. The traditional, intermediate levels of government, if they did not cooperate fully, were by-passed. Committees formed everywhere to enforce the Association, and sympathetic men volunteered to assist in its enforcement. In some places, like Peterborough, the same men who were enrolled in the militia became the strong right arm of the local committee; reluctant militia officers were ignored because, after all, not the militia as such but a voluntary association of militia members was taking the action. In other places, like parts of the Hudson valley and Long Island, reluctance was so widespread that men opposed to the Association actually tried to take over the committee system in order to kill it; when meetings were called to form the new armed organization of Associators, loyal militiamen packed the meetings and re-elected the old, royally commissioned lieutenants and captains.[10] But even where the Association encountered heavy opposition, it effectively dissolved the old military structure and created a new one based on consent, and whose chief purpose was to engineer consent, by force if necessary. The new revolutionary militia might look very much like the old colonial militia, but it was, in its origins, less a draft board and a reserve training unit than a police force and an instrument of political surveillance. Although the boycott could be defended to moderate men as a constitutional, non-violent technique, its implementation had radical consequences. Adoption by Congress gave it a legitimacy and a unity that it could have gained in no other way. Ordinary men were forced to make public choices, and thus to identify themselves with one side or the other. Not until the Declaration of Independence clarified the hazy status of the traditional levels of government did the local committees, acting through the new militia, relinquish some of their truly revolutionary power.

It is difficult to overestimate the importance of what happened in 1775 to engage mass participation on the side of the Revolution. The new militia, which was repeatedly denying that it was in rebellion and proclaimed its loyalty to the Crown, enforced a boycott intended to make Britain back down; Britain did not back down, but the attempt drew virtually everyone in-to the realm of politics. Enlistment, training, and occasional emergencies were the means whereby dissenters were identified, isolated, and dealt with. Where the new militia had trouble getting organized, there revolutionary activists could see that forceful intervention from outside might be needed. Connecticut units moved into the New York City area; Virginia troops moved

10. Force, 4th series, III, 696, for example, on Dutchess County, New York.

into the Delmarva peninsula; in Pennsylvania, men from Reading and Lancaster marched into Bucks County. Once established, the militia became the infrastructure of revolutionary government. It controlled its community, whether through indoctrination or intimidation; it provided on short notice large numbers of armed men for brief periods of emergency service; and it found and persuaded, drafted or bribed, the smaller number of men needed each year to keep the Continental army alive. After the first months of the war, popular enthusiasm and spontaneity could not have sustained the struggle; only a pervasive armed organization, in which almost everyone took some part, kept people constantly, year after year, at the hard task of revolution. While Scott and his sons, the indigent, the blacks, and the otherwise socially expendable men fought the British, James and Samuel Cunningham, Henry Ferguson, John Gray, William McNee, Benjamin Mitchell, Robert Morison, Alexander and William Robbe, Robert Swan, Robert Wilson, and four or five men named Smith—all militiamen, but whose combined active service hardly equalled that of "Long Bill" Scott alone—ran Peterborough, expelling a few Tories, scraping up enough recruits for the Continental army to meet the town's quota every spring, taking time out to help John Stark destroy the Germans at the battle of Bennington.

The mention of Tories brings us, briefly, to the last aspect of our subject. Peterborough had little trouble with Tories; the most sensational case occurred when the Presbyterian minister, the Reverend John Morrison, who had been having trouble with his congregation, deserted his post as chaplain to the Peterborough troops and entered British lines at Boston in June, 1775. But an informed estimate is that about a half million Americans, about a fifth of the population, can be counted as loyal to Britain.[11] Looking at the absence of serious Loyalism in Peterborough, we might conclude that Scotch-Irish Presbyterians almost never were Tories. That, however, would be an error of fact, and we are impelled to seek further for an explanation. What appears as we look at places, like Peterborough, where Tories are hardly visible, and at other places where Toryism was rampant, is a pattern—not so much an ethnic, religious, or ideological pattern, but a pattern of raw power. Wherever the British and their allies were strong enough to penetrate in force—along the seacoast, in the Hudson, Mohawk and lower Delaware valleys, in Georgia, the Carolinas, and the transappalachian west—there Toryism flourished. But geographically less exposed areas, if population density made self-defense feasible—most of New England, the Pennsylvania hinterland, and piedmont Virginia—where the enemy hardly appeared or not at all, there Tories either ran away, kept quiet, even serving in the rebel armies, or occasionally took a brave but hopeless stand against revolutionary committees and their gun-

11. Smith, "American Loyalists...," 259-77.

men.[12] After the war, of course, men remembered their parts in the successful revolution in ways that make it difficult for the historian to reconstruct
accurately the relationship between what they thought and what they did.

The view which I have presented of how armed force and public opinion
were mobilized may seem a bit cynical—a reversion to Thomas Hobbes. True,
it gives little weight to ideology, to perceptions and principles, to grievances
and aspirations, to the more admirable side of the emergent American
character. Perhaps that is a weakness; perhaps I have failed to grasp what
really drove Bill Scott. But what strikes me most forcibly in studying this
part of the Revolution is how much in essential agreement almost all Americans were in 1774, both in their views of British measures and in their feelings about them. What then is puzzling, and thus needs explaining, is why so
many of these people behaved in anomalous and in different ways. Why did
so many, who did not intend a civil war or political independence, get so
inextricably involved in the organization and use of armed force? Why did
relatively few do most of the actual fighting? Why was a dissenting fifth of
the population so politically and militarily impotent, so little able to affect
the outcome of the struggle? Answers to these questions cannot be found in
the life of one obscure man, or in the history of one backwoods town. But
microscpoic study does emphasize certain features of the Revolution: the
political structuring of resistance to Britain, the play of social and economic
factors in carrying on that resistance by armed force, and the brutally direct
effects on behavior, if not on opinions, of military power.

12. Nelson, *The American Tory*, ch. 5, sep. p. 91.

Revolution and Change in America

PAULINE MAIER

Change is the essence of revolution. To understand the American Revolution, to grasp the ways in which it moved beyond a conservative movement for the protection of traditional rights and privileges, it is necessary to see how it effected a fundamental redirecting of American life. It is necessary, in short, to consider colonial development in the pre-Revolutionary era and to examine the kinds of reforms the old order inspired, then to contrast these with the demands of the mid-1770s, which went far beyond what leaders of American resistance to Britain had either foreseen or desired at the outset of conflict. The aims of revolutionary Americans were not accomplished in a day or even a decade. In a real sense, they are being worked out in the United States today—but again, ironically, in ways that few advocates of independence either foresaw or desired.

Change is always with us. But in the first two centuries of American life change was particularly dramatic. The small, fragile settlements of the early seventeenth century gave way to an established and thriving American community that spanned the eastern seaboard and by the early eighteenth century was pushing into the interior. But the direction of change, as it has emerged from recent historical studies, is perhaps surprising: for as America progressed through time, it seems in many respects to have increasingly resembled England. Provincial life was furthest from that in Europe, it seems, in the earliest years of American history, when the sparseness of population and problems of sustaining civilized life on the edge of a great wilderness prompted innovation, when the possibilities of beginning anew in a land "even as God made it," in William Bradford's phrase, recasting human society into new and better forms, produced a great diversity of institutions and practices in the various colonies along the coast. Mobility, too, was the order of the day, not just geographically, but socially: the authority of old elites proved difficult to sustain through generational changes, and were challenged with remarkable success by new contenders for power until the late 1700s.[1]

Within the eighteenth century a new stability emerged. As population increased, society became more stratified: wealth was increasingly concentrated within fewer hands at the upper end of the social scale, while the number of poor and propertyless, whether in town or country, increased.[2] Eighteenth-century America also contained forces that interrupted the authority of elites, and Europeans continued to marvel at the familiarity between social groups, at the relative lack of social distance between the "upper" and "lower" orders.[3] But it remained possible to interpret these "disorderly" attributes as anachronisms left from the childhood of America that would disappear with increasing maturity. By the 1770s, James Henretta notes, residential patterns had begun to separate Boston's merchant princes from the propertyless laborers of the North End. Meanwhile such titles as "merchant" became more exclusive, suggesting that "occupations and titles were regaining some of their traditional distinctiveness and meaning."[4]

These demographic developments correlate with the "Anglicization" of the militia, church, and other Massachusetts institutions recently studied by John Murrin. Law courts, for example, were increasingly modeled upon their British counterparts; English laws and precedents were cited more frequently; even the livery of British judges and lawyers was adopted in Massachusetts on the eve of Revolution.[5] In retrospect, all of this was natural enough: as the population grew and the colonial economy became more complex, problems arose for which—unlike those of the settlement years—the Mother Country offered natural solutions.

This process of "Anglicization," as Murrin calls it, touched politics as well, suggesting that the tendency was not simply an automatic response to historical change, but was in some areas deliberate, founded also on the affections and convictions of colonists in general. The bedlam of provincial institutions that distinguished, say, the Carolinas from New York or Pennsylvania in the 1680s was reduced in the late seventeenth and early eighteenth centuries as more royal colonies were created and governments became characteristically composed of a governor, council, and elected assembly. Each pro-

1. Bailyn, "Politics and Social Structure in Virginia," 135-159; Bailyn, *New England Merchants.*
2. Henretta, "Economic Development and Social Structure in Colonial Boston," 450-465; and Lockridge, 466-491; Land.
3. Bailyn, *Ideological Origins,* 303 and n.
4. Henretta in Katz, ed., 457-58, 460.
5. Murrin, "Anglicizing an American Colony..."; Murrin, "The Legal Transformation...," 415-449.

vincial government seemed to be modeled on England's own constitution, so praised by enlightened writers for its ability to protect freedom. Like the British constitution, these provincial constitutions were "mixed," with power shared by the king, or governor; the House of Lords, or council; and the Commons, or, as the colonists saw it, their own assemblies. With affection for English institutions came reverence for England's Glorious Revolution of 1688-89 at which, writers claimed, the monarchical power of the Stuart kings had been constrained, and the survival of freedom made possible by a balancing of monarchy, aristocracy, and democracy within the British constitution. This conception had little relation to the actual functioning of the Mother Country's government on the eve of the American Revolution, and the colonists' image of the Glorious Revolution owed as much to Whig writers as it did to actual events of the late seventeenth century. Yet a belief in English liberty, and in the historical process by which it had been preserved, united colonists in provinces so distinct in other regards as South Carolina and Massachusetts. It explains, moreover, how Americans of the 1760s and 1770s could resist their current English rulers in the name of a more fundamental British heritage. The preservation of freedom, and of the constitution that protected it, was a historic obligation shared by all the British, whether at home or in the colonies.[6]

There were, of course, important differences between provincial governments and that of England. Before the revolutionary period these differences were often identified as defects, and so awoke the most important movement for reform of the late colonial period. This effort sought further to approximate colonial and British institutions and, beyond that, to strengthen Anglo-American political ties. Active movements for the end of charter or proprietary rule and the establishment of royal government were, for example, under way in both Rhode Island and Pennsylvania in the early 1760s. The movement for uniformity in provincial government was perhaps championed most articulately by Governor Francis Bernard of Massachusetts: "the most perfect form of government for a dependent," he wrote, was that "which approaches the nearest to that of the sovereign state, and differs from it as little as possible." From this perspective he concluded that "every American Government is capable of having its constitution altered for the better." Some colonists disagreed. Samuel Adams, for example, praised the British constitution as beyond all contenders in its ability to preserve liberty, yet found the Massachusetts charter preferable because it secured for the people "all the English liberties" and "some additional privileges which the common people there have not." Any effort to make Massachusetts government further resemble that of Britain entailed for him, then, an implicit threat to popular freedom.

6. Bailyn, *Ideological Origins*, 70-73, 79-83.

But many Americans shared Bernard's concern. The colonial councils above all worried not just Bernard but future revolutionaries like Richard Henry Lee, for of all governmental agencies they seemed the most jarringly unlike their British equivalent, and most responsible for operational differences between politics in America and England. As a result proposals were made to increase the tenure of councillors, making them, in effect, life peers, so they would be more independent—more capable of assuming the constitutional functions attributed to the House of Lords.[7]

A more extensive field for innovation lay in the limbo between England and the separate colonies. Distracted by internal ferment, England had never defined the relationship of the Mother Country with her "plantations" during the settlement years, and later efforts foundered. As a result so basic an issue as whether the dominions were subject to the Crown or the English nation was still debatable 160 years after Jamestown. Proposals for strengthening Anglo-American ties were regularly made through the eighteenth century, but increased dramatically after the Seven Years' War. The advocacy of reform here in no way reflected the divisions of 1776: British officeholders like Thomas Pownall participated, as did future Loyalists like William Smith or Joseph Galloway, along with others who came to champion independence such as Benjamin Franklin, Stephen Sayre, Samuel Adams, Arthur Lee. In one regard the colonists were the more creative: it was they, Richard Koebner has demonstrated, who first used the word "empire," which for them implied a partnership of equals, all of whom would exercise significant power of self-government, and so implicitly rejected the British assumption that colonies were subordinate to the Mother Country. In retrospect, however, the similarities that link the proposers of imperial reform seem as important as their differences. All reformers were concerned with the same problems—the need for effecting territorial adjustments, for coordinating military actions, for involving colonists in questions of taxation, and, above all, with averting American independence. Colonists as well as Englishmen discussed American representation in a widened "Imperial Parliament." Both considered carefully the possibility of creating new institutions between the Mother Country and the separate provinces—whether a government of captain general and bicameral "plantation parliament," as Martin Bladen, a Commissioner for trade and plantations, proposed in 1739; an elected American "Board of Trade" at New York, such as the colonist merchant Stephen Sayre suggested; a legalization of the already existent Continental Congress or the adoption of Joseph Galloway's plan of union, which specified a new Continent-wide government under a royally appointed President General and

7. Bernard quoted in Koebner, 139; Adams quoted in Wells, I, 21-22; Bailyn, *Ideological Origins*, 274-77.

a Grand Council of delegates from the various colonies. Either of the last two were acceptable to Benjamin Franklin in 1774. No union was possible for colonial radicals like Arthur Lee and Samuel Adams without some guarantee of colonial rights, so they discussed an American Bill of Rights, like the English document of 1689. But even this proposal was not original. The Englishman Thomas Pownall had raised the possibility five years earlier.[8]

These advocates of imperial reform had, however, no significant effect upon official policy. When Britain did attempt to tighten Anglo-American ties, she emphasized not those policies upon which English and American reformers agreed, but precisely the issues of jurisdiction and right that separated them. The exclusive right of local assemblies to tax was denied; the sovereign authority of Parliament was declared to extend over the colonies "in all cases whatsoever," and finally a frontal attack upon traditional rights and institutions was mounted through what the Americans called the "Intolerable Acts."

On virtually every point, moreover, British actions of the late 1760s and early 1770s, whether towards America, Ireland, France, or the Wilkesites in England, awoke memories of Stuart despotism and inspired resistance—not for a new order, but to protect the heritage of the Glorious Revolution. Even the name taken on by the Stamp Act resisters, the Sons of Liberty, emphasized this quality: colonial insurgents acted to protect the English constitution of their fathers "according to its true form and original texture" against "unjust force and usurpation." Guidelines for resistance were taken from England's own revolutionary tradition; the seventeenth century was scanned for opposition techniques. Colonial resistance was shaped, too, by the Americans' new notion of empire. They understood that there could be no lasting union without parity between England and her overseas dominions, and so active efforts were taken to coordinate resistance in England and Ireland with that in America. But even here the precedent of 1688-89 was relevant, for, as the colonists understood it, uprisings in America had been as fully a part of the Glorious Revolution as those at home. Activism and eloquence were inspired by the great need of averting independence by teaching the Mother Country to respect colonists' rights and privileges: "Torn from the body, to which we are united by religion, liberty, laws, affections, relation, language and commerce," John Dickinson wrote, "we must bleed at every vein." Accommodation, not separation, was the goal even of Samuel Adams, who actively explored possible solutions for the Anglo-American conflict as late as 1774. According to surviving documentary evidence, he first advocated

8. Koebner, 86-90, 105-49; J. Greene, "Martin Bladen's Blueprint...," 516-530, 516n; Calhoon, 105-118; Galloway, 391-393; Stephen Sayre, undated proposal, Earl of Dartmouth Papers, Wm. Salt Library, Stafford, England, D1778/2/1079; Maier, *From Resistance to Revolution,* 245.

independence in late 1775, months after the war had begun. In July 1776, when independence had finally been declared, Adams claimed the move would have been "justified in the Sight of God and Man" nine months earlier—but then scratched out the nine and substituted three![9]

Colonists accepted independence only as an absolute necessity. While Britain's rulers appeared intent on reversing Britain's heritage of freedom, Englishmen remained sunk in an "unaccountable supineness." Only the colonists seemed to retain the virtue and dedication of their forebears. Continued membership in the empire promised to make of America another Ireland. And so independence was accepted, but not without regret. "We might have been a free and great people together," Thomas Jefferson recalled in his "original rough draught" of the Declaration of Independence, but:

...a communication of grandeur and of freedom it seems is below their dignity. Be it so, since they will have it: the road to glory and happiness is open to us too; we will climb it in a separate state, and acquiesce in the necessity which pronounces our everlasting Adieu![10]

Independence was not the culmination, but a beginning of the American Revolution. Before 1776 agitation had been, for the most part, conservative in conception: it sought to preserve the achievement of 1688-89. But as the struggle with Britain developed, it became increasingly clear that the British constitution was "imperfect...and incapable of producing what it seems to promise," the preservation of liberty. Its flaws, it seemed, were monarchy and hereditary aristocracy, two of the three traditional parts of the British constitution. And so to eliminate the potential for despotism from their institutions, Americans set about erecting governments in which "the whole road to promotion" would be "through the affection of the people," governments that they came to call "republican." This development was critical: separation alone, Thomas Paine recognized, "would have been a matter but of little importance, had it not been accompanied by a revolution in the principles and practice of governments."[11]

Republicanism was by its nature innovative—even utopian—in the age of the American Revolution. Had one ever succeeded, particularly in governing a country so large as the United States? However attractive in theory, republics were considered impractical, always ending in anarchy and despotism. Kings and nobles were essential for good order: if the people rule, who would be ruled? Yet with the surprising willingness of colonists to obey those elected committees and congresses that emerged in the two years before independence, some revolutionaries dared to reject traditional wisdom and

9. Providence, R. I. Sons of Liberty to N. Y. Sons of Liberty, 24 May 1776, Belknap Papers, 61.c.121, Massachusetts Historical Society; Dickinson, 18; Samuel Adams, III, 295.
10. Jefferson, *Papers*, I, 427; Maier, *From Resistance to Revolution*, 145-270.
11. Paine, I, 7, 354; Frothingham, 483.

argued that popular government was more successful in maintaining internal order than even regular British government had been. What then of previous republics—above all that of Rome? Their failure lay, it was said, not in their popular base, but in the imperfections of their republicanism—in the crumbs of privilege and nobility that remained embedded in their walls. The remedy for the ills of republics was then more republicanism—a purer, yet more unadulterated pursuit of popular self-government than the world had yet seen.[12]

The past suddenly became irrelevant. History was not, of course, banished from American thought. Even the most wild of revolutionaries—such as the anonymous author who suggested in 1776 that Americans should form new state governments "just as if we had never any form of Government before" —used historical examples to illustrate faults that must be avoided. But the focal point of historical consciousness was shifting from 1689 to 1776; and the bank of useful historical references was accordingly reduced. By 1789 William Maclay of Pennsylvania argued that "within the space of twenty years back more light had been thrown on the subject of governments and on human affairs in general than for several generations before." And two years later, in *The Rights of Man*, Thomas Paine claimed that "the case and circumstances of America present themselves as in the beginning of the world," and so inquiries into the origins of government could safely render only "to the facts that have arisen in our own day":

We have no occasion to roam for information in the obscure field of antiquity, nor hazard ourselves upon conjecture. We are brought at once to the point of seeing government begin, as if we had lived in the beginning of time. The real volume, not of history, but of facts, is directly before us, unmutilated by contrivance or the errors of tradition.[13]

Government, the core of Maclay's and Paine's concern, was fundamentally altered. Republican institutions were established for the states, and finally for the federal jurisdiction. This achievement was complex: constitutional conventions evolved as institutional expressions of the people's power to "compact" together in forming fundamental law; representation was extended from the assembly through all other segments of government; a new system of majoritarian democracy made its appearance; separation of powers was substituted for the old English idea of "mixed government"; the traditional "truth" that sovereignty was unitary was challenged, allowing the development of modern federalism. These and other revolutionary developments in political science evolved slowly over decades of intense argument and experimentation. So momentous was this outpouring of creative energy, so far-reaching in its implications, that the final achievement of the federal consti-

12. Maier, "The Beginnings of Republicanism...," 106-113.
13. Force, ed., 4th ser., VI, 842; Maclay, 22; Paine, I, 376.

tution seemed to many the conclusion of revolution. Even Benjamin Rush spoke of the revolution as something already accomplished in 1788; and Thomas Paine referred to the American Revolution as already established in 1792.[14]

Change was, however, not easily confined to governmental institutions. "There is such a spirit of innovation gone forth as I am afraid will throw us into confusion," John Winthrop, the Harvard scientist, complained in June 1776: it seemed as if everything was to be altered. Noah Webster claimed in 1789 that the Americans' recent experiences had put them "in a situation the most favorable for great reformations": men's minds had been weaned from the lethargy of tradition as the need for "new expedients called forth the powers of invention." The possibility of change seemed heightened, moreover, by the character of the American, which became idealized even as the British constitution was demythologized. All the marks of provincialism that signalled backwardness in the colonial era suddenly became assets, proof that the American was the simple man of nature, more primitive and free from the corruptions of "civilization" than he had ever in fact been, even at Jamestown and Plymouth. "The human mind here is like clay," Benjamin Rush claimed in the mid-1780s:

It has as yet received but few impressions but what are derived from nature. Our love of liberty is the effect of instinct rather than education. Religion and science will have no prejudice or errors to encounter among us.[15]

In this atmosphere of expanded possibilities, innovations of widely differing character were effected or proposed. Mechanics and poor farmers, who had served with dignity on the committees of the resistance movements or in the army, often demanded a new importance in the young republic. "It is a rare thing to meet with any body here without some lofty titles to declare their merit," the Rev. John Eliot complained from Boston in January 1777: "Colonel A., Major B., Captain C., denominates every puppy that 'bays at the moon'." Even those without military titles belonged "to some Committee of Correspondence, of Safety, or Supply...and therefore must be treated with complaisance." To call someone a "mechanic" was an affront:

We are all obliged to go barefoot and ragged, for you may as well fish for pearls in Oyster River, or look for the planet Venus at midday, as seek for such creatures in Boston as a taylor or shoemaker.[16]

With dignity came insistence upon fuller political participation, a refusal

14. Bailyn, *Ideological Origins*, 160-229; Wood, *Creation of the American Republic*; Pole; Dietze, 76-77, n.5; Paine, I, 347.

15. Winthrop to John Adams, *Massachusetts Historical Society Collections*, 5th ser., IV, 308; N. Webster, *Dissertations on the English Language*, 405-406; Rush quoted in Hawke, 279.

16. Eliot to Jeremy Belknap, *Massachusetts Historical Society Collections*, 6th ser., IV, 103-104.

to yield decision-making power to the privileged few. Fo
ers of western Massachusetts, a rigorously democratic s
greater attention to their interests and problems, which cc
of the commercialized seaboard. Urban artisans were also
of how their economic interests conflicted with those
and determined that their separate voices be heard in
making. The doctrine of equality, asserted in the Declaration of Independence, provided ideological justification for the new politics: "In *these*
days," Charleston's William Hornsby noted, "we are equal citizens of a
DEMOCRATIC REPUBLIC, in which *jealousy* and *opposition* must naturally
exist, while there exists a difference in the minds, interests, and sentiments
of mankind." Accordingly, black Americans played an important role in
their own emancipation; dissenters fought for religious freedom; a plea was
even heard that revolutionary lawmakers "Remember the Ladies, and be
more generous and favourable to them than your ancestors." "Do not put
such unlimited power into the hands of the Husbands," Abigail Adams
wrote John on March 31, 1776; "Remember all Men would be tyrants if
they could," so the "vicious and Lawless" should be denied power "to use
us with indignity and impunity."[17]

Social change of this sort was unanticipated by many revolutionary
leaders of 1776, who had struggled over a decade to effect an orderly revolution. And order implied hierarchy, with chains of command and subordination arranged according to social position. How appropriate that the
eighteenth century spoke of not classes but social "orders"—the "upper
order," or "lower orders," terms that reflected not sharp and substantive
societal divisions founded on contrary economic interests, but groups related to each other in a more graduated hierarchy of authority. The continuation of order in this sense seemed all the more important in a republic,
which promised to ameliorate the condition of mankind, but could do so only
if it survived the disease of anarchy. Republics were weak from an institutional inability to impose order from above; stability had to emerge from
within the society itself—in a willingness of the citizens to sacrifice private
indulgences for the common good, which included a willingness among the
able to forego the pleasures of private life for the responsibilities of command, and among the members of the "lower orders" to accept with good
spirit a stance of subordination and obedience. The lower people would, of
course, participate in the selection of office-holders; they might even—as they
had during the colonial period—hold minor offices. Such involvement in
fact strengthened the willingness of people to respect public authority.[18]

17. Patterson; Olten; Maier, "Charleston Mob...," including quote from Hornsby,
p. 194; *Adams Family Correspondence*, I, 370.
18. Zuckerman, "Social Context of Democracy in Massachusetts," 226-245, esp. 231.

But there were limits: Charleston's Christopher Gadsden, a popular leader before Independence, was appalled when his old followers continued to meet, and tried to control the public actions of legislators they had helped elect. All men—whatever their station during the war—should go "cheerfully into the ranks again," he demanded, in the name of *true genuine Republicanism.*" Nor did the problem stop with mechanics: the "able" seemed increasingly reticent to hold office after the opening years of the nation ("Where are the men who filled these seats in 1774?" Benjamin Rush asked of the Continental Congress in 1779), although they were never more needed. Reports reached Congress that the whole of society was becoming unhinged: "That Children and Apprentices were disobedient—that schools and Colledges were grown turbulent—that Indians slighted their Guardians and Negroes grew insolent to their Masters." On receiving his wife's plea that he "Remember the Ladies," John Adams concluded—playfully, perhaps—that "another Tribe more numerous and powerfull than all the rest were grown discontented."[19]

If the people were not republican in their habits, then they must be made so: it became necessary, as Benjamin Rush wrote in 1787, to effect "a revolution in our principles, opinions, and manners so as to accommodate them to the forms of government we have adopted." Rush and some of his fellow reformers sought no less than a cultural revolution: selfishness and contentiousness were imports, the habits of the Old World. America must be purged of European customs along with traditional ideas of government. Reform for such men consisted above all in ridding America of "barbarous usages, corrupt society, and monarchical principles," emphasizing instead what was distinctive to a "new country" of "simple manners, and a popular form of government." And so Samuel Adams and other revolutionaries of '76 waged a remorseless war against the frivolousness of insurgent democracy, condemning theatres, idleness, gaming, ostentatious dress. Even the "practices of swimming, sliding, and skating, which prevail so universally on Sundays in most cities of the United States" seemed to threaten "destruction." In the name of republicanism old causes like antislavery were quickened, while new proposals multiplied. For Benjamin Rush, who advocated every reform from antislavery through temperance, as well as penal and educational reform, even handwriting demanded modification:

...the Italian and inverted hands which are read with difficulty, are by no means accommodated to the active state of business in America, or to the simplicity of the citizens of a republic.

And slavery was attacked not just because it dishonored free government,

19. Gadsden, *Writings*, 206; Maier, "Charleston Mob...,"; Rush, *Letters*, I, 231; Hawke, 231; *Adams Family Correspondence*, I, 382.

but because it supported "luxury, vice, and indolence," and encouraged among slaveholders "a haughty, unsocial, aristocratic temper" that was "inconsistent with that equality which is the basis of our governments and the happiness of human society."[20]

It was through education, above all, that these reformers sought to set off their society from that of Europe, raising the people from the ignorance of less enlightened ages, while at the same time affirming students in republican habits of austerity and order. Under monarchies education might be elitist, but in a republic where the people ruled, knowledge had to be universally distributed by means of public schools. The need for universal education was one consideration behind Noah Webster's proposal for a new "American language," which was a perfect model of republican reform. Webster sought to eliminate from the English language all its faults and abuses, that is, the spelling irregularities that witnessed its complex historical development, and to reduce all words to their simple phonetic elements. The introduction of "order and regularity into the orthography of the AMERICAN TONGUE" would "facilitate the learning of the language" and "render the pronunciation uniform" in different parts of the country and among different ranks of persons so as to "remove prejudice, and conciliate mutual affection and respect."[21]

Particularly in his proposals for educational institutions Rush hoped to demonstrate the possibility of converting men into "republican machines." Indeed, he thought this "must be done, if we expect them to perform their parts properly, in the great machine of the government of the state." The pupil must be taught:

That he does not belong to himself, but that he is public property. Let him be taught to love his family, but let him also be taught...that he must forsake, and even forget them, when the welfare of his country requires it.

Self-sacrifice would be made a life style: the students' diets would be temperate, "consisting chiefly of broths, milk and vegetables," their bodies subjected to "physical discipline," and Christianity would be emphasized because it inculcated "humility, self-denial, and brotherly kindness." Academic subjects, even amusements would be rigorously measured against the criterion of usefulness—pleasure alone was insufficient. The logic of his behaviorism drove Rush to a cause far in advance of his time: in America even women must be educated, he argued, because they exercised a greater responsibility than European women over their husbands' property, and because, for lack

20. Rush, *Letters*, I, 388; *An Account of the State Prison...in the City of New York*, 9; Wells, *Samuel Adams*, III, esp. 156-158, 290-291; Rush quoted in Hawke, 359; Rush, "Thoughts upon Female Education," 79; Webster, *Sketches of American Policy*, 46.

21. Webster, *Dissertations on the English Language*, 393-95, 397.

of capable servants, they presided over their sons' education during the earliest, formative years of the boys' lives. Here, as in his educational plans in general, Rush conceived of knowledge as uplifting all it touched, while retaining intact—even reaffirming—the lines of command and subordination that separated individuals from each other. "If men believe that ignorance is favourable to the government of the female sex, they are certainly deceived," he wrote, "for a weak and ignorant woman will always be governed with the greatest difficulty"—implying, poor man, that an educated woman would be ruled more easily.[22]

Not all reform proposals were successful. Those that reached fullest fruition in the late eighteenth century—religious freedom, for example—had in fact been begun before the Anglo-American conflict. Beginnings were made in abolishing slavery; legal codes were liberalized; and the foundations of a participatory democracy were laid. But Webster's suggestions for language reform were never adopted, and Rush himself abandoned the cause of reform in 1790 after a stunning dream in which he saw himself as a madman, attempting like God to command nature, then complaining of "refractory elements" when his failure was manifest.[23] Yet many causes that failed, or that produced only limited results in the earliest years of the republic, were revived in the nineteenth century. Abigail Adams would have been at home in the Seneca Falls convention of 1848; and Rush's belief that a systematic educational system could control the intellectual and moral development of children predicted the work of Horace Mann, who saw common schools as "buttresses to hold our fabric firm," fitting the masses for republicanism, assuring that the revolution "will not go backward." Mann, as well as the early nineteenth century founders of penitentiaries, orphanages, and workhouses lately studied by David Rothman, saw in their institutional innovations the same dream Rush had harbored, of a new and orderly world, freed from the vice and crime that had plagued mankind through history, won through the mechanism of arduous discipline.[24]

The continuation of reform, even the doubts about the new democratic-republican society that prompted so many schemes for change, suggest the long-term significance of the Revolution of 1776. America's first revolutionary tradition, that of 1688, was conservative in character because it assumed that an ideal state had been achieved in the past. Future generations were above all to preserve that historic achievement. The Revolution of '76 is today sometimes described in similar terms, but it was in fact the

22. Rush, "Thoughts upon Female Education," 14-15, 10-11; "Of the Mode of Education...," 77, 92.
23. Hawke, 381-82.
24. Messerli, 442; Rothman.

opposite: a step into the dark, founded on a hope that by eliminating English ways, Americans could make way for a "novus ordo seclorum" founded upon the authority of the people and constructed for the betterment of all men.

The results were revolutionary in that they changed the course of American history. The theories and forms of government were transformed, and independence was clearly a prerequisite for the economic diversity and development that reshaped the country in the nineteenth century. The social effects of the revolution are perhaps more limited. The war against hereditary nobility failed to become, as some feared, a war against wealth, and so the eighteenth century trend toward economic stratification continued after the Revolution. Rather than attack economic privilege, so complicated by the question of property rights, Americans instead moved against arbitrary barriers to preferment—for equality of opportunity. But this deceitfully modest goal has never been won without pain. If Christopher Gadsden was appalled by the Charleston mechanics' demand for power in the name of equality, if many of his fellows from the resistance movement died seeing anarchy around them, convinced that popular insurgency witnessed the Revolution's failure, they were only the first to feel the pressure of the tradition they founded. Demands by, or on behalf of blacks were no more pleasant for slaveholders of the Old South, or for the beneficiaries of white privilege today. Nor are the demands of women welcomed by men whose status or livelihoods rest upon the preference and power traditionally conceded them for their sex alone.

The American Revolution instituted, in this sense, a tradition of innovation, demanding an expansion of freedom over time as prejudices give way— with "all deliberate speed," or, in Abraham Lincoln's words, "as fast as circumstances should permit." In the assertion that "all men are created equal," the revolutionaries, Lincoln claimed:

Set up a standard maxim for free society, which should be...constantly labored for, and even though never perfectly attained, constantly approximated, and thereby constantly spreading and deepening its influence, and augmenting the happiness and value of life to all people of all colors everywhere.[25]

And all sexes, Mr. Lincoln.

25. Fehrenbacher, 91.

Loyalists and Non-Participants

WALLACE BROWN

In the beginning there were no Loyalists, or rather everybody was loyal. Most scholars treat Loyalism as an aberration, but rebellion was the aberration.[1] In the beginning everybody was loyal and everybody was also Whig. Most future Loyalists opposed the controversial British legislation from the Stamp Act onwards. Indeed many important ones, for example John J. Zubly of Georgia and William Smith of New York, led the colonial opposition. Loyalists differed with patriots over the *mode* of opposition, holding that constitutional protest was preferable to the anarchy that would inevitably accompany secession. The essential similarity of both sides is highlighted by the razor's edge that separated Peter Van Schaack from his friend John Jay.[2] William H. Nelson's conclusion in *The American Tory* that the Loyalists represented an organic conservatism is belied by the body of his book.[3] And it has recently been plausibly argued that even the genteel preacher of Annapolis, Jonathan Boucher, was Lockean. If Boucher was, who wasn't?[4]

Although the Stamp Act was opposed from Quebec to the Leeward Islands, when war came most of the inhabitants of Quebec, Nova Scotia, the Floridas and the British West Indies (a numerical majority of the involved colonies) remained loyal. In the area that became Canada the people generally resisted rebel blandishments and deserve the appellation "Loyalists" as much as the loyal denizens of the "old thirteen."[5] At least one of the thirteen,

1. Nelson, *The American Tory*; Norton; Van Tyne; W. Brown, *The Good Americans.*
2. Becker, *Everyman his own Historian*, 284-98. For other instances see Benton; and Maier, xv, *From Resistance to Revolution.*
3. Bell; Nelson, "The Last Hopes of the American Loyalists."
4. Zimmer and Kelly; M. Clark; Gummere.
5. Kerr; Lanctôt; Stewart and Rawlyk; P. Smith, "American Loyalists."

120

Georgia, was a reluctant participant, and particularly substantial Loyalist strength must be noted in New York, South Carolina and various urban centres.[6] The area that became Vermont was loyal to itself, seeking advantage from both sides.[7]

Just as World War I did not break out in 1905 or 1911 the American Revolution did not occur in 1765 or 1770, and there is no reason to suppose that British concessions between 1774 and 1776 could not have permanently prevented a rupture as later happened in Canada, Australia and elsewhere. Rebels and Loyalists were fundamentally similar, but not when it came to independence.

This leads to two simple questions with complex answers. How do you define a Loyalist (including who were they) and how many were there? Their enemies variously define them as "the timid," those of "weak parts," "Rottin' sheep," even scatologically as the "ordure of 5,000 years." Many agreed that the first Loyalist was Cain, and that, "A Tory is a thing whose head is in England, and its body in America, and its neck ought to be stretched."[8] The Loyalists usually described themselves as men of honour, devotedly loyal to the British constitution, particularly as practised in the colonies, to good orderly government, genuine freedom and evolutionary reform. Clearly as in any large group of people everything from the most noble to the most base can be found. Clearly a common sense definition of a Loyalist is one who opposed independence and the war necessary to maintain it. But many difficulties arise. What of those colonists who changed sides, sometimes more than once, as a result of such pressures as the fortunes of war? What of those who joined the king opportunely, overawed by seemingly invincible power, or attracted by salaries and supplies?—"able body'd beef devourers...eating up the...Royal Bounty," as one Loyalist official complained.[9] Frequently a colonist was branded a Loyalist simply because he traded with the British army for strictly non-ideological cash and became permanently compromised. What of the numerous Americans who hated the Revolution but through fear of reprisal never expressed their sentiments beyond their intimates? In defining a Loyalist I'm inclined to the analogy of the English definition of "gentleman." There isn't any, but if people think you are one you are one!

Perhaps a footnote on nomenclature is fitting. The Loyalists called themselves Loyalists. They also used refugees, friends of the government, King's friends, and even Sgnik Sdneirf! (cf. Serutan and Aksarben.) Their enemies the patriots or Whigs, to use their own terms, called the Loyalists Tories, a pejorative term implying, unjustly, an affinity with the English high Tories

6. W. Brown, *The King's Friends, passim.*
7. Williamson, *Vermont in a Quandary.*
8. W. Brown, "The Loyalists of the American Revolution," 151; Williamson, 70.
9. Pemberton, 95-96.

who opposed the revolutionary settlement of 1689. The Loyalists dubbed the Whigs rebels. Each side called the other banditti. What's in a name? Quite a lot!

Who were the Loyalists? The gamut of society from slaves and indentured servants to the richest in the land from the first immigrants, Indians like Joseph Brant, to scions of ancient families such as William Byrd III to recent arrivals like the Scottish heroine Flora MacDonald. Statistically the typical Loyalist was a yeoman farmer (as were most Americans of that time), but the rich, the urban, the official, the conservative, the immigrant contributed more heavily than other parts of society.

As for talent it is true that Whig ranks are more glittering, but the loyal exodus from Massachusetts has been aptly likened to the Huguenot migration from France, and everywhere the colonies lost a remarkable segment of talent, to name only a handful: Joseph Galloway of Pennsylvania, distinguished politician and prolific pamphleteer; J. S. Copley of Massachusetts and Peter Harrison of Rhode Island, respectively the greatest American painter and architect of the time; Count Rumford of New Hampshire, a scientist whose reputation was second only to Franklin's; Thomas Hutchinson of Massachusetts, a distinguished historian; William Smith, outstanding jurist of New York and Quebec; Jonathan Odell of New Jersey, possibly the best American poet of the era; Jonathan Boucher of Maryland, Anglican cleric and writer; David Fanning, a ferocious soldier from North Carolina who became lieutenant-governor of Prince Edward Island; Dr. Alexander Garden of South Carolina (*vide* gardenias) who became vice president of the Royal Society. These names have subsequently been lost to American memory. Loyalists became nonpersons almost in the familiar manner of individuals falling into disfavor under communist regimes.[10] A good example of a victim of American amnesia is the poet Jonathan Odell, forgotten by his alma mater, Princeton, to this day.

The intractability of definition plus the impossibility of accurate counting means the question of Loyalist numbers will never be completely resolved. However, some useful comments can be made. If the notion, attributed to John Adams, that America, like Gaul, was divided into thirds (Whig, Tory and neutral) is discredited we must also dismiss the myth of patriot unanimity.[11] Active Loyalists probably numbered one fifth (half a million) of the white population. They were of sufficient number to prolong the war. About 19,000 of them "formally took up arms...to suppress the American rebellion" compared with perhaps 100,000 enlisted rebels. It is claimed that in 1780 roughly 8,000 Americans were fighting for George III while 9,000

10. W. Brown, "The View at Two Hundred Years."
11. P. Smith, "American Loyalists," 260 and n.; W. Brown, *King's Friends*, 250; John Adams, *Works*, 87; Evans, 189-190 and n.

were fighting for George Washington. In addition Loyalists were widely employed as guerillas, propagandists, counterfeiters, spies, guides, pilots, foragers, pioneers and other civil aids.[12] Between sixty and eighty thousand Loyalists went into permanent exile which is proportionately at least five times as many as fled the French Revolution, and certainly proportionately more than fled Castro's revolution.[13] Two conclusions are evident. Whatever the precise numbers, there were a lot of Loyalists, and they made the Revolutionary war a genuine civil war.[14] More so than the Civil War of a century later which, in a sense, was a war between two nationalities, North and South. The Loyalists were distributed right across the board—by geography, religion, nativity, occupation and status.[15] As a contemporary put it, "Nabour was against Nabour."[16] Particularly vicious internecine fighting may be noted in upstate New York, the vicinity of New York City, and in the Carolina backcountry. Families, friendships, businesses, faculties and students, legal partnerships, even marriages were split. Few Americans today remember that Benjamin Franklin's son William was an active Loyalist. It is interesting in this context to note that such American historians as Charles Beard and Louis Hacker have often called the Civil War the second American Revolution whereas Canadian writers, more accurately in my opinion, call the Revolution the First Civil War.

Committed Loyalists were certainly not "non-participants." But, unfortunately for their cause, early Loyalist participation was usually on the Whig side, and with the outbreak of fighting it was necessarily subordinated to broader British strategy that wavered from a contempt for the Loyalists to a widely misconceived belief in their superior numbers based on the Loyalists' own overestimation,[17] evidenced by the final disastrous campaign ending at Yorktown.

It is odd that historians have put much more effort into defining and analyzing Loyalists than Whigs.[18] There were more active rebels than Loyalists, but the largest group of all was the grey middle, including quietist Loyalists, apathetic Whigs, various neutrals. This bulk of the population, "insipids" or "mongrels", to use John Adams' words, has been the least analysed of all.[19]

12. P. Smith, "American Loyalists," 264, 267, 269; Peckham, 200; Alden, 87n.

13. Palmer, I, 188; Draper, 60; W. Brown, *Good Americans*, 227.

14. P. Smith, *Loyalists and Redcoats*; Mackesy.

15. W. Brown, *King's Friends, passim*.

16. Zeichner, 235.

17. P. Smith, *Loyalists and Redcoats*; Mackesy; Isaac Ogden to Joseph Galloway, 22 November 1778, *Balch Papers*, New York Public Library.

18. For the correct broad approach see Allan; McKirdy; also see Martin, Sosin, *Revolutionary Frontier*, ch. 7; Waters, ch. 9.

19. Esmond Wright, 88.

Neutrality and trimming were the order of the day. Samuel Miles, a Connecticut farmer, echoed a common sentiment when he said he "kept as much out of the way as possible," as did the Long Island innkeeper who when asked which side he was on replied, "I was for peace." For caginess there is Matthew Lymburner of Penobscot who "affected to be neutral in political disputes...but in private was a Loyalist," for deviousness Francis Pemart of Peekskill who served as a rebel forage master but with "an intention of serving the Loyalists"! And there was Vermonter Thomas Johnson of whom it was said he was "a rebel among rebels, a loyalist among loyalists." Francis Hopkinson in his poem "The Birds, the Beasts, and the Bat," likened the trimmer to the bat, "always ready to proclaim himself all bird when the birds were in luck, and as all beast when the beasts seemed likely to win."[20] A classic case of expediency is afforded by Benjamin Towne whose *The Pennsylvania Evening Post* was a Whig paper until late 1777 when the arrival in Philadelphia of the British army was hailed as "the dawn of returning liberty." With the departure of the army King George again became the "British tyrant" and Towne reverted to his Whig stance.[21]

The well known example of America's less than total dedication to the Revolution is the plight of Washington's army at Valley Forge contrasted with the easy circumstances of Howe's, well supplied with specie, at Philadelphia. Even the very Whiggish Rhode Islanders rushed to trade with the British forces in 1775. At one point Washington complained that lack of public support was "infinitely more to be dreaded than the whole [British] force."[22] Perhaps half the rebel militia and one third of the Continental Line deserted during the war.[23]

A close connection between allegiance and military success occurs repeatedly as shown by the way large areas of the south appeared restored to loyalty when the British swept northwards in 1780 only to return to rebellion as the patriot army followed behind. Lord Howe "relentlessly rolled Washington back from Whig positions on Long Island, in New York City, and in New Jersey. Everywhere in the area where Washington had so recently and thoroughly applied rebel loyalty tests royal forces received ardent popular welcome."[24] Jared Sparks told an amusing story: In June, 1775, the provincial congress of New York was alarmed to learn that George Washington and William Tryon, the royal commander in chief, were expected in New

20. Tyler, II, 150; American Loyalists: Transcripts, XII, 127; XX, 102; XV, 555; (Hereafter cited as ALT); W. Brown, *King's Friends*, 252; Williamson, *Vermont in a Quandary*, Ill.

21. Ousterhout, 139-141.

22. J. Miller, 476.

23. Bowman, 70, 72.

24. Hyman, 99. For an instance in Georgia where there was little changing of sides see Ellefson, 347-356.

York City on the same day. The congress dispatched a force prepared to welcome "either the General, or Governor Tryon, whichever should first arrive, and wait on both sides as well as circumstances would allow."[25]

Many Americans took a position reluctantly as a result of coercion. It is unlikely that Georgia would have joined the Revolution without the coercion of South Carolina. The efficient work of Whig committees with recalcitrants is notorious and in my opinion took on aspects of an American "terror."[26]

This usually produced "patriots." But not always. James Moody, a native-born "happy farmer" in New Jersey was politically uninvolved, tried to remain "silent," "not to give offense." However he was "harrassed" by Whig committees, even shot at, and finally, his dander up, fled to the British with seventy-three neighbours and became a daring soldier and spy.[27] A recent Loyalist study concludes that rebel persecution was the single most important motivation in creating active Loyalists.[28] Although Jacob Bailey, Anglican minister at Pownalborough, Massachusetts, could not in conscience violate his oath he tried to be neutral, but was assailed by the Whigs. "And pray, Gentlemen, what have I done to injure the American cause?" he asked his accusers. He had neither taken up arms nor attended meetings to aid England. He added, "I sincerely wish to see the Prosperity of my country and am willing to submit to the Authority of the present government." But he was forced out of his homeland and became a dedicated frontier missionary in Nova Scotia. Another moderate, Tench Coxe, Philadelphia merchant and political economist, disliked both British legislation and the violent opposition to it. He became a victim of a patriot witch-hunt and was forced to flee Philadelphia in December, 1776. His *cri de coeur*, "I am (if permitted) likely to become a good American," was to be answered when he lived down his equivocal past and eventually became a prominent government official in the 1790s and finally a Jeffersonian Republican.[29] One Vermonter wrote, "I endeavoured to be quiet, but it would not do."[30] Daniel Parent of Long Island tried to stay out of things, was twice whipped by the rebels and accordingly fled to the British lines and eventually to New Brunswick.[31]

As lines hardened from 1774 onwards, neutrality became increasingly difficult. James Allen of Philadelphia complained that though neutral, he

25. W. Brown, *Good Americans*, 59.

26. W. Brown, *Good Americans*, ch. 5.

27. W. Brown, *King's Friends*, 123-24; MacNutt, "The Narrative of Lieutenant James Moody," 72-90.

28. Sloan, 97-98.

29. Ross; Cooke, 88 and 48-88; See also Slaski, 1-4, 38-39, 165, 221, 252, 256, 258-59, 268.

30. Williamson, *Vermont in a Quandary*, 72.

31. "Daniel Parent," Saunders Papers, Box 1, Archives, University of New Brunswick.

was branded a Tory "under which name is included every one disinclined to Independence tho' ever so warm a friend to constitutional liberty and the old cause." As patriot clergyman Nathaniel Whitaker wrote, "those who are not for us, must be against" us.[32] An open press disappeared and in Whig-controlled areas all but the most courageous Loyalists and neutralists lay low.

After the war the equivocal nature of American allegiance continued to be demonstrated. W. S. MacNutt in his book *The Atlantic Provinces* has reminded us of the "commercial character" of the migration of "scores of traders from New York to Kennebec [who] slipped their moorings and sailed north for Nova Scotia" in the autumn of 1783 following the news that the Navigation Acts, excluding foreigners from the West Indian trade, would apply to the U.S.[33] There was the ease with which many Loyalists émigrés were able to return to the young republic or send their children there for an education. There was the alacrity with which thousands of American specu-lators and frontiersmen, so-called "late Loyalists," deserted their homeland in response to Simcoe's offer of crown land in Upper Canada and their sub-sequent opposition to the U.S. invasion during the War of 1812. A dramatic example of the dubious nature of this immigration is the executioner of Major John André, unfortunate go-between of the equally dubious Benedict Arnold, who was given a land grant at Kingston before "he was recognized... and was whipped out of the community."[34]

Many Americans were non-participants or *faux amis* because of apathy, weakness, fear, selfishness and ignorance, but there were some who were neutral on doctrinal grounds, who could not see events in Manichaean terms. Some individuals were simply becalmed by events, like John Dickinson, "Penman of the Revolution," who could not for a time sanction revolution-ary violence or independence,[35] but most important were religious pacifists of whom the Quakers are the most significant.

The Whigs generally scorned the Quakers, branding them Loyalists. The Friends suffered considerable persecution, but to a degree most other neutrals lacked they had the spiritual fortitude to avoid trimming. A few "Free Qua-kers" (all disowned) ignoring the teaching "that the setting up and putting down Kings and Government is God's Peculiar Prerogative"[36] actually fought on one side or the other. Rather more passively favoured one side or the other (particularly the Tory). Certainly Quakers were conservative[37] and by

32. Nelson, *American Tory*, 147; Upton, *Revolutionary Versus Loyalist*, 121.
33. MacNutt, *Atlantic Provinces*, 92.
34. Burt, II, 81n; Morton, *Kingdom of Canada*, 201.
35. W. Brown, *King's Friends*, 151-152; Allen, "Diary," 176-196, 278-296, 424-441.
36. Thorne, 323.
37. Brock, 255n.

simply remaining aloof—refusing military service, supplies and taxes—they helped the British, but most were genuinely neutral.[38] The same may be said of the German pacifists, the Mennonites, Dunkers and Schwenkfelders.

The Moravians were ambiguous. Their leader, John Ettwein, and many other older brethren were inclined to Loyalism at first, though they eventually became reconciled to the Revolution.[39] In 1775 John Wesley told his missionaries "to be peace-makers" and to join "no party". Following this policy, and in view of Wesley's public condemnation of independence, Methodists became "stamped...as Loyalists," to quote a contemporary. They are problematical, produced no outstanding Tory, and like their leader Francis Asbury, most came to accept the Revolution.[40]

The "Black Studies" movement threatens to become overemphasized but we cannot ignore the one American in five who was black. It might be expected that this group, so uneducated and subordinated, would be most genuinely "non-participant". This is probably true, but given these handicaps it is surprising how involved blacks were. They seem to have been on one or both sides of every major battle of the war. Numbers are only guesses but maybe 5,000 of the 100,000 patriot troops were black, while "thousands" were in the British forces.[41] A great many more served as auxiliaries. It may be questioned how many blacks joined either side of their own volition, but the same may be asked of whites.

When Benjamin Harrison was about to go as a Virginia representative to the First Continental Congress he was visited by a group of his "respectable, but uninformed" neighbours whose leader said: "You assert that there is a fixed intention to invade our rights and privileges; we own that we do not see this clearly, but since you assure us that it is so we believe the fact. We are about to take a very dangerous step, but we confide in you, and are ready to support you in every measure you shall think proper to adopt."[42]

It is true the majority of enslaved blacks, at least outwardly, remained unaffected by the Revolution and many, as in the Civil War, continued genuinely attached to benevolent masters of all political persuasions. It is also true that thousands of slaves were taken overseas as mute property by Loyalist masters. But similarly on the Loyalist side Carolina Highlanders followed their chiefs, New York tenants their landlords, and miscellaneous whites their political and religious leaders.

38. Mekeel, "The Society of Friends (Quakers) and the American Revolution"; Brock, 258; W. Brown, *Good Americans*, 268; Archer; James, "Impact of the...Revolution on Quakers' Ideas..."; Wainwright, "Diary of Trifling Occurences...," 411-465; Mekeel, "The Quaker-Loyalist Migration..."; Oaks; Dorland, ch. 3 and 47-50, 308-309.

39. Brock, 259, 303-304; Dollin.

40. Stokes, 95-96.

41. Quarles, *The Negro in the American Revolution*, ix; Peckham, 99; W. Brown, "Negroes in the American Revolution"; Quarles, "Lord Dunmore as Liberator."

42. Bridenbaugh, *Seat of Empire*, 16-17.

There is evidence that a substantial minority of blacks were far from being mere ciphers. There is their response to British offers of freedom for deserting slaves of rebel owners. This offer was first made by Virginia's governor, the earl of Dunmore in 1775 and was extended throughout the colonies by General Clinton in 1779. It has been estimated that very large numbers fled.[43] I would estimate their number to be proportionately larger than those fleeing to Union lines during the Civil War. Two thousand slaves alone, including many belonging to Washington, joined Cornwallis at Yorktown in the hope of freedom. One may note also the active role played by articulate Negroes in promoting the abolition of slavery in the northern states during the revolutionary period.[44]

About 3,000 blacks fled to Nova Scotia as free Loyalists, about 1,000 went to Britain and an unknown number went to the rest of British North America and elsewhere. A likely estimate of the proportions of the white population that emigrated to the proportion of black population that emigrated is 3 to 1—a respectable comparison given restrictions on black opportunity. The black émigrés were probably the cream of the black Loyalists. They certainly continued to show initiative in Nova Scotia where as elsewhere they met severe prejudice and even re-enslavement. Conditions grew so "extremely irksome" that early in 1792 Thomas Peters, a North Carolina war veteran, led more than 1,000 to a new life in Sierra Leone where he is still honoured as a founding father.[45]

It is not easy to enter the minds of the blacks at this time because illiteracy resulted in a lack of records—even Thomas Peters was probably illiterate. What records there are suggest that when blacks did become deliberately involved in the Revolution their motivation was clearer than the whites'. They did not care directly about the great religious, constitutional and economic issues, even when they understood them. The hypocrisy of both sides was plain. For example, on the one hand British officers sold stolen slaves to the West Indies; on the other there was the way some patriot soldiers were paid in slaves. Blacks wanted freedom and advancement and, like Vermonters, were prepared to become either "Whigs" or "Loyalists." Thus, John Twine of Virginia was at first a wagoner with the Whigs, but "was kept very bare in Cloths and little Money and therefore he ran away from home when he heard there was more Money and better Usage in the British Army."[46] Crèvecoeur was probably right when he wrote that blacks were inclined to be Tories. The rebels, at least in the South, could never

43. Aptheker, 19-21.

44. J. Miller, *Triumph of Freedom*, 609; Litwak; W. Brown, "Negroes in the American Revolution," 559.

45. Peters, Petition in the *Foreign Office Papers*, 4/1, 419-423; W. Brown, *Good Americans*, 203; Spray, 9-41.

46. ALT, LVIII, 236.

match the British offers of freedom. The southern dread of black uprising remained paramount. As early as August, 1775, it was reported that "a Tory Negro was hanged, and burnt at Charlestown for endeavouring to excite Negroes to sedition."[47] William Prince said that though born free he had been "cheated" into slavery in Georgia. Accordingly when the British army arrived he escaped to it and regained his freedom by serving in the 60th Regiment. The British Claims Commissioners to whom he told his story would grant him no compensation, declaring that he had been "a great gainer by the troubles...for being in a situation in which he could loose [*sic*] nothing, he has gained everything...his Liberty."[48] Unsympathetic words, but they sum up the Negro's position.

With the end of the war, adjustment to independence was normal for Loyalists and neutrals. Even the Anglican church, so tainted with Toryism in the north, adjusted and the appointment of the formerly dreaded bishop caused little fuss. Persecution of Loyalists often continued in defiance of the Peace Treaty, but generally reconciliation was remarkably quick. Although some individuals like Galloway were permanently refused re-entry to the U.S., by 1790 anti-Loyalist action was a thing of the past. A very few eccentrics like the charming Byles sisters in Boston, continued to flaunt their Toryism,[49] but there was no Loyalist revival as happened after the French Revolution. Indeed, some Loyalists, especially with implementation of the constitution in 1789, came to admit that the Revolution had turned out to be "a good thing,"[50] and a few even had successful political careers in the young republic, usually it seems as Federalists.[51]

The story of the ex-Loyalists who remained in the United States awaits its historian.[52] Here I will concentrate on the minority 80,000 who, by choice or compulsion, became permanent émigrés and whose great achievements contrast dramatically with the almost unrelieved failures of earlier years. I offer only a few random comments on a complex theme.

The Loyalist diaspora of refugees, or "displaced persons" as we might call them, enriched the host countries around the globe as surely as it impoverished "the revolted colonies."[53] About 10,000[54] settled in the British

47. *Boston Gazette*, Sept. 18, 1775.
48. ALT, V, 194-195; W. Brown, *Good Americans*, 90, 99; Sosin, "The Use of Indians...," 101-21; Graymont.
49. W. Brown, *King's Friends*, 41-42.
50. Watson, 399-400; W. Brown, *Good Americans*, 249; MacKinnon, "Changing Attitudes...," 13.
51. E. Green, 307.
52. L. F. S. Upton, University of British Columbia, is working on it.
53. For effects of loss of Loyalists to the U. S. see W. Brown, *Good Americans*, 245-254; for exiles see W. Brown, "Escape from the Republic"; "American Loyalists in Britain"; *Good Americans*, chs. 6 and 7.
54. Figure supplied by Mary Beth Norton of Cornell University.

Isles (plus a handful in Europe). They were assimilated and are lost to view with the exception of a few who achieved some prominence such as Daniel Leonard, the former *Massachusettensis*, who died the senior member of the bar, Benjamin Thompson (Count Rumford) who founded the Royal Institution, J. S. Copley whose career reached a popular if not artistic pinnacle, and Isaac Coffin who became a well-known admiral. Many Loyalists or their sons died for Britain during the Napoleonic wars and many served the Empire in a variety of capacities.

Bermuda and the Caribbean attracted many immigrants, especially Southerners, who sought a warm climate for themselves and their slaves. The greatest number, about 3,000 whites, went to Jamaica, where as in England, they were swallowed up by a larger society. Many attained success as planters and businessmen.[55] About 2,000 whites fled to the Bahamas where they outnumbered the old inhabitants, expanded settlement, and generally began the modern era of those islands, including it is to be feared, as in Jamaica, a stiffened opposition to slave emancipation.[56]

Most important of all was the migration to what remained of British North America, which became a sort of equivalent to Ulster after Irish independence.[57] About 35,000 arrived in Nova Scotia doubling the population and resulting in 1784 in the creation, by partition, of New Brunswick where perhaps 14,000 swamped the few "pre-Loyalists" in the largely virgin wilderness. Extensive settlement also occurred in Prince Edward Island and Cape Breton, with a few Loyalists even reaching Newfoundland. Today in Saint John, New Brunswick, "the Loyalist city," the anniversary of the Loyalist landing of 1783 is celebrated with a fervour accorded in Plymouth to the Pilgrim landing. Few Americans know this. Even fewer know that until recently a similar celebration took place in Sierra Leone, marking the 1791 arrival of the black Maritime Loyalists, who, Christopher Fyfe concludes, were essential to the success of that British philanthropic forerunner of Liberia. Nova Scotian tradition is still alive and many of the non-political elite are proud of their Loyalist descent.[58]

In the ancient province of Quebec a maximum of 10,000 (including part of the Six Nations) arrived, occasionally moving to such French areas as the Gaspé, but usually going to the western wild where they settled Upper Canada (the future Ontario) formed in effect by Pitt's Constitutional Act of 1791.

The Loyalists created several American colonies before the traditional

55. Gardner, 211-212.
56. W. Brown, *Good Americans*, 219.
57. W. Brown, *Good Americans*, ch. 7; MacNutt, *New Brunswick*; *Atlantic Provinces*; Craig, ch. 1; Talman; MacKinnon, "Nova Scotia Loyalists...,"; Conrad; Burt, ch. 15; Nelson, "Last Hopes," 36.
58. Fyfe, 25, 42; Winks, ch. 2 and 3.

ones of the late nineteenth century. I say American because it cannot be stressed too much that the Loyalists were essentially American, rarely docile Tories. Just as they sometimes brought their American houses in sections to their new lands across the St. Croix River so they brought their "prefabricated" ideas. Even before the war ended refugees in Britain were shocked when their dreams met reality. One bluntly dubbed the place "Sodom." Samuel Curwen of Salem, Massachusetts, was very disappointed with "these conceited islanders," and even the arch-Loyalist Thomas Hutchinson, wrote plaintively, "I would rather die in a little country farm house in New England than in the best nobleman's seat in old England."[59] The Loyalists were pro-English yet often hated England; they were anti-American, yet often loved America.

In the Maritime provinces one thinks of the rambunctious Whiggishness demonstrated by the Loyalists in Saint John during the first New Brunswick election of 1785, and of Benjamin Marston who in May, 1783 complained of the "curs'd Republican Town meeting Spirit" that characterized Shelburne, the temporary Loyalist boom-town of Nova Scotia.[60] The best modern authority concludes that the legislative history of Nova Scotia and New Brunswick was firmly, in the "traditions of the lost thirteen colonies," that "provincial governors were subjected to the same strains that had finally destroyed the first British Empire," and that "replicas of the constitutional struggles ...of New York and Massachusetts were...the common lot of the two provinces."[61] It is fitting that it was a son and a grandson of Loyalists who were most important in the advance of Nova Scotia and New Brunswick to self-government in the mid-nineteenth century. Joseph Howe, whose father had run the *Massachusetts Gazette*, was a flamboyant Halifax newspaperman and statesman who combined a passionate feeling for colonial democracy with Loyalism and anti-republicanism. Lemuel Allan Wilmot was a similar reform politician in New Brunswick whose grandfather, Lemuel Wilmot, was a Poughkeepsie warrior-Loyalist sprung from an old New England family. In the Bahamas the story was similar. Governor Maxwell, before he fled in disgust, found the Loyalists no more congenial than did his counterpart Governor Parr of Nova Scotia complaining that they "almost wish to take over the government." The old inhabitants regarded the newcomers as semi-republican revolutionaries.[62]

It has nurtured the self-esteem of New Brunswickers to consider themselves descendants of American colonial aristocrats in the same way it has flattered Virginians to consider themselves the progeny of Cavaliers. The fact

59. "Letters of Jonathan Sewel," 423; Curwen, 90, quoted in Winsor, VIII, 208n.
60. Marston, Diary, May 8, 1783.
61. MacNutt, *Atlantic Provinces*, 123.
62. Quoted in W. Brown, *Good Americans*, 219.

that as usual the elite, the Winslows, the Odells *et allii* wrote the records and left the evidence, has helped this image. Further it has suited some New Brunswickers (and other Canadians) to brand the nineteenth century "Family Compacts" as Loyalist inspired. This is a myth in Upper Canada and only partly true in New Brunswick where Loyalists were part of the opposition to the Compact. The Loyalist tradition has, however, been used primarily as a conservative force. Today, for example, the title Loyalist is used by some groups to oppose biculturalism. But it is clear that most New Brunswick Loyalists were modest farmers from the middle colonies rather than the well-to-do Harvard graduates of myth, tradition and the Saint John Chamber of Commerce.[63] A similar plebeian character must also be given to the bulk of Loyalist settlers in the rest of Canada.

Without denying the elite Loyalists' real contributions to the upbuilding of British North America especially in politics, commerce, the professions and the church, it was the yeomen and artisans, aided by government grants of land and supplies, who were most fitted for the daunting, arduous task of taming the wilderness. Indeed, the influence of the elite was often evanescent and sometimes even baleful. In the 1790s Sergeant-Major William Cobbett noticed the slightly ludicrous side of early New Brunswick society. Although he admired the "able Yankee farmers," the "Yankee Loyalist" society shattered his English view of the class structure. He found "Thousands of captains...without soldiers, and of squires without stockings or shoes." At home he "had never thought of approaching a squire without a most respectful bow: but in this new world, though I was but a corporal, I often ordered a squire to bring me a glass of grog and even take care of my knapsack."[64] Another British visitor was amazed to find General John Coffin, of the distinguished Nantucket family, a huckster on the Saint John Wharf. In short New Brunswick suffered from too many generals, too few privates. It comes as no surprise that some of the gentlemen Loyalists, for whom there were no jobs or fees and who did not relish swinging an ax or serving grog, returned to the United States. A most conspicuous example was Dr. William Paine, a founder of the University of New Brunswick who soon returned permanently to Massachusetts and became a founder of the American Antiquarian Society. No less than six members of New Brunswick's first assembly which met in 1785 had returned to the U.S. before the session was completed! So much for evanescence. Now for balefulness. The Loyalist tradition has been blamed in New Brunswick for encouraging politics too devoted to office, patronage, and elitism, and a general lack of enterprise (particularly industrial). Even Edward Winslow, distinguished descendant of the Pilgrims,

63. Esther Wright.
64. Cobbett, 35; W. Brown, "William Cobbett in North America."

noted: "Those who had [government] salaries made their calculations to eat, drink, and vegetate to the exact amount of their income."[65]

The Loyalists deserve admiration for pointing out that the Revolution was not of unalloyed righteousness, and foreseeing the dangers of American lawlessness and republicanism. As the Reverend Mather Byles put it as he watched the hysteria accompanying the funeral of Crispus Attucks: "They call me a brainless Tory; but tell me...which is better to be ruled by one tyrant three thousand miles away, or by three thousand tyrants one mile away?"[66] Or, in the words of Clergyman Samuel Seabury, "If I must be devoured let me be devoured by the jaws of a lion, and not *gnawed* to death by rats and vermin."[67]

The Loyalists deserve admiration for being less parochial and more cosmopolitan than the patriots. Thus they contributed to the Canadian concept of the "cultural mosaic," which, even when allowances are made for Canadian romanticizing, does contrast with the American melting-pot. Their devotion to the "Unity of Empire," their anticipation of Confederation and the ideal of a federated Empire, or even Commonwealth, beginning with Galloway's plan, and the constitutional efficacy of monarchy, was not ignoble.[68]

The Revolution not only made Americans free, but also Canadians who despite initial tightening of imperial control, never surrendered the basic principle of "No taxation without representation" won by the rebellion. The Loyalists secured Canadian integrity, what both French and English call the "miracle" of survival or *survivance*, physically as well as psychologically. An important step was their contribution to the disaster at Saratoga which brought France into the war opposed to American capture of the north. By expanding Canadian settlement within the powerful British Empire the Loyalists produced a country strong enough to withstand Manifest Destiny. French-Canadian integrity, begun by the Quebec Act of 1774, was also assured because without the advent of the Loyalists it is difficult to see how Quebec any more than Louisiana could have survived American imperialism. And within the union it is difficult to see how *le fait français en Amerique du Nord* could have continued. At the same time the Loyalists made a reality of the basic Anglicising of British North America begun in the 1750s with the Acadian expulsion and Wolfe's victory on the Plains of Abraham.

The Loyalists are important in the development of Canadian nationalism which so often reflects their own love-hate for the United States and the

65. Winslow Papers, 709; J. Davidson, 162-172.
66. Quoted in W. Brown, *Good Americans*, 74.
67. Quoted in Bailyn, *Pamphlets*, I, 197.
68. Upton, *The Loyal Whig*, 220; Craig, 6; Norton, ch. 3.

rancour peculiar to civil war. Canadians combine strong desires for emulation with the fear that "Satan's Kingdom"[69] will *"Yankifier le Canada."*[70] Loyalist hostility has been intense enough to convert outsiders. Thus John Strachan arrived in Upper Canada from Scotland in 1799 with strong pro-American attitudes, but by 1809 was fully convinced that "true liberty" did not exist in the U.S.[71] Despite the vaunted "undefended border" Canadian militia defence included plans for an American attack until the 1920s![72]

I will only hint at the Loyalists' further role in shaping Canadian history and national character, so perhaps surprisingly different from American. Note Canada's relatively peaceful western advance and Indian policies (the King's Peace!);[73] her attitude to minorities; her partial acceptance of socialism (creeping republicanism is the equivalent of creeping socialism in the U.S.); her more evolutionary, hierarchical and less democratic, but also less violent, doctrinaire development; her more cosmopolitan foreign policy.[74]

In conclusion let me say that as the American Revolutionary bicentennial approaches the auguries are good both for Canadians and the long-dead Loyalists. Loyalist studies, with an international scholarly committee that reflects, I'm sure, a burgeoning general interest, are a "growth stock." Loyalists are ceasing to be disquieting phantoms hovering at the founders' banquet like Banquo's ghost. Scholars of Loyalism are ceasing to feel like the Ancient Mariner collaring the guests at the wedding feast. In Canada the task is to make the national memory more realistic, in America the task is to restore it. Americans seem to be in a masochistic mood, ready to admit that Benedict Arnold does not epitomize the Loyalists, ready to accord the losers of the First Civil War the respect (hopefully devoid of the sentimentalism) given the losers of the second. Respect for the Loyalists in the United States should produce a needed increased respect for Canada.

69. Quoted in MacKinnon, "Changing Attitudes...," 2.
70. *Le Canadien*, December 24, 1808, quoted in Wise and Brown, 26.
71. Wise and Brown, 19.
72. Wise and Brown, 9.
73. Morton, *The Canadian Identity*, 47.
74. McCrae; Horowitz; Lipset; S. Clark; Underhill.

The Strange Case of the "Revolutionary" Establishment

The key concept to be kept in mind in understanding the development of American governments after Independence is that at ground zero virtually nothing happened when the King's writ ceased to run. Since the 17th century, America had been a "do-it-yourself" enterprise. The British were far too busy fighting continental wars—and settling their own civil war—to involve themselves at the *operational* level in the government of these remote colonies. Except for protection from the French in Canada, all most Americans wanted was to be left alone. And they were largely left alone to create their own governmental institutions. (As Richard B. Morris pointed out forty years ago in his neglected classic, *Studies in the History of American Law*, law reforms not achieved in Britain until the 1830s were incorporated in the Massachusetts Body of Liberties [1641] and in colonial legislation which simply hacked away the jungle of writs that provided the essence of common law litigation.)

Curiously enough John Calvin spotted this phenomenon incredibly early, presenting in his *Commentary on Deuteronomy* (c. 1535) the nub of what later became known as the "safety valve thesis". Justifying capital punishment for blasphemy, Calvin observed: "Some object that since the offense consists only in words, there is no need for such severity. But we muzzle dogs, and shall we leave men free to open their mouths as they please? Those who object are like dogs and swine. *They murmur that they will go to America where nobody will bother them.*" (Italics mine.)

No commentator in his sense would argue that American institutions in the 17th and 18th centuries were "democratic" in the modern sense of the word. However, the level of citizen participation in the decisions of his governments was certainly greater here than anywhere else in the contemporary world. One found here an open society with closed enclaves: the Anglican oppressed by the Bay Colony could move to Virginia and get his licks in against the local Puritans.[1] To put it differently, there was a high level of consensual authoritarianism: it was hardly necessary to employ Dr. Gallup to find out how a Puritan felt about Quakers (it would be comparable to polling Israelis on their view of anti-Semites).

What these scattered communities along the coast of North America shared, then, was not a common ideology in substantive terms, but a complete conviction that it was their business to define whatever ideology might be relevant and applicable. As Royal Governor after Royal Governor (to say nothing of excisemen) learned the hard way, the Americans simply took for granted precisely the question allegedly at issue: Who ran the colonies? (Those interested in the colonists' talents at attrition are referred to the hilarious adventures of Edward Randolph in his efforts to enforce the customs laws against various provinces in the late 17th century. And who but the Marx Brothers could master the political scenarios that the good citizens of "Rogues" Island later mounted?)[2]

To an average American very little changed after independence was declared—except when British troops turned up to inconvenience him. The town meetings kept in business, the legislatures shifted ground (as from Boston to Salem under Gage's duress), the same justice of the peace with the same veniremen ran the "hundreds". In short, the social system retained its integrity.

A number of eccentrics opted for the Crown, either because they did not discern the strength of the American civic religion or—more frequently—because they were personal enemies of the local elite. But they were handled with an efficiency that Lenin might well have envied: they were outlawed under sentence of death and their goods and chattels confiscated by their "conservative" (or were they "radical"?) neighbors. It was clear that any opposition to the American order would be located in Britain, Canada or the West Indies, not on its home ground.[3]

What was the American rationale for this assumption of *de facto* sovereignty? Did a careful reading of John Locke lead to this universal upsurge of "radical Whiggery"? Obviously, as the *Declaration of Independence* evidences, John Locke's concepts were useful things to have on the shelf. But then there are some sticky precedents that have to be explained. Listen to Edward Winslow, Governor of Plymouth Colony, writing in 1646: "If the Parliaments

1. Roche, "American Liberty."
2. Hall, *Edward Randolph*; and Lovejoy, *Rhode Island Politics*.
3. For statistics on refugees see Palmer, 188.

of *England* should impose Lawes upon us having no Burgesses in their house of Commons, nor capable of a summons by reason of the vast distance of the Ocean being three thousand miles from *London*, then wee should lose the libertie and freedome I conceived of *English* indeed."[4] (Italics in original.)

This was not idle rhetoric. In 1661, when the Restoration of Charles II threatened a wholesale reorganization of colonial government, the Great and General Court of Massachusetts Bay rejected the British right to reimpose the Navigation Acts, but then—in as neat a legal ploy as one can imagine—the legislature passed *in its own right* statutes enforcing the Navigation measures.[5] (An interesting reversal of the technique was employed by the British Parliament a century later when the Stamp Act was repealed but accompanied by a Declaratory Act stating Parliament's rights in premises.)

"No taxation without representation" was thus rattling around in the American arsenal a century before it became a *mot d'ordre*. There are other interesting coincidences which suggest that John Locke was in some respects a codifier of the majoritarian view of sovereignty rather than its author.[6] For instance, in dealing with the reach of colonial authority the 1648 Massachusetts *Laws and Liberties* provided that anyone entering the province "doe(s) tacitly submit to this Government and to all the wholesome laws thereof." A third of a century later John Locke in his *Second Treatise* (Sec. 119) presented a virtually identical definition of "tacit consent".

This is not the place to set out the innumerable techniques that the various American assemblies devised to circumvent the day to day jurisdiction of the Crown. Or, for the matter, the way the good Quakers of Pennsylvania dealt with their Proprietor when the latter, deciding to collect his quit-rents, sent Captain John Blackwell of Philadelphia to institute law and order.[7] It was not that Americans were disloyal; they just insisted on defining for themselves the outward and visible manifestations of fealty. The latter, needless to say, did not include payment of taxes except those enacted by their provincial legislatures. Because of Royal preoccupation with crises of a far higher order (the "Second Hundred Years War", for example), and simple administrative inefficiency, the Americans by and large got away with their autonomy.

Indeed, by 1765 I think it is legitimate to say that Americans were simply habituated to self-government. This did not mean that the majority of the population were actual participants, but there is no reason to suspect that the largest group of non-participants—women—held different views from their husbands. Indeed, there were those in the British government who favored

4. P. Miller, *Orthodoxy in Massachusetts*, 307.
5. P. Miller, *New England Mind*, 125-126.
6. Laslett, Introduction to Locke.
7. Wainwright, "Governor John Blackwell."

leaving the French in Canada as a means of keeping the colonies attached to the homeland. On May 9, 1761, for example, the Duke of Bedford wrote that he wondered if "the neighborhood of the French to our Northern Colonies was not the greatest security of their dependence on the Mother Country who I fear will be slighted by them when their apprehensions of the French are removed."[8]

When you recall that there was no civil list for support of the Crown in the American colonies, that the royal governors were dependent for their salaries on the provincial assemblies, and that a navy is hardly the ideal instrument for what we today call "pacification", it is immediately obvious the extent to which the British had in all but symbolic terms waived their rights to sovereignty. In each province the political class effectively ran public affairs. This political class could be elected on a quite broad franchise as in Watertown, Massachusetts, in 1757 where there was a bitterly contested election to the General Court in which of 135 qualified voters 131 voted,[9] or on a narrow franchise. Or this "establishment" could simply hold its position by deference. But there it was in place assuming without argument the legitimacy of its authority.

Of course, the pamphleteers were out in force arguing all sorts of Talmudic questions ("When is a tax not a tax? When it's a regulation." Etc.), but this was icing on the cake. As Mary Beth Norton has recently suggested,[10] the poor Loyalists never understood what hit them. They thought they were loyal, only to discover as they were dispossessed and exiled that, properly understood, they were "rebels".

These poor folks had plenty of time in the wilds of Canada to meditate on the problem, but they never did grasp the difference between loyalty to a symbol and loyalty to a social system. Concededly, the political class had some unique definitions: in March, 1775, for example, the Newport, Rhode Island, Committee of Inspection demanded the banning of a newspaper in the name of freedom of the press—which it defined as "the diffusion of liberal sentiments on the administration of Government."[11] Equally unnerving was the political class' views on law and order on which Lieutenant Governor Thomas Hutchinson of Massachusetts was something of an authority: After a 1768 "tumult", he had the attorney general lay the facts before the grand jury, but to no avail since, as he caustically noted to the Lords of Trade, the foreman of the jury had been the instigator of the affair.[12]

Civil libertarians who look back to a "Golden Age" of American Liberty

8. Namier, 276.
9. S. Greene.
10. Norton.
11. Roche, "American Liberty."
12. *Pennsylvania Chronicle*, July 5, 1773.

which—in their view—has been replaced by an era of "repression" might meditate briefly on the "chilling effect" of the following resolution of the Continental Congress, passed in October, 1775:

"Resolved, That it be recommended to the several provincial Assemblies
or Convention, and councils or committees of safety, to arrest and secure
every person in their respective colonies, whose going at large may, in their
opinion endanger the safety of the colony, or the liberties of America."[13]

What this adds up to is the hardly novel thesis that (as John Adams later
wrote Mercy Warren) "the Revolution was over before the War began." But
beyond that I would contend that far too much time and energy has been
expended by scholars on taxonomic exercises in the realm of political
theory.[14] The Americans did not inch their way towards a theory of
autonomy: they took autonomy for granted and turned the high theorists
loose to make the brief. ("No taxation without Representation," for example,
sounded pretty good until a canny anonymous critic "F. L." in the *Pennsylvania Journal*, March 13, 1766, spotted the joker—suppose the Royal
authorities got clever and passed out some seats? The Americans would be
sawed off at the knees: "represented" but outvoted.[15] John Adams later
made the same point. So it was back to the drawing board with the ultimate
design of a federal theory of the British Empire.) As Jack Greene has shown
in his fine *Quest for Power*, the colonial elite was constantly on the alert for
ways of moving in on the prerogative, and once some commanding height or
other had been effectively seized, a scribe could be found to prove that, in
fact the action was fully justified by Sec. 31 of *Magna Carta*, or the Assize of
Clarendon, or both.

Which is not to say that the debate was not sharp and interesting. John
Dickinson, for example, was a grand master of the art of circular reasoning:
Conceding the Parliament could regulate trade but not lay internal taxes, he
set himself the question, "When is a regulation actually a disguised tax?"
Answer: "When it has the impact of a tax."

On the other side of the hill Soame Jenyns was a superb dialectician—
indeed, at the risk of confiscation of goods and chattels and exile to Nova
Scotia, I think his *The Objections to the Taxation of Our American Colonies
...briefly consider'd* merits first prize in the trans-Atlantic dispute. Jenyns,
with a cold eye, went right to the central weakness of the colonial position.
"It has been moreover alleged," he commented, "that though Parliament may
have power to impose taxes on the colonies, they have no right to use it, because it would be an unjust tax; and no supreme or legislative power can have

13. Ford, III, 280.
14. Colbourne, *Lamp of Experience*; Maier, *From Resistance to Revolution*.
15. J. Adams, *Novanglus*, March 6, 1775, 78-94.

a right to enact any law in its nature unjust. To this, I shall make only this short reply, that if Parliament can impose no taxes but what are equitable, and if the persons taxed are to be the judges of that equity, [Parliament] will in effect have no power to lay any tax at all."

But this exchange of polemics was at the fundamental level trivial because it burked the real issue, namely, who has the ultimate authority to draw the boundary lines between conflicting claims to sovereignty? Each side took for granted its right to define its own rights leaving an "Appeal to Heaven" (Locke's euphemism for war) as the inexorable solution.

The theoretical model perfectly designed for American use was that provided in John Locke's *Second Treatise* which combined legislative supremacy with majority rule. However, crucial to the employment of Locke's design was the determination that the provinces were the *units of sovereignty*. To turn the proposition around, before one proclaimed the sovereignty of the legislature, Parliament had to be expelled from the premises and replaced by the provincial assemblies. Once this feat was accomplished, the rest was easy: the King had betrayed his trusteeship and, *ipso facto*, destroyed his own claim to jurisdiction. George III, in short, was in revolt against the good people of Massachusetts, New York, *et al*, as represented in their sovereign legislatures. Note carefully the superbly functional character of this logic: it left the fabric of the community intact. Everything was distinctly *not* up for grabs.

Take New Hampshire, for example, where the colonial legislature in December 21, 1775, regretted that the Royal Governor John Wentworth had let them down by departing and promptly went on to write a constitution. They wasted no time establishing their jursidiction: "We, the members of the Congress of New Hampshire, chosen and appointed by the free suffrages of the people of said colony, and authorized and empowered by them to meet together and use such means and pursue such measures as we should judge best for the public good; and in particular *to establish some form of government....*"[16] (Italics added.)

But the application of Locke which doubtless had that worthy spinning in his grave was the *Declaration of Independence*, for he had taken a very dim view of the application of his doctrines against British Parliamentary authority: when his disciple Thomas Molyneux applied the logic of Ireland in the *Case of Ireland*, 1698, Locke disowned the argument completely. The *Declaration of Independence* was a masterpiece of political warfare. An innocent observer reading its indictment of Royal abuses would understandably tuck George III into the same category as Henry VIII or Elizabeth I—a Tudor monarch ravaging the rights of Englishmen. The authors of the *Declaration* were quite aware, of course, that the source of their discontent was

16. Thorpe, IV, 2451.

not George III engaged in tyrannical use of the prerogative but the British Parliament. Yet Parliament *qua* Parliament was egregiously downgraded.

What we find are two references: 1) "He [George III] has combined with others to subject us to a jurisdiction foreign to *our constitution* (italics added), and unacknowledged by our laws; giving his assent to their acts of pretended legislation." And 2) "We have warned [our British brethren], from time to time, of attempts by their legislature to extend an unwarrantable jurisdiction over us." The implication of (1) is that Parliament was a kind of Star Chamber working in tandem with the king; the implication of (2) is that Parliament was simply the British equivalent of the Massachusetts Great and General Court, i.e., an "internal legislature."

This was a breath-taking application of the technique of *petitio principi*, of assuming one's conclusions in his premises and moving on from there. For once it was settled that George III stood in precisely the same relationship to the General Court in his capacity as King of Massachusetts Bay as he did to Parliament in his role as King of England, the ideological battle was won. All one now had to do was turn to Locke and find the appropriate citations for coping with a usurping executive; Sec. 238 of the *Second Treatise* was made to order.

Asking himself in Sec. 237 when the people can resist a king, Locke replies that "The People therefore can never come by a Power over him, unless he does something that makes him cease to be a King." In Sec. 238 he elaborates an example: "When a King makes himself dependent of another, and subjects his kingdom...and the People put free into his hands, to the Dominion of another." Thus when George III turned his American "kingdoms" over to "a jurisdiction foreign to our constitution", the British Parliament, he automatically *unkinged himself*.

When I was young, and historians learned Latin tags instead of calculus, there were great controversies over the "legality" of these various American scenarios. The followers of Charles McIlwain were at daggers drawn with the acolytes of Robert Livingston Schuyler on whether the American Revolution was based on a correct or incorrect reading of various esoteric precedents—I recall wrestling for a week with the arcane intricacies of Poynings' Act. For the benefit of those who have not similarly suffered, Poynings' Act, passed by the *Irish* Parliament in 1495 under English duress, gave the King and Council what amounted to an absolute, pre-emptive veto over any measures passed by that body. An Irish Parliament could not be held until the King and Council had approved in advance of its legislative purpose! Moreover, the Act proclaimed that every Royal writ under the Great or Privy seal had the same status in Ireland as in England, and that statutes "lately" passed by the English Parliament were in Ireland the law of the land. "Lately" was subsequently construed to include any measure passed before 1495.

Stark and simple as this may seem, it opened up a dispute similar to that occasioned by the Roman *lex regia*. Was this an irretrievable gift of power by the Irish legislature, what the Roman lawyers would have deemed a *cessio*? Or was it merely a revocable delegation, a *translatio*? The implications for the American colonies hardly need elaboration. However, a quarter of a century later I look back on this exercise with some amusement for it is crystal clear that—with the exception of a few ill-fated sceptics—the Americans took the legality of their actions as a given in the equation.

In a formal sense, just about everything that happened from the Stamp Act Congress, the First and Second Continental Congresses onwards to the Federal Constitution was "illegal". Provincial legislatures converted themselves into state legislatures and constitutional conventions, or called separate constitutional conventions, or (as in Connecticut and Rhode Island) simply made minor amendments in their colonial charters. As far as law enforcement was concerned, the various states provided that the common and statutory law of England should remain in force as altered by the legislature. Judges and juries—purged of course of Tories—continued their business. Fundamentally the definition of legality hinged on the outcome of the War: *inter arma leges silent*.

As noted above, each of the newly independent states took action to provide formal legitimation for its jurisdiction. Since Gordon S. Wood has in *The Creation of the American Republic* provided us with a fascinating exploration of this period in what might be called the history of ideas metier, I will concentrate more on what the "Fathers" did than what they said. As anyone who has closely compared the work of the Constitutional Convention in Philadelphia with its *a posteriori* justification in *The Federalist* will suspect, there is no necessary connection between rhetoric and reality.

Putting aside for the time being the question of a "national" government, let us turn to the states—where until at least the mid-1780s lay the locus of action.[17] Since executive despotism had been the rationale for independence, it is hardly surprising that the states in their new constitutions virtually demolished executive power. The casual reader may be disconcerted by a recurring statement to the effect that "the legislative, executive and judiciary department, shall be separate and distinct, so that neither exercises the powers that properly belong to the other" (Virginia, 1776). Similar formulations appeared elsewhere (e.g., Georgia, North Carolina) and it was finally cast in concrete by John Adams in Section I, Article 30 of the Massachusetts Constitution of 1780.

The "separation of powers" thus became enshrined as one of the fundaments of American constitutionalism, that is, until you take a closer look at

17. Richardson, "Early American Political Authority" is the source of most of the specific material on state constitutions incorporated herein.

those documents themselves. Then you realize with a shock that (with a few exceptions to be noted later) the new governments were built around a radical version of Locke's supreme legislative. True, as in Maryland, some checking and balancing could be introduced by the creation of a second *legislative* chamber. But these two houses elected the governor, denied him a veto, supervised his appointments, and the like. In short, we are dealing here with a parliamentary model. The so-called "radical" Pennsylvania Constitution of 1776 went even further: the executive was a body of 12 elected from various counties who, in conjunction with the unicameral legislature, chose a president from their number. Since the legislature retained the right to appoint all important officials, and the President had no veto, he was simply a figurehead.

This catalogue could be continued at some length, but the crux of the matter is that except in Massachusetts and New York, there was nothing resembling an executive veto power (and in New York the governor's power was limited by a Council of Revision). Where the governors or presidents had appointing power, it was hedged about with legislative checks: in New York a Council of Appointments; in Massachusetts, the Governor's Council of nine "annually chosen...by the joint ballot of the Senators and Representatives assembled..." Only in Massachusetts, Rhode Island, Connecticut, and New York was the governor publicly elected, which in political terms meant that he could develop an independent constituency. (New Hamsphire revised its Constitution in 1784 to include an elected "President," but circumscribed his authority far more strictly than that of his legislatively selected predecessor!) Most judges, who in the British tradition, and in Locke, were considered agents of the executive, were chosen by legislative ballot.

So much for the "separation of powers". It was a precept much honored but virtually ignored. It is interesting in this context to anticipate by noting that the Randolph Plan presented by James Madison to the Philadelphia Convention as the preliminary model for the new federal government was built around the total supremacy of the legislature.[18] (The Articles of Confederation created a legislative supremacist pseudo-government, but its problems were of a different order: it had no power.)

The second major characteristic of the new state governments was their dedication to the principle of "power to the people". Again recall that the legitimacy of the legislative power in Locke rested on its representative character (Sec. 140, *Second Treatise*) and on the application of the majority principle (Sec. 96). Here the trick question had always been the majority of *whom*? That is, the extent of the political class to which the majority rule proposition was applied. Writing of the English electorate in the 1640s the British historian J. H. Plumb has observed that "the situation in the counties

18. Roche, "Founding Fathers...," 804-805.

as well as the boroughs had changed out of all recognition from Elizabethan times, and we witness the birth of a political nation, small, partially controlled, but no longer co-extensive with the will of the gentry."[19]

It is my contention that the American Revolution legitimized the birth of a "political nation", that throughout the colonies-turned-states there was a great awakening of political consciousness. Indeed, in 1777 the Constitution of Georgia not only awarded the franchise to virtually every freeman but also included a mandatory voting provision: "Every person absenting himself from an election, and shall neglect to give in his or their ballot at such election, shall be brought to a penalty not exceeding five pounds."!

Ultimate power lay in the "People" and every state constitution contained a more or less elaborate "Bill of Rights" or declaration of the residual jurisdiction of the populace, plus certain procedural guarantees against arbitrary exercises of power. But, and this is vital, the underlying assumption was that these rights were to be protected from an arbitrary executive—few precautions were taken against what Tocqueville later described as the "tyranny of the majority", or more specifically, the tyranny of a representative legislature. Indeed, the bill of rights in a number of these early constitutions darkly warned against speaking "slanderously" of the government, i.e., the legislature!

The legislature was supreme and was kept on a very tight leash through the mechanism of short terms "to the End that those who are unfit for their Posts may be easily dropped, and such as are Worthy as they come on the stage Elected."[20] One almost visualizes the Rousseauistic ideal of the annual session of the community as a whole deciding whether or not to retain its governors, though in point of fact this ideal had existed for over a century in the New England town meetings.

Moreover, the concept of instructions to legislators was common; that is, in its paradigmatic form, the town meeting of Barnstable, or Belchertown, Massachusetts, had no reservations about telling its representatives in the General Court what to do,[21] and the same practice applied in other states. The Burkean view of the conscientious autonomy of the legislator was considered part and parcel of the old "aristocratic" order. (It was perhaps on this ground that most constitutions barred clergymen from office-holding: there were real risks that men of the cloth would refuse to confuse *vox populi* with *vox Dei*.) State delegates to the Congress under the Articles of Confederation were, excepting in Connecticut, Rhode Island, and New Hampshire, chosen by the legislatures, and expected to get instructions from home: in essence, they were ambassadors.

19. Plumb, "Growth of the Electorate."
20. Handlin, 47.
21. Handlin, 47.

On the eve of the Constitutional Convention, then, we can summarize the governmental situation in the United States in the following terms: the fiercely independent states had created governments on the unitary, parliamentary model with a supreme legislative and subordinate executive and judicial branches. That is, they implemented (with partial deviations here and there, notably in New York and Massachusetts) John Locke's ideal. Paradoxically, the American response to the growth of Parliamentary power in England was to create in miniature precisely the system they saw as the source of their woes. At the "national" level, there was the United States government under the *Articles* which substantively had no power and procedurally also followed the parliamentary model: the Chairman of the Committee on Foreign Affairs was *de facto* Secretary of State.

I have in my essay "The Founding Fathers" explored in considerable, even excruciating detail the political and social forces that led to the Federal Convention.[22] Suffice it for our purposes here to say that the leading reformer, James Madison, wanted to enact a constitution that would incorporate the Lockean model. If anybody can find a trace of the "separation of powers" in the "Randolph Plan", he has second-sight. Not only did Madison's model establish a supreme legislative in the federal government, but it conferred decisive powers over the states. To make a long story short, what later emerged as the great American doctrine of "federalism" was a set of improvisations, compromises between those delegates who wanted to strengthen the center and those who felt that if they took Madison's plan home, they would probably be lynched.[23]

Eventually things worked out, the compromise was adopted by the popularly elected conventions, and Madison, Hamilton and Jay provided one of the great works of American political fiction, *The Federalist*. While all this was taking place, while the states were writing their constitutions and the war was winding along in its desultory fashion, what was the reaction of the "average" American? This is a lovely question because it is subject neither to proof, nor to disproof, but my hunch is that—to revert to my original theme—he just went about his business (more accurately, his farming) with the unarticulated assumption that there was no great crisis. The elite (with few defectors) remained incredibly stable over a quarter of a century. Were they "radicals"? Were they "conservatives"? This strikes me as a foolish question, one based on the supposition that they had extensive access to the writings of Karl Marx and V. I. Lenin. Their sole concern was to maintain the social system: their didactic descendants could figure out the appropriate labels.

22. Roche, "Founding Fathers..."
23. Roche, "Constitutional Law..."

The American Revolution as a Precedent

STAUGHTON LYND

I suspect that my intended function is to add a dash of twentieth-century relevance to the solid eighteenth-century bill of fare you have been consuming thus far.

If so, I shall disappoint you. I shall not compare the ever-glorious spirit of Don't Tread On Me to the equally glorious spirit of Freedom Now and We Won't Go. Nor shall I dwell on parallels—obvious though they may be—between George III and Richard Nixon.

Before we can talk about the American Revolution as a precedent we have to decide what kind of revolution it was, if indeed that term was not a semantic mistake. The basic answers to this question are few and were all suggested before the year 1800. I shall denote them Answers A, B, C, and D.

Answer A was advanced by the Revolution's leaders and echoed by their friends in England, such as Edmund Burke: *The American Revolution was a struggle for constitutional rights.*

Answer B was that of the Revolution's opponents, again both in America and England: *The American Revolution was a struggle for economic independence from the British Navigation Act and trade laws.*

Answers C and D were put forward in a second round of controversy in the 1790s, as Americans tried to determine their proper relationship to the French Revolution. Answer C was that of the Jeffersonians: *The American Revolution was a democratic movement essentially similar to the French Revolution.* Their Federalist opponents responded with Answer D: *The American Revolution was a colonial independence movement essentially different from the French Revolution.*

On the whole subsequent scholars of the Revolution have fallen into two groups. There have been A-D men and women, holding that the Revolution was an independence movement on behalf of constitutional rights. This position has been referred to as Whig, or in its most recent variants, neo-Whig. And there have been B-C iconoclasts, who contended that the Revolution was an internal social conflict, economically motivated. This position is associated with historians who wrote during the Progressive period before the first World War, such as Carl Becker and Charles Beard, and is therefore often denominated as the attitude of Progressive historians.

With all appropriate qualifications, I am a B-D man. I think the American Revolution was basically an independence movement, but that the reasons for it were fundamentally economic.[1] I shall make a case for this position, and then return to the question, What kind of precedent does this kind of Revolution provide?

Please bear in mind, as this discussion proceeds, that economic interpretation can be narrow or broad. An example of a narrow economic interpretation is Charles Beard's argument that many of the men who drafted the United States Constitution stood to benefit personally from its adoption. Economic interpretation can be more subtle than this. George Bancroft, for instance, is generally considered the very prototype of filiopietistic Whiggery. Yet it was Bancroft who wrote: "American independence, like the great rivers of the country, had many sources; but the head-spring which colored all the stream was the Navigation Act."[2] If the American Revolution had fundamentally economic causes it is not thereby demeaned, for our own era of colonial independence movements should have retaught us something about the many-sided meaning of economic sovereignty for developing nations.

I

How may the truth or falsity of an economic interpretation of the Revolution be tested? One approach was suggested by Edmund Burke in 1775. As quoted approvingly by Oliver Dickerson toward the close of his *The Navigation Acts and the American Revolution*, Burke stated in his House of Commons speech on conciliation:

One fact is clear and indisputable. The public and avowed origin of this quarrel was on taxation. This quarrel has indeed brought on new disputes on new questions; but certainly the least bitter and the fewest of all, on the trade laws. To judge which of the two to be the real radical cause of the quarrel we have to see whether the commercial dispute did, in order of time, precede the dispute over taxation. There is not a shadow of evidence for it.[3]

1. This essay elaborates theses outlined in Lynd, *Class Conflict, Slavery and the U. S. Constitution*, 13-14. See Egnal and Ernst; and Olton for essays that have encouraged me to resume the discussion.
2. Bancroft, V, 159.
3. Dickerson, 284-285.

Burke was demonstrably wrong. The commercial dispute began in 1760 during the "French and Indian" war when the question of taxing the colonies had not yet been raised. In that year the British government started to use its navy to suppress illegal trade between the North American colonies and the French West Indies. The stated intention was military: to deprive the French forces of "Provisions, and other Necessities whereby they are, principally, if not alone, enabled to sustain, and protract, this long and expensive War."[4] The new British policy flew in the face of the deep conviction of New England merchants that the survival of their economy required the export of fish and other produce to the foreign as well as to the British West Indies, and the import of molasses from the foreign West Indies duty-free, or very nearly so. They considered the 6d. a gallon import duty on molasses from outside the British empire imposed by the Molasses Act of 1733 to be economically prohibitive. If they could not evade the duty by smuggling, they would fight it.

This was the background of two legal actions brought by James Otis on behalf of Boston merchants directed against effective enforcement of the Molasses Act. The first sought to claim from customs house officers for the Massachusetts legislature a portion of sums forfeited under the Molasses Act which these officers had illegally retained. The practice had enabled the customs house officers to offer larger sums to informers than the law allowed. The second legal action was the celebrated protest against general search warrants (writs of assistance). The writs were necessary to the British because, as Thomas Hutchinson explained, "a writ, or warrant, to be issued only in cases where special information was given upon oath, would rarely, if ever, be applied for, as no informer would expose himself to the rage of the people."[5] It was, of course, during this pleading that Otis declared that an act of Parliament against the constitution and natural equity was void, thus adopting the ultimate natural law argument against British authority before taxation was an issue at all.

When war with France ended in 1763, rigorous enforcement of the trade laws continued. The French government, responding to the fact that cession of Canada to England deprived the French West Indies of any source of supply within the French empire, issued an order in April 1763 to the governors of all French colonies in the Americas to permit foreign vessels to import horses, mules, lumber of all kinds, bricks, furniture and a wide variety of foodstuffs in exchange for molasses.[6] Reciprocally, the British govern-

4. Pitt to the governors of the American colonies, August 23, 1760, quoted in Gipson, *The Coming of the American Revolution, 1763-1775*, 33. See also Gipson, "The American Revolution as an Aftermath...," 100-101; "Aspects of the Beginning of the American Revolution...," 11-32.
5. Hutchinson, 68.
6. Goebel, 331-372.

ment issued orders from the customs houses of the Northern colonies in December 1763 to enforce the Molasses Act "in all its parts," that is, to see to it that all the molasses imported from the French West Indies paid the full duty of 6d. a gallon. Governor Bernard of Massachusetts stated that the publication of these orders "caused a greater alarm in this country than the taking of Fort William Henry did in 1757," an observation later confirmed by John Adams.[7]

Americans had the more reason to be distressed in 1763 because of the post-war depression. An influx of goods from England caused specie to drain to the mother country which in turn produced a general inability to pay debts, both foreign and domestic. These circumstances provided new economic reasons for opposing a policy which had initially been opposed largely on economic grounds.

The Molasses Act was due to expire in 1764, and during 1763-1764, while the British government tightened enforcement of the old law, merchants in New England and New York petitioned Parliament through their respective legislatures against its reenactment. Their statements emphasized the economic distress of the colonies. The action was ineffective, because the Sugar Act passed Parliament before the colonial remonstrances arrived. But this "first intercolonial movement of the pre-Revolutionary period designed to exert political pressure in England"[8] set a precedent which could readily be resurrected when, with the passage of the Sugar Act, the right to tax finally became an issue.

Among modern scholars there is really no disagreement that until the spring of 1764 public protest against British policy ran along economic lines. Bernard Bailyn writes: "The most striking fact about these addresses and petitions is their entire devotion to economic arguments: nowhere do they appeal to constitutional issues; nowhere was Parliament's right to pass such laws officially questioned."[9] Bailyn's formulation separates economic and constitutional argument too sharply. A good example of the way constitutional argument grew out of economic is the instructions of the town of Boston to its representatives in the Massachusetts legislature, written by Samuel Adams and others in May, 1764. After lengthy admonition "to support our commerce in all its just Rights," the document more briefly but quite intensely poses the danger of taxation without representation.[10] Edmund and Helen Morgan add that economic considerations weighed more heavily than constitutional in the initial protests against the Sugar Act itself: "Undoubtedly the drastic economic effects the colonists anticipated from the

7. Schlesinger, *Colonial Merchants*, 48 and n.
8. Knollenberg, 148.
9. Bailyn, *Pamphlets*, I, 358-359.
10. Samuel Adams, I, 3-5.

Sugar Act prompted the alarm they felt, but it was natural for them to inquire into the right of the matter."[11]

The question is what this means. Those, like Bailyn and the Morgans, who feel that the constitutional controversy became the heart of the matter, consider the economic arguments of 1763-1764 a sort of prelude. After the passage of the Stamp Act, they say or imply, debate settled into a constitutional pattern.

The difficulty with this reasoning is that it has to be used too often. When Parliament repealed the Stamp Act, it also lowered the duty on imported foreign molasses from 3d. a gallon to 1d. a gallon, a burden New England merchants appear to have felt that they could live with. And when Parliament imposed new import duties in the Townsend Acts of 1767 the initial agitation against this legislation, too, was again primarily economic.

Charles M. Andrews, the closest student of the non-importation movement against the Townsend Acts, states flatly: "The non-importation movement was at first a protest against commercial restraints and financial impositions and was initiated chiefly by the merchants."[12] A good illustration of Andrews' point is the text of the non-importation agreement entered into by Boston merchants on August 1, 1768. The preamble recited the difficulties of trade, scarcity of money, trade acts, new duties, taxes for the late war, a bad corn crop and poor prospects for whale fisheries, "by which our principal sources of remittance are likely to be greatly reduced, and we thereby rendered unable to pay the debts we owe the merchants in Great Britain, and to continue the importation of goods from thence."[13] It may be said that the non-importation movement had been developing for some time by August, 1768. Here is Professor Schlesinger's summary of its beginnings: "The first phase of the movement originated in the fall of 1767 in New England where evidences of hard times had at once become apparent, and had for its primary object a reduction in the cost of living....The movement received its first impulse from the action of a Boston town meeting on October 28, 1767. A form of subscription was adopted, which attributed the prevailing commercial depression to the high war taxes, the loss of trade in late years and the many burdensome trade restrictions, the money stringency and the unfavorable balance of trade with England."[14] Clearly the October 1767 and August 1768 statements struck essentially the same note. It is apparent that in the second great pre-Revolutionary crisis as well as in the first, economic complaints preceded constitutional.

This is equally the case for the third such crisis occasioned by the Tea Act

11. Morgan and Morgan, 51.
12. Andrews, *The Colonial Period*, IV, 427.
13. Becker, *The History of Political Parties*, 61n.; text in Andrews, "The Boston Merchants...," 205.
14. Schlesinger, *Colonial Merchants*, 106-107.

of 1773. It cannot be emphasized too much that, constitutional scruples not-withstanding, Boston merchants imported large quantities of dutied tea in the years immediately preceding the Tea Act. Dickerson notes that the average imports at Boston actually increased from 110,471 pounds a year in the five-year period before the adoption of the Townsend Acts to 179,169 pounds a year in the five-year period 1768-1772.[15]

What changed in 1773? Nothing constitutional: no new duty was laid, no new enforcement procedures were elaborated, no new inflammatory assertion of right was insisted on by Parliament. What was new was the bestowal on the East India Company of a monopoly of one of the colonies' most lucrative imports. Contemporary historians on both sides of the constitutional argu-ment agree that the merchants were once more the first to act, and once more for economic reasons. Thomas Hutchinson states: "The only apparent dis-content was among the importers of tea, as well those who had been legal importers from England (principally in Boston because of the concentration of enforcement machinery there), as others who had illegally imported from Holland (principally in New York and Philadelphia); and the complaint was against the East India Company for monopolizing a branch of commerce which had been beneficial to a great number of particular merchants."[16] David Ramsay concurs that "the opposition originated in the selfishness of the merchants."[17] Once again base economic metal was transformed into constitutional gold, and by mid-October, when mass meetings began to call on American consignees to resign, it was undoubtedly true that "the decisive opposition was based on the issue of the Townsend duty."[18] But the evi-dence supports the judgment of Arthur Schlesinger, Sr. in 1917: "These meetings, however, were the flowering, not the roots, of the tree that had been carefully planted and nourished by the beneficiaries of the existing business order."[19]

Thus Edmund Burke's call for inquiry into the "real radical cause" of American discontent produces results discomfiting not only to his Whig thesis of 1775, but also to its latter-day, epicyclical, neo-Whig variants. In each of the major pre-Revolutionary crises agitation was initiated by mer-chants for primarily economic reasons. The commercial dispute preceded the constitutional, not just once, but again and again throughout these years.

II

The constitutional or neo-Whig view of the Revolution is based on the belief that the colonial population shared an intellectual consensus. Assuming

15. Dickerson, 89.
16. Hutchinson, 303.
17. Ramsay, *History of the American Revolution*, I, 97.
18. Labaree, 96.
19. Schlesinger, "The Uprising against the East India Company," 79.

that everyone thought pretty much alike, this approach cannot deal effectively with the questions of who took the lead in resistance and why some groups persisted longer than others.

If it could be shown that the groups which most strongly and persistently resisted British policy were the groups most damaged by the British economy, the entire train of events would appear in a new light. The hypothesis could then be ventured that a political break with England came to be desired by those who sought an economic break, who (for instance) wanted to limit the flow of British imports into American markets or to find markets for American exports outside the British empire. The groups which in crisis situations took a hard line toward England would be those which preferred to cut themselves off entirely from the British economy rather than continue existing patterns of Anglo-American trade. And conversely, the groups which most ardently sought political conciliation would also be those which, for economic reasons, "strove to obtain the most favorable terms possible within the empire but not to leave it."[20]

A *locus classicus* for testing this hypothesis is the debate over continuing non-importation in 1770.

Andrews, Schlesinger, and Becker characterize the two sides in this debate in essentially the same way. Andrews believes that the constitutional issue was of secondary importance in initiating non-importation, but that "as the commercial and financial complaints dwindled in importance with the failure of the non-importation movement, it became the leading issue after 1770." Continuation of non-importation became the cause of a vaguely defined group of radicals whose concerns were chiefly political.[21] Schlesinger agrees: "As the political agitators and turbulent agitators gained the upper hand, the contest began to assume more clearly the form of a crusade for constitutional rights."[22] Becker, too, states at the conclusion of his chapter on the Townsend Acts that the "radicals" were unable to prevent the "merchants" from renewing importation.

However, all three authors provide evidence for a different assessment of the division between those who wished to continue non-importation and those who wished to end it. In this view three economic interests were involved in non-importation: merchants who imported dry goods from Great Britain; merchants who smuggled from the West Indies, and whose business continued as usual under the non-importation agreement; and artisans. At one point Becker puts the matter in just this way:

But by the spring of 1770, the unity of the industrial interest had disappeared; the merchants and importers of wealth and standing were pre-

---

20. Schlesinger, "American Revolution Reconsidered," 70.
21. Andrews, *The Colonial Period*, IV, 427.
22. Schlesinger, "American Revolution Reconsidered," 70.

pared to take a frankly conservative attitude; the mechanics and artisans, the merchants and importers whose profits were largely identified with smuggling, held fast to the radical program, and constituted the rank and file of the Sons of Liberty.[23]

One might have expected Becker to go on to say that while the importers of dry goods from Great Britain, for economic reasons, desired to end non-importation, the importers from the West Indies and the artisans, for economic reasons, were happy to see it continue. For the dry goods merchants, especially the larger ones, one year of non-importation made good economic sense. The glut of dry goods on the American market was reduced, existing stores were sold off at higher prices. Thereafter, however, the dry goods merchant began to hurt. The importers of wines and molasses, on the other hand, remained undisturbed in their traffic. Usually late-comers to the mercantile scene, and for this reason forced into the more risky and less capitalized West Indian trade, they saw their share of the community's business expand the longer non-importation continued.

The thesis almost advanced by Carl Becker has now been stated and developed by Charles Olton. In Philadelphia, he says, there were "two factions— dry goods merchants on the one hand, and mechanics and radical West Indies merchants on the other hand." The conflict of dry goods and West Indian merchants is detailed. Especially important is Olton's exposition of the posture of the Philadelphia artisans, which corroborates Schlesinger's evidence for Boston and New York. Of all colonial economic groups the artisans came most directly into conflict with the British economy. "During the 1760s, they complained incessantly about the ruinous competition of foreign wares." Non-importation appealed to these native manufacturers. "One Philadelphia tradesman later testified that those mechanics who suffered from non-importation were 'but few, when compared to the number of those who have received great benefit from it'." Accordingly, Olton finds, mechanic support of non-importation in early 1770 was practically unanimous.

Indeed—and here we return to the larger question of the dynamics of the Revolutionary movement—Olton suggests that the mechanics self-consciously intruded themselves into colonial politics, not because they were disfranchised (they were not), but because they wanted to make sure that a policy of economic nationalism initially sponsored by the merchants was carried through to the end. "Because the merchants hesitated, mechanics began to organize."[24] Schlesinger notes in the division of opinion in Massachusetts

23. Becker, *The History of Political Parties*, 83.
24. Olton, 317, 319, 320, 320n, 321. See also Andrews, "The Boston Merchants...," 208-9, 257; Schlesinger, *Colonial Merchants*, 218, 230; Brunhouse, 369-370; Harrington, ch. 9, sep. 350.

after the destruction of the tea the artisans were among the party which wished not to pay for the tea and to renew non-importation, and cites artisan support for non-importation in New York, Charleston, and Philadelphia as well.[25]

This finding squares with everything that we know of the artisans during and after the Revolution. Becker, viewing the artisan as the carrier of democratic ideology, is calamitously at a loss to explain how it happened that in 1787-1788 the artisans of every major American city enthusiastically supported a purportedly counter-revolutionary Constitution.[26] If, however, the artisans are understood as first and foremost defending their livelihoods, they assume a new role and even a new dignity as the most passionate and consistent proponents of American economic sovereignty from the 1760s to the 1790s. When the military struggle was over and political independence was assured, the struggle for economic independence continued in resistance to what then became British neocolonialism. The end of the war in 1783 brought a depression remarkably like that which followed the end of the war in 1763. Once again imports from Great Britain flooded the American market. Once again specie was drained from the country, and the scarcity of money was universally bemoaned. Once again merchants and artisans set aside other quarrels to work together on behalf of economic protection; and, this time, a new Constitution.

A third group of colonists who had strong economic reasons to resist British policy were the tobacco planters of Virginia and Maryland. Unlike the Northern merchants, the planters were damaged not so much by the particular acts passed after 1763 as by England's mercantilist orientation expressed in the Navigation Act itself. The original passage of the Navigation Act a century before the Revolution had ended the direct trade between Virginia and Holland, driven down the price of tobacco, and led to the large-scale importation of slaves. Forced to sell their tobacco in a single market, and to buy imported dry goods from a single source of supply, the Virginians fell into debt to British merchants. Economists have tried to measure the burden of the Navigation Act by asking how much the colonists would have gained had they been able to trade freely. If the burden is distributed over all thirteen colonies the per capita loss due to the Navigation Act is small. But 90 percent of the burden fell on the South.[27] In a similar vein, the potent Treasury official Charles Jenkinson contended in the midst of the Revolutionary war that the British should make sure of securing the Southern colonies because

25. Schlesinger, *Colonial Merchants*, 175, 220, 224, 219-220, 236n.
26. Lynd, *Class Conflict*, chs. 4 and 5.
27. Ransom, 427-435.

the export of tobacco was the only function of the American economy worth the effort of monopolizing by trade laws.[28]

Years before 1763 the Virginia legislature was trying to find ways to lighten the burden of private debt borne by the planters. The famous Parson's Cause, in which Patrick Henry questioned the British government's right to veto colonial legislation, arose from the legislature's passage of a law to permit debts to be paid in tobacco whose value was set by the legislature above the current market price.

These circumstances led Progressive historians to suggest that a main motive for independence in Virginia was the desire to repudiate debts. Neo-Whigs have indignantly denied this. It may be that both arguments miss the point. Thoughtful and honorable Virginians sought to recover control over the destiny of their economy by breaking ties with England and seeking a market for their tobacco in France and Holland. A passionate Francophilism persisted among Virginians long after the winning of political independence. Jefferson, for instance, as American representative to France and Secretary of State devoted "a decade of unremitting activity to develop a national system of political economy independent of Britain, tied to France."[29]

Becker, in this respect, may require less to be rejected than to be revised. He wrote at the outset of his study of colonial politics:

The American Revolution was the result of two general movements; the contest for home-rule and independence, and the democratization of American politics and society. Of these movements, the latter was fundamental; it began before the contest for home-rule, and was not completed until after the achievement of independence.

To come a little closer to how it really was, perhaps we need only substitute "the struggle for economic sovereignty" for the struggle over who should rule at home. The passage would then read: The American Revolution was the result of two general movements; the contest for political home-rule and independence, and the struggle for economic sovereignty. Of these movements, the latter was fundamental; it began before the political home-rule, and was not completed until after the achievement of independence.

III

And the precedent? It may seem elusive. Clearly this is no longer a developing economy, contending against the colonialism and neocolonialism of stronger foreign powers. The roles are now reversed: it is we who are imperial England, crushing with napalm and fragmentation bombs, not to speak of

28. Mackesy, 158-159.
29. Peterson, 585.

whatever Hessians we can still find to fight for us, the spirit of the American Revolution wherever it may raise its head.

My point is this: Of course there *is* an anti-authoritarian spirit abroad in the land. The students, the blacks, the draft resisters of the 1960s, the women of the 1970s need make no apologies to Massachusetts minute men. All are part of a continuing tradition of struggle for participation in the decisions that affect one's life. And there *is* a trend toward executive usurpation in the United States today, even toward classical 18th century corruption, which can be compared rather minutely to the efforts of the British government to pass laws for people unrepresented in the law-making process, to disregard the will of the colonial legislatures, and the rest.

But in my opinion the subjective discontent on the one hand, the objective provocation on the other, will never create a mass movement like the movement for American independence until a third factor is added, a factor which I have sought to show was abundantly present in 1760-1776: namely, a set of economic circumstances which bring potent sectors of the population increasingly into conflict with the government which also robs them of their more abstract liberties.

Briefly, I believe that such economic conflicts are in the making. For the first time in a generation American working people, the artisans if you will, are being thrust into head-on collision with the American government.

After World War II the American economy forestalled a recurrence of depression like that of the 1930s by a program of massive military spending: a permanent war economy. The price of thus forestalling unemployment has been to create structural inflation, especially in periods when the cold war becomes hot, as after 1965. The result was that in the late 1960s the real wages of American working people began to go down for the first time since 1945 as prices rose faster than wages. We too, one might say, are being taxed to support a standing army.

More significantly, after World War II the American economy forestalled socialism in Western Europe and Japan by a program of massive economic aid and investment. Having been saved for capitalism, these economies—rebuilt with the latest technology from the ruins our bombers made—are now beginning to undersell American industry and even to take away a portion of the domestic market, as in automobiles and steel. The result is that American industry and government have begun to assault the wages and working conditions of American workers, controlling wages while prices and profits spiral, speeding-up work and taking away jobs under the guise of "job enrichment" and "productivity," moving toward compulsory arbitration. Like the Philadelphia artisans, American workers are trying to protect their jobs from foreign imports.

Like the colonists in 1776, many American workers are property owners. Like the colonists, they are not utopian visionaries but are concerned first and foremost with their own livelihoods, and with constitutional rights on which a livelihood may depend, such as the right to strike. Like the colonists, their initial motivation is to protect what they already have rather than to seek something new. But if property-owning, pragmatic common people made a revolution then, they can also make another—should it be needed—now.

References

Abernethy, Thomas P. *Western Lands and the Revolution*. New York: Appleton-Century Co., 1937.

An Account of the State Prison or Penitentiary House, in the City of New York. By one of the Inspectors. New York: Isaac Collins, 1801.

Adams, John. *The Adams-Jefferson Letters*. Edited by Lester J. Cappon. 2 vols. Chapel Hill: University of North Carolina Press, 1959.

Adams, John and Sewall, Jonathan. *Novanglus and Massachusettensis; or Political Essays published in the years 1774 and 1775*. Boston: Hews & Goss, 1819.

Adams, John. *The Works of John Adams*. Edited by Charles Francis Adams. 10 vols. Boston: Little, Brown, 1856.

Adams, Samuel. *The Writings of Samuel Adams*. Edited by Harry Alozo Cushing. 4 vols. New York and London: G. P. Putnam, 1904-08.

Adams Family Correspondence. Edited by Lyman H. Butterfield. 4 vols. Cambridge, Mass.: Harvard University Press, 1963-73.

Akagi, Roy H. *The Town Proprietors of the New England Colonies: A Study of Their Development...1620-1770*. Philadelphia: University of Pennsylvania Press, 1924.

Alberts, Robert C. *The Golden Voyage: The Life and Times of William Bingham, 1752-1804*. Boston: Houghton-Mifflin, 1969.

Alden, John R. *The American Revolution*. New York: Harper and Row, 1954.

Allan, Anne A. "Patriots and Loyalists: The Choice of Political Allegiances by Members of Maryland's Elite." *Journal of Southern History* 38 (1972):283-292.

Allen, James. "Diary of James Allen, esq., of Philadelphia, Counsellor at Law, 1770-1778." *Pennsylvania Magazine of History and Biography* 9 (1885-1886):176-196, 278-296, 424-441.

Almond, Gabriel A. and Powell, G. Bingham, Jr. *Comparative Politics: A Developmental Approach*. Boston: Little, Brown, 1966.

American Loyalists: Transcripts of the Manuscript Books and Papers of the Commission of Enquiry into the Losses and Services of the American Loyalists. Microfilm, 60 reels, New York Public Library.

Andrews, Charles M. "The Boston Merchants and the Non-importation Movement." Colonial Society of Massachusetts *Publications* 19 (1917):159-259.

Andrews, Charles M. *The Colonial Period of American History*. 4 vols. New Haven: Yale University Press, 1934-1938.

Aptheker, Herbert. *The Negro in the American Revolution.* New York: International, 1940.

Archer, Adair P. "The Quaker Attitude towards the Revolution." *William and Mary Quarterly* 2d ser. 1 (1921):167-182.

Argenson, René Louis de Voyer de Paulmy. *Considérations sur le Gouvernement Ancien et Présent de la France.* Amsterdam: Marc Michel Rey, 1765.

Bailyn, Bernard. "Education as a Discipline: Some Historical Notes." In *The Discipline of Education,* edited by John Walton and J. L. Kuethe. Madison: University of Wisconsin Press, 1963.

Bailyn, Bernard. *Ideological Origins of the American Revolution.* Cambridge, Mass.: Harvard University Press, 1967.

Bailyn, Bernard. *New England's Merchants in the Seventeenth Century.* Cambridge, Mass.: Harvard University Press, 1954.

Bailyn, Bernard. *The Origins of American Politics.* New York: Knopf, 1968.

Bailyn, Bernard, ed. *Pamphlets of the American Revolution, 1750-1776.* Cambridge, Mass.: Harvard University Press, 1965.

Bailyn, Bernard. "Politics and Social Structure in Virginia." In *Seventeenth-Century America: Essays in Colonial History,* edited by James Morton Smith. Chapel Hill: University of North Carolina Press, 1959; Also in *Colonial America: Essays on Politics and Social Development,* edited by Stanley N. Katz. Boston: Little, Brown, 1971.

Baker, Norman. *Government and Contractors: The British Treasure and War Supplies, 1775-1783.* London: Athlone Press, 1971.

Bancroft, George. *History of the United States from the Discovery of the American Continent.* 6 vols. Boston: Little, Brown, 1852.

Barker, Charles A. *The Background of the Revolution in Maryland.* New Haven: Yale University Press, 1940.

Barnwell, Robert W., Jr. "Loyalism in South Carolina, 1765-1785." Ph.D. dissertation, Duke University, 1941.

Baugh, Daniel A. *British Naval Administration in the Age of Walpole.* Princeton: Princeton Univerity Press, 1965.

Beard, Charles A. *An Economic Interpretation of the Constitution of the United States.* New York: Macmillan, 1913.

Becker, Carl L. *Everyman His Own Historian.* New York: Crofts, 1935.

Becker, Carl L. *The History of Political Parties in the Province of New York, 1760-1776.* Madison: University of Wisconsin Press, 1960.

Bell, David V. J. "The Loyalist Tradition in Canada." *Journal of Canadian Studies* 5 (1970):22-33.

Benton, William A. *Whig-Loyalism.* Rutherford, N. J.: Fairleigh Dickinson University Press, 1969.

Billias, George A., ed. *Law and Authority in Colonial America: Selected Essays.* Barre, Mass.: Barre Publishers, 1965.

Binney, John Edward Douglas. *British Public Finance and Administration, 1774-1792.* Oxford: Clarendon Press, 1958.

Bjork, Gordon C. *Private Enterprise and the Public Interest: The Development of American Capitalism.* Englewood Cliffs: Prentice Hall, 1969.

Blackburne, Francis. *Memoirs of Thomas Hollis, Esq.* 2 vols. London: 1780.

Bonomi, Patricia. *A Factious People: Politics and Society in Colonial New York.* New York: Columbia University Press, 1971.

Boston Gazette. September 18, 1775.

Bowman, Allen. *The Morale of the Revolutionary Army.* Port Washington, N. Y.: Kennikat, 1964.

Boxer, Charles R. *The Dutch Seaborne Empire: 1600-1800.* London: Hutchinson, 1965.

Bradford, William. *Of Plymouth Plantation, 1620-1647.* Edited by Samuel E. Morison. New York: Knopf, 1952.

Breen, T. H. *The Character of the Good Ruler: A Study of Puritan Political Ideas in New England, 1630-1730*. New Haven: Yale University Press, 1970.

Bridenbaugh, Carl. *Mitre and Sceptre*. New York: Oxford University Press, 1962.

Bridenbaugh, Carl. *Seat of Empire*. Charlottesville: Dominion, 1963.

Brock, Peter. *Pacifism in the United States, from the Colonial Era to the First World War*. Princeton: Princeton University Press, 1968.

Brown, Richard D. *Revolutionary Politics in Massachusetts: The Boston Committee of Correspondence and the Towns, 1772-1774*. Cambridge, Mass.: Harvard University Press, 1970.

Brown, Richard M. "The American Vigilante Tradition." In *The History of Violence in America*, edited by Hugh Graham and Ted Gurr. New York: F. A. Praeger, 1969.

Brown, Richard M. *The South Carolina Regulators*. Cambridge, Mass.: Harvard University Press, 1963.

Brown, Robert E. and Brown, Katherine. *Virginia, 1705-1786: Democracy or Aristocracy?* East Lansing: Michigan State University Press, 1964.

Brown, Wallace. "American Loyalists in Britain." *History Today* 19 (1969):672-678.

Brown, Wallace. "Escape from the Republic." *History Today* 22 (1972):94-102.

Brown, Wallace. *The Good Americans*. New York: Morrow, 1969.

Brown, Wallace. *The King's Friends*. Providence: Brown University Press, 1965.

Brown, Wallace. "The Loyalists of the American Revolution." *History Today* 12 (1962):149-157.

Brown, Wallace. "Negroes in the American Revolution." *History Today* 14 (1964): 556-563.

Bruchey, Stuart. *The Roots of American Economic Growth, 1607-1861: An Essay in Social Causation*. New York: Harper & Row, 1965.

Brunhouse, Robert Levere. "The Effect of the Townshend Acts in Pennsylvania." *Pennsylvania Magazine of History and Biography* 54 (1930):355-373.

Buel, Richard, Jr. "Democracy and the American Revolution: A Frame of Reference." *William and Mary Quarterly* 3d ser. 21 (1964):165-190.

Buel, Richard, Jr. *Securing the Revolution: Ideology in American Politics, 1789-1815*. Ithaca: Cornell University Press, 1972.

Burnett, Edmund C., ed. *Letters of Members of the Continental Congress*. 8 vols. Washington, D. C.: Carnegie Institution, 1921-1936.

Burt, Alfred L. *The Old Province of Quebec*. 2 vols. Toronto: McClelland and Stewart, 1968.

Bushman, Richard. "Corruption and Power in Provincial America." In *The Development of a Revolutionary Mentality: Papers presented at the First Library of Congress Symposium on The American Revolution*. Washington, D. C.: Library of Congress, 1972.

Bushman, Richard. *From Puritan to Yankee: Character and the Social Order in Connecticut, 1690-1765*. Cambridge, Mass.: Harvard University Press, 1967.

Calhoon, Robert M. "William Smith, Jr.'s Alternative to the American Revolution." *William and Mary Quarterly* 3d ser. 22 (1965):105-118.

Cassinelli, C. W. "Some Reflections on the Concept of the Public Interest." *Ethics* 69 (1958):48-60.

Champagne, Roger. "New York Politics and Independence, 1776." *The New York Historical Society Quarterly* 46 (1962):281-303.

Clark, Michael D. "Jonathan Boucher: The Mirror of Reaction." *The Huntington Library Quarterly* 33 (1969):19-32.

Clark, Samuel D. *Movements of Political Protest in Canada, 1640-1840*. Toronto: University of Toronto Press, 1959.

Clive, John and Bailyn, Bernard. "England's Cultural Provinces: Scotland and America." *William and Mary Quarterly* 3d ser. 11 (1954):200-213.

Cobb, Richard. "The French Revolution and Private Life." *Historical Studies* 8 (1971 [Dublin 1969]):3-30.

Cobbett, William. *Life and Adventures of Peter Porcupine*. Port Washington, N. Y.: Kennikat, 1970.

Colbourn, H. Trevor. *The Lamp of Experience*. Chapel Hill: University of North Carolina Press, 1965.

Colbourn, H. Trevor, ed. "A Pennsylvania Farmer at the Court of King George: John Dickinson's London Letters, 1754-1756." *Pennsylvania Magazine of History and Biography* 86 (1962):241-286, 417-453.

Condon, Thomas J. *New York Beginnings: The Commercial Origins of New Netherland*. New York: New York University Press, 1968.

Conrad, Harold E. "The Loyalists in New Brunswick." Ph.D. dissertation, University of Toronto, 1934.

Cook, Edward Marks, Jr. "Local Leadership and the Typology of New England Towns, 1700-1785." *Political Science Quarterly* 86 (1971):586-608.

Cooke, Jacob E. "Tench Coxe: Tory Merchant." *Pennsylvania Magazine of History and Biography* 96 (1972):48-88.

Corbett, Julian S. *Drake and the Tudor Navy*. 2 vols. London: Longmans, Green, and Co., 1899.

Craig, Gerald M. *Upper Canada: The Formative Years, 1784-1841*. Toronto: McClelland and Stewart, 1963.

Cremin, Lawrence A. *American Education: The Colonial Experience, 1607-1783*. New York: Harper & Row, 1970.

Curwen, Samuel. *Journal and Letters, 1775-1784*. Edited by G. A. Ward. New York: C. S. Francis, 1842.

Daniell, Jere R. *Experiment in Republicanism: New Hampshire Politics and the American Revolution, 1741-1794*. Cambridge, Mass.: Harvard University Press, 1970.

Davidson, John. "The Loyalist Tradition in Canada." In *The United Empire Loyalists: Men and Myths*, edited by L. F. S. Upton. Toronto: Copp Clark, 1967.

Davidson, Philip. "The Southern Backcountry on the Eve of the Revolution." In *Essays in Honor of William E. Dodd,* edited by Avery Craven. Chicago: University of Chicago Press, 1935.

Davis, David B. "Some Themes of Counter-Subversion: An Analysis of Anti Masonic, Anti Catholic, and Anti Mormon Literature." *Mississippi Valley Historical Review* 47 (1960):205-224.

De Armond, Anna Janney. *Andrew Bradford*. Newark: University of Delaware Press, 1949.

DeMond, Robert O. *The Loyalists in North Carolina During the American Revolution*. Durham, N. C.: Duke University Press, 1940.

Demos, John. *A Little Commonwealth: Family Life in Plymouth Colony*. New York: Oxford University Press, 1970.

Diamondstone, Judith. "Philadelphia's Municipal Corporation, 1701-1776." *Pennsylvania Magazine of History and Biography* 90 (1966):183-201.

Dickerson, Oliver M. *The Navigation Acts and the American Revolution*. New York: A. S. Barnes, 1963.

Dickinson, John. "Letters from a Farmer in Pennsylvania." In *Empire and Nation*, edited by Forrest McDonald. Englewood Cliffs, N. J.: Prentice-Hall, 1962.

Dietze, Gottfried. "Benjamin Rush and the American Revolution." In *Early Dickinsoniana: The Boyd Lee Spahr Lectures in Americana, 1957-1961*. Carlisle, Pa., Dickinson College, 1961.

Dollin, Norman. "The Schwenkfelders in Eighteenth Century America." Ph.D. dissertation, Columbia University, 1971.

Dorland, Arthur G. *A History of the Society of Friends (Quakers) in Canada*. Toronto: Macmillan, 1927.

Dorman, John Frederick, compiler. *Virginia Revolutionary Pension Applications*. 16 vols. to date. Washington, D. C.: 1958- .

Douglass, Elisha P. *The Coming of Age of American Business: Three Centuries of Enterprise, 1600-1900*. Chapel Hill: University of North Carolina Press, 1971.

Douglass, Elisha P. *Rebels and Democrats: The Struggle for Political Equality and Majority Rule During the American Revolution*. Chapel Hill: University of North Carolina Press, 1955.

Draper, Theodore. "Cubans and Americans." *Encounter* 17 (1961):59-77.

Duarte, Nestor. *A Ordem Privada e a Organização Politica Nacional*. São Paulo: Companhia Editoria Nacional, 1939.

Dyckman, John W. "The Public and Private Rationale for a National Urban Policy." In *Planning for a Nation of Cities*, edited by Sam Bass Warner, Jr. Cambridge, Mass.: M. I. T. Press, 1966.

Egnal, Marc, and Ernst, Joseph. "An Economic Interpretation of the American Revolution." *William and Mary Quarterly* 3d ser. 29 (1972):3-32.

Elkins, Stanley M. *Slavery: A Problem in American Institutional and Intellectual Life*. Chicago: University of Chicago Press, 1959.

Ellefson, C. Ashley. "Loyalists and Patriots in Georgia During the American Revolution." *The Historian* 24 (1962):347-356.

Ellis, Richard E. *The Jeffersonian Crisis: Courts and Politics in the Young Republic*. New York: Oxford University Press, 1971.

Evans, Geraint N. D. *Allegiance in America*. Reading, Mass.: Addison-Wesley, 1969.

Fanning, Samuel J. "The King's Purse and the Absentee's Pocket in Eighteenth-Century Ireland." In *Crisis in the "Great Republic": Essays Presented to Ross J. S. Hoffman*, edited by Gaetano L. Vincitorio. New York: Fordham University Press, 1969.

Fehrenbacher, Don E., ed. *Abraham Lincoln: A Documentary Portrait Through His Speeches and Writings*. New York: New American Library, 1964.

Ferguson, Elmer James. *The Power of the Purse: A History of American Public Finance, 1776-1790*. Chapel Hill: University of North Carolina Press, 1961.

Fleming, Thomas J., ed. *Benjamin Franklin. A Biography in His Own Words*. New York: Harper and Row, 1972.

Flick, Alexander C. *Loyalism in New York During the American Revolution*. New York: Columbia University Press, 1901.

Force, Peter, ed. *American Archives*, 4th ser. Washington, D. C., 1837-1846.

Ford, Worthington C. et al., eds. *Journals of the Continental Congress*. 34 vols. Washington: Government Printing Office, 1904-1937.

Fortes, Meyer. "Descent, Filiation, and Affinity." *Man: A Monthly Record of Anthropological Science* 59 (1959):206-212.

Foster, Stephen. *Their Solitary Way: The Puritan Social Ethic in the First Century of Settlement in New England*. New Haven: Yale University Press, 1971.

Franklin, Benjamin. *The Writings of Benjamin Franklin*. Edited by Albert Henry Smyth. 10 vols. New York: Macmillan, 1905-07.

Franklin, Benjamin. *The Papers of Benjamin Franklin*. Edited by Benjamin W. Labaree. 17 vols. New Haven: Yale University Press, 1959-1973.

Frantz, Joe. "The Frontier Tradition: An Invitation to Violence." In *The History of Violence in America*, edited by Hugh Graham and Ted Gurr. New York: F. A. Praeger, 1969.

Friedrich, Carl J., ed. *The Public Interest*. New York: Lieber-Atherton Press, 1962.

Frothingham, Richard. *The Life and Times of Joseph Warren*. Boston: Little, Brown, 1865.

Fyfe, Christopher. *A History of Sierra Leone*. London: Oxford University Press, 1962.

Gadsden, Christopher. *The Writings of Christopher Gadsden*. Edited by Richard Walsh. Columbia: University of South Carolina Press, 1966.

Galloway, Joseph. "A Candid Examination of the Mutual Claims of Great Britain and the Colonies..." In *Tracts of the American Revolution, 1763-1776*, compiled by Merrill Jensen. Indianapolis: Bobbs-Merrill, 1967.

Gardner, William J. *A History of Jamaica*. London: E. Stock, 1873.

Gaustad, Edwin S. *The Great Awakening in New England.* New York: Harper, 1957.

Gibbon, Edward. *Autobiography.* London: J. N. Dent & Co., 1939 (first published in 1796).

Gipson, Lawrence Henry. "The American Revolution as an Aftermath of the Great War for the Empire, 1754-1763." *Political Science Quarterly* 65 (1950):86-104.

Gipson, Lawrence Henry. "Aspects of the Beginning of the American Revolution in Massachusetts Bay, 1760-1762." *Proceedings of the American Antiquarian Society* 67 (1957):11-32.

Gipson, Lawrence Henry. *The Coming of the Revolution, 1763-1775.* New York: Harper, 1954.

Goebel, Dorothy Burne. "The 'New England Trade' and the French West Indies, 1763-1774: A Study in Trade Policies." *William and Mary Quarterly* 3d ser. 20 (1963): 331-372.

Goldman, Perry M. "Political Virtue in the Age of Jackson." *Political Science Quarterly* 87 (1972):46-62.

Gooch, Sir William. "Some Remarks on a Paper Transmitted into America, Entitled a Short Discourse on the Present State of the Colonies in America with Respect to Great Britain." In *History of the Dividing Line, and Other Tracts,* by William Byrd. 2 vols. Richmond: 1866.

Grant, Charles S. *Democracy in the Connecticut Frontier Town of Kent.* New York: Columbia University Press, 1961.

Graymont, Barbara. *The Iroquois in the American Revolution.* Syracuse: Syracuse University Press, 1972.

Greene, Evarts B. *The Revolutionary Generation, 1763-1790.* New York: Macmillan, 1943.

Greene, Jack P. "Changing Interpretations of Early American Politics." In *The Reinterpretation of Early American History,* edited by Ray A. Billington. San Marino, Calif.: Huntington Library, 1966.

Greene, Jack P. "Foundations of Political Power in the Virginia House of Burgesses, 1720-1776." *William and Mary Quarterly* 3d ser. 16 (1959):485-506.

Greene, Jack P., compiler. *Great Britain and the American Colonies, 1606-1763.* New York: Harper and Row, 1970.

Greene, Jack P. "Martin Bladen's Blueprint for Colonial Union." *William and Mary Quarterly* 3d ser. 17 (1960):516-530.

Greene, Jack P. "Political Mimesis: A Consideration of the Historical and Cultural Roots of Legislative Behavior in the British Colonies in the Eighteenth Century." *American Historical Review* 75 (1969):337-360.

Greene, Jack P. *The Quest for Power: The Lower Houses of Assembly in the Southern Royal Colonies, 1689-1776.* Chapel Hill: University of North Carolina Press, 1963.

Greene, Jack P. Review of *Papers of George Mason,* edited by Robert A. Rutland. *South Atlantic Quarterly* 72 (1973):159-162.

Greene, Jack P. "Search for Identity: An Interpretation of the Meaning of Selected Patterns of Social Response in Eighteenth-Century America." *Journal of Social History* 3 (1970):189-220.

Greene, Jack P. "An Uneasy Connection: An Analysis of the Preconditions of the American Revolution." In *Essays on the American Revolution,* edited by Stephen G. Kurtz and James H. Hutson. Chapel Hill: University of North Carolina Press, 1973.

Greene, Susan N. Honors thesis, Brandeis University, n.d.

Greven, Philip J., Jr. *Four Generations: Population, Land, and Family in Colonial Andover, Massachusetts.* Ithaca: Cornell University Press, 1970.

Grigsby, Hugh Blair. *The Virginia Convention of 1776.* Richmond: J. W. Randolph, 1855.

Gummere, Richard M. "Jonathan Boucher, Toryssismus." *Maryland Historical Magazine* 55 (1960):138-145.

Gunn, John A. W. *Politics and the Public Interest in the Seventeenth Century.* London: Routledge & K. Paul, 1969.

Halévy, Elie. *A History of the English People.* London: T. R. Unwin, Ltd., 1924.

Hall, Michael G. *Edward Randolph and the American Colonies, 1676-1703.* Chapel Hill: University of North Carolina Press, 1960.

Hamilton, Alexander. *The Papers of Alexander Hamilton.* Edited by Harold C. Syrett. 19 vols. New York: Columbia University Press, 1961- .

Handlin, Oscar and Handlin, Mary. *The Popular Sources of Political Authority.* Cambridge, Mass.: Harvard University Press, 1966.

Hanna, William S. *Benjamin Franklin and Pennsylvania Politics.* Stanford: Stanford University Press, 1964.

Hanson, Donald W. *From Kingdom to Commonwealth: The Development of Civic Consciousness in English Political Thought.* Cambridge, Mass.: Harvard University Press, 1970.

Haraszti, Zoltán. *John Adams & the Prophets of Progress.* Cambridge, Mass.: Harvard University Press, 1952.

Harrington, Virginia D. *The New York Merchant on the Eve of the Revolution.* New York: Columbia University Press, 1935.

Hart, Freeman H. *The Valley of Virginia in the American Revolution, 1763-1789.* Chapel Hill: University of North Carolina Press, 1942.

Hawke, David F. *Benjamin Rush, Revolutionary Gadfly.* Indianapolis: Bobbs-Merrill, 1971.

Hawley, Ellis W. *The New Deal and the Problem of Monopoly: A Study in Economic Ambivalence.* Princeton: Princeton University Press, 1966.

Heitman, Francis B., compiler. *Historical Register of Officers of the Continental Army.* 2d ed. Washington, D. C.: Rare Book Shop, 1914.

Henretta, James A. "Economic Development and Social Structure in Colonial Boston." In *Colonial America: Essays on Politics and Social Development,* edited by Stanley N. Katz. Boston: Little, Brown, 1971.

Henretta, James A. *"Salutary Neglect": Colonial Administration Under the Duke of Newcastle.* Princeton: Princeton University Press, 1972.

Hobsbawm, E. J. "From Social History to the History of Society." *Daedalus* 100 (1971):20-45.

Hollis, Thomas. Manuscript Diary in the Houghton Library, Harvard.

Hollis, Thomas. *Memoirs.* See Blackburne, Francis.

Hollis Papers, 1759-1771, in the Massachusetts Historical Society. MSS Hollis, f. 91-92.

Horowitz, G. "Conservatism, Liberalism, and Socialism in Canada: An Interpretation." *The Canadian Journal of Economics and Political Science* 32 (1966):143-171.

Howe, John R. *The Changing Political Thought of John Adams.* Princeton: Princeton University Press, 1966.

Hunter, Robert. *Androboros: A Biographical Farce.* New York: Bradford, 1714.

Huntington, Samuel P. *Political Order in Changing Societies.* New Haven: Yale University Press, 1968.

Hutchinson, Thomas. *The History of the Colony and Province of Massachusetts-Bay.* Edited by Lawrence Shaw Mayo. Cambridge, Mass.: Harvard University Press, 1936.

Hutson, James H. *Pennsylvania Politics, 1746-1770: The Movement for Royal Government and Its Consequences.* Princeton: Princeton University Press, 1972.

Hyman, Harold M. *To Try Men's Souls: Loyalty Tests in American History.* Berkeley and Los Angeles: University of California Press, 1959.

Jacobson, David L., ed. *The English Libertarian Heritage.* Indianapolis: Bobbs-Merrill, 1965.

James, Sydney V. "Colonial Rhode Island and the Beginnings of the Liberal Rationalized State." In *Essays in Theory and History: An Approach to the Social Sciences,* edited by Melvin Richter. Cambridge, Mass.: Harvard University Press, 1970.

James, Sydney V. "The Impact of the American Revolution on Quakers' Ideas about Their Sect." *William and Mary Quarterly* 3d ser. 19 (1962):360-382.

Jefferson, Thomas. *The Complete Jefferson*. Edited by Saul K. Padover. New York: Duell, Sloan & Pearce, 1943.

Jefferson, Thomas. *The Life and Selected Writings of Thomas Jefferson*. Edited by Adrienne Koch & William Peden. New York: Modern Library, 1944.

Jefferson, Thomas. *The Papers of Thomas Jefferson*. Edited by Julian Boyd. 19 vols. Princeton: Princeton University Press, 1950- .

Jellison, Charles A. *Ethan Allen: Frontier Rebel*. Syracuse: Syracuse University Press, 1969.

Johnson, Sir William. *The Papers of Sir William Johnson*. Edited by James Sullivan. 14 vols. Albany: University of the State of New York, 1921-1965.

Judd, Jacob. "Lord Bellomont and Captain Kidd." *The New York Historical Society Quarterly* 47 (1963):67-74.

Kammen, Michael. *Deputyes & Libertyes: The Origins of Representative Government in Colonial America*. New York: Knopf, 1969.

Kammen, Michael. *Empire and Interest: The American Colonies and the Politics of Mercantilism*. Philadelphia: Lippincott, 1970.

Kammen, Michael G. "Intellectuals, Political Leadership, and Revolution." *New England Quarterly* 41 (1968):583-593.

Kammen, Michael. *People of Paradox: An Inquiry Concerning the Origins of American Civilization*. New York: Knopf, 1973.

Kammen, Michael. *A Rope of Sand: The Colonial Agents, British Politics, and the American Revolution*. Ithaca: Cornell University Press, 1968.

Katz, Stanley. *Newcastle's New York: Anglo-American Politics, 1732-1753*. Cambridge, Mass.: Harvard University Press, 1968.

Kemmerer, Donald L. *Path to Freedom: The Struggle for Self-Government in Colonial New Jersey, 1703-1776*. Princeton: Princeton University Press, 1940.

Kerr, Wilfred B. *Bermuda and the American Revolution: 1760-1783*. Princeton: Princeton University Press, 1936.

Kirby, J. B. "Early American Politics—The Search for Ideology: An Historiographical Analysis and Critique of the Concept of Deference." *Journal of Politics* 32 (1970): 808-838.

Knollenberg, Bernhard. *Origin of the American Revolution: 1759-1766*. New York: Macmillan, 1960.

Knox, William. "Considerations on the Great Questions, What is to be Done with America? Part Second." In the Germane Papers, 27, William L. Clements Library, Ann Arbor, Michigan.

Koebner, Richard. *Empire*. Cambridge, England: Cambridge University Press, 1961.

Kramnick, Isaac. *Bolingbroke and His Circle*. Cambridge, Mass.: Harvard University Press, 1968.

Labaree, Benjamin Woods. *The Boston Tea Party*. New York: Oxford University Press, 1964.

Lambert, Sheila. *Bills and Acts. Legislative Procedure in Eighteenth-Century England*. Cambridge, England: Cambridge University Press, 1971.

Lanctôt, Gustave. *Le Canada et la Revolution Americaine*. Montreal: Beauchemin, 1965.

Land, Aubrey C. "Economic Base and Social Structure: The Northern Chesapeake in the Eighteenth Century." *The Journal of Economic History* 25 (1965):639-654.

Laslett, Peter, ed. Introduction to *Two Treatises of Government*, by John Locke. London: Cambridge University Press, 1960.

Laslett, Peter. *The World We Have Lost*. 2d ed. London: Methuen, 1971.

Leder, Lawrence H. *Robert Livingston (1654-1728) and the Politics of Colonial New York*. Chapel Hill: University of North Carolina Press, 1961.

Leder, Lawrence H., ed. " 'Dam'me Don't Stir a Man': Trial of New York Mutineers in 1700." *The New York Historical Society Quarterly* 42 (1958):261-283.

Leder, Lawrence H. "Dongan's New York and Fletcher's London: Personality and Politics." *New York Historical Society Quarterly* 55 (1971):28-37.

Lefler, Hugh T. and Newsome, Albert R. *North Carolina: The History of a Southern State*, rev. ed. Chapel Hill: University of North Carolina Press, 1963.

Le Goff, Jacques. "Is Politics Still the Backbone of History?" *Daedalus* 100 (1971): 1-19.

Lemisch, Jesse. "Jack Tar in the Streets: Merchant Seamen in the Politics of Revolutionary America." *William and Mary Quarterly* 3d ser. 25 (1968):371-407.

Lemon, James T. *The Best Poor Man's Country: A Geographical Study of Early Southeastern Pennsylvania*. Baltimore: Johns Hopkins Press, 1972.

Lemon, James T. and Nash, Gary B. "The Distribution of Wealth in Eighteenth-Century America: A Century of Changes in Chester County, Pennsylvania, 1693-1802." *Journal of Social History* 2 (1968):1-24.

A Letter to a Member of Parliament on the Present Unhappy Dispute between Great Britain and her Colonies. London: J. Walter, 1774.

Lincoln, Charles Z., ed. *State of New York. Messages from the Governors...* Albany: J. B. Lyon, 1909.

Lipset, Seymour Martin. *The First New Nation: The United States in Historical and Comparative Perspective*. London: Basic Books, 1964.

Litwak, Leon F. *North of Slavery*. Chicago: University of Chicago Press, 1961.

Lockridge, Kenneth. "Land, Population and the Evolution of New England Society, 1630-1790." In *Colonial America: Essays on Politics and Social Development*, edited by Stanley N. Katz. Boston: Little, Brown, 1971.

Lossing, Benson John. *Biographical Sketches of the Signers of the Declaration of American Independence*. New York: George F. Coolidge & Bro., 1848.

Lovejoy, David S. *Rhode Island Politics and the American Revolution, 1760-1776*. Providence: Brown University Press, 1958.

Lovejoy, David S. *The Glorious Revolution in America*. New York: Harper and Row, 1972.

Lowi, Theodore J., ed. *Private Life and Public Order. The Context of Modern Public Policy*. New York: Norton, 1968.

Lucas, Paul. "A Note on the Comparative Study of the Structure of Politics in Mid-Eighteenth-Century Britain and Its American Colonies." *William and Mary Quarterly* 3d ser. 28 (1971):301-309.

Lynd, Staughton. *Class Conflict, Slavery, and the United States Constitution*. Indianapolis and New York: Bobbs-Merrill, 1967.

Lynd, Staughton. "Who Should Rule at Home? Dutchess County, New York, in the American Revolution." *William and Mary Quarterly* 3d ser. 18 (1961):330-359.

Mackesy, Piers. *The War for America, 1775-1783*. London: Longmans, 1964.

MacKinnon, Neil. "The Changing Attitudes of Nova Scotia Loyalists Toward the United States, 1783-1791." Paper read at the Loyalist Symposium, University of New Brunswick, October 14, 1972.

MacKinnon, Neil. "Nova Scotia Loyalists, 1783-1785." *Social History/Histoire Sociale* (1969):17-48.

Maclay, William. *The Journal of William Maclay, United States Senator from Pennsylvania, 1789-1791*. Edited by Charles A. Beard. New York: Boni, 1927.

MacNutt, William Stewart. *New Brunswick, A History, 1784-1867*. Toronto: Macmillan, 1963.

MacNutt, William Stewart. *The Atlantic Provinces*. Toronto: McClelland and Stewart, 1965.

MacNutt, William Stewart, ed. "The Narrative of Lieutenant James Moody." *Acadiensis: Journal of the History of the Atlantic Region* 1 (1972):72-90.

Madison, James. *The Papers of James Madison.* Edited by William T. Hutchinson and W. M. E. Rachal. 2 vols. Chicago: University of Chicago Press, 1962-1973.

Maier, Pauline. "The Beginnings of American Republicanism, 1765-1776." In *The Development of a Revolutionary Mentality: Papers presented at the First Library of Congress Symposium on the American Revolution.* Washington: Library of Congress, 1972.

Maier, Pauline. "The Charleston Mob and the Evolution of Popular Politics in Revolutionary South Carolina." *Perspectives in American History* 4 (1970):173-196.

Maier, Pauline. *From Resistance to Revolution: Colonial Radicals and the Development of American Opposition to Britain, 1765-1776.* New York: Knopf, 1972.

Maier, Pauline. "Popular Uprisings and Civil Authority in Eighteenth-Century America." *William and Mary Quarterly* 3d ser. 27 (1970):3-35.

Main, Jackson T. "Government by the People: The American Revolution and the Democratization of the Legislatures." *William and Mary Quarterly* 3d ser. 23 (1966): 391-407.

Mark, Irving. *Agrarian Conflicts in Colonial New York, 1711-1775.* New York: Columbia University Press, 1940.

Marston, Benjamin. Manuscript Diary in the Archives, University of New Brunswick.

Martin, James Kirby. "A Model For the Coming American Revolution: The Birth and Death of the Wentworth Oligarchy in New Hampshire, 1741-1776." *Journal of Social History* 4 (1970):41-60.

Marty, Martin E. *Righteous Empire: The Protestant Experience in America.* New York: Dial Press, 1970.

Mason, Bernard. *The Road to Independence: The Revolutionary Movement in New York, 1773-1777.* Lexington: University of Kentucky Press, 1966.

Massachusetts Historical Society Collections, 5 ser. 4 (1878).

Massachusetts Historical Society Collections, 6 ser. 4 (1891).

Massachusetts Soldiers and Sailors of the Revolutionary War. 17 vols. Boston: Wright and Potter, 1896-1908.

McCrady, Edward. *The History of South Carolina in the Revolution, 1780-1783.* New York: Macmillan, 1902.

McCrae, Kenneth D. "The Structure of Canadian History." In *The Founding of New Societies: Studies in the History of the United States, Latin America, South Africa, Canada and Australia,* edited by Louis Hartz. New York: Harcourt, Brace and World, 1964.

McKirdy, Charles R. "A Bar Divided: The Lawyers of Massachusetts and the American Revolution." *The American Journal of Legal History* 16 (1972):205-214.

Mekeel, Arthur J. "The Quaker-Loyalist Migration to New Brunswick and Nova Scotia in 1783." Friends' Historical Association *Bulletin* 32 (1943):65-75.

Mekeel, Arthur J. "The Society of Friends (Quakers) and the American Revolution." Ph.D. dissertation, Harvard University, 1940.

Merivale, Herman. *Lectures on Colonies and Colonization.* 2 vols. London: Longman, 1841-42.

Messerli, Jonathan. *Horace Mann: A Biography.* New York: Knopf, 1972.

Miller, John C. *Triumph of Freedom: 1775-1783.* Boston: Little, Brown, 1948.

Miller, Perry. *The New England Mind: From Colony to Province.* Cambridge, Mass.: Harvard University Press, 1953.

Miller, Perry. *Orthodoxy in Massachusetts, 1630-1650.* Boston: Beacon, 1959.

Montgomery, Morton L. *History of Berks County, Pennsylvania, in the Revolution, from 1774 to 1783.* Reading, Pennsylvania: C. F. Haage, 1894.

Morgan, Edmund S. and Morgan, Helen. *The Stamp Act Crisis.* Chapel Hill: University of North Carolina Press, 1953; New York: Collier, 1963.

Morison, Samuel E. *Builders of the Bay Colony.* Boston: Houghton Mifflin, 1930.

Morse, Richard. "Some Characteristics of Latin American Urban History." *American Historical Review* 67 (1962):317-338.

Morton, William Lewis. *The Kingdom of Canada*. Toronto: McClelland and Stewart, 1963.

Morton, William Lewis. *The Canadian Identity*. Madison: University of Wisconsin Press, 1961.

Murrin, John M. "Anglicizing an American Colony: The Transformation of Provincial Massachusetts." Ph.D. dissertation, Yale University, 1966.

Murrin, John M. "From Corporate Empire to Revolutionary Republic: The Transformation of the Structure and Concept of Federalism." Paper read at the Annual Meeting of the American Historical Association, New York City, December 30, 1966.

Murrin, John M. "The Legal Transformation of the Bench and Bar of Eighteenth-Century Massachusetts." In *Colonial America: Essays on Politics and Social Development*, edited by Stanley N. Katz. Boston: Little, Brown, 1971.

Murrin, John M. "The Myths of Colonial Democracy and Royal Decline in Eighteenth-Century America." *Cithara* 5 (1965):53-71.

Namier, Sir Lewis. *England in the Age of the American Revolution*. 2d ed. New York: St. Martins, 1961.

Nash, Gary B. *Quakers and Politics: Pennsylvania, 1681-1726*. Princeton: Princeton University Press, 1968.

Nelson, William H. *The American Tory*. Oxford: Clarendon, 1961.

Nelson, William H. "The Last Hopes of the American Loyalists." *Canadian Historical Review* 32 (1951):22-42.

Norton, Mary Beth. *The British Americans: The Loyalist Exiles in England, 1774-1789*. Boston: Little, Brown, 1972.

Oaks, Robert F. "Philadelphians in Exile: The Problem of Loyalty During the American Revolution." *Pennsylvania Magazine of History and Biography* 96 (1972):298-325.

O'Callaghan, Edmund B., ed. *Documentary History of New York*. 4 vols. Albany: Weed, Parsons, 1850-1851.

O'Callaghan, Edmund B., ed. *Documents Relative to the Colonial History of the State of New York*. 15 vols. Albany: Weed, Parsons, 1853-87.

Oliver, Peter. *Origin & Progress of the American Rebellion*. Edited by Douglass Adair and John A. Schutz. San Marino: Huntington Library, 1961.

Olson, Alison and Brown, Richard M., eds. *Anglo-American Political Relations, 1675-1775*. New Brunswick: Rutgers University Press, 1970.

Olton, Charles S. "Philadelphia's Mechanics in the First Decade of Revolution 1765-1775." *Journal of American History* 59 (1972):311-326.

Ousterhout, Anne McCabe. "The Forgotten Antagonists: Pennsylvania Loyalists." Ph.D. dissertation, Michigan State University, 1972.

Paine, Thomas. *The Complete Writings of Thomas Paine*. Edited by Philip S. Foner. 2 vols. New York: Citadel, 1969.

Palmer, Robert. *The Age of the Democratic Revolution*. Princeton: Princeton University Press, 1959.

Papenfuse, Edward C. and Stiverson, Gregory A. "General Smallwood's Recruits: The Peacetime Career of the Revolutionary War Private." *William and Mary Quarterly* 3d ser. 30 (1973):117-132.

"Parent, Daniel." In the Saunders Papers, Archives, University of New Brunswick.

Patterson, Stephen E. *Political Parties in Revolutionary Massachusetts*. Madison: University of Wisconsin Press, 1973.

Peckham, Howard H. *The War for Independence*. Chicago: University of Chicago Press, 1958.

Pemberton, Ian C. B. "Justus Sherwood, Vermont Loyalist, 1747-1798." Ph.D. dissertation, University of Western Ontario, London, Ontario, 1972.

Pennsylvania Archives. 3d ser. vol. 18 (1897) Harrisburg, and 5th ser. vol. 1-4 (1906) Harrisburg.

Pennsylvania Chronicle. July 5, 1773.

Peters, Thomas. Petition in the *Foreign Office Papers*, Public Record Office, 4/1, 419-423.

Peterson, Merrill D. "Thomas Jefferson and Commercial Policy, 1783-1793." *William and Mary Quarterly* 3d ser. 22 (1965):584-610.

Philbrick, Francis S. *The Rise of the West, 1754-1830*. New York: Harper and Row, 1965.

Plumb, John H. "The Growth of the Electorate in England from 1600 to 1715." *Past and Present* 45 (1969):90-116.

Plumb, John H. *The Origins of Political Stability: England, 1675-1725*. Boston: Houghton Mifflin, 1967.

Plumstead, A. W., compiler. *The Wall and the Garden: Selected Massachusetts Election Sermons, 1670-1775*. Minneapolis: University of Minnesota Press, 1968.

Pocock, John G. A. *Politics, Language and Time: Essays on Political Thought and History*. New York: Atheneum, 1971.

Pocock, John G. A. "Virtue and Commerce in the Eighteenth Century." *The Journal of Interdisciplinary History* 3 (1972):119-134.

Pole, Jack R. *Political Representation in England and the Origins of the American Republic*. New York: St. Martin's, 1966.

Potter, David. "The Historical Perspective." In *The Meaning of Commercial Television*, edited by Stanley T. Donner. Austin: University of Texas Press, 1967.

Potter, J. "The Growth of Population in America, 1700-1860." In *Population in History*, edited by David V. Glass and D. E. C. Eversley. Chicago: Aldine, 1965.

Powell, William S., ed. *The Regulators in North Carolina: A Documentary History, 1759-1776*. Raleigh: State Department of Archives and History, 1971.

The Privileges of the Island of Jamaica Vindicated with an Impartial Narrative of the late Dispute between the Governor and the House of Representatives. London: J. Williams, 1766.

Providence, R. I., Sons of Liberty to New York Sons of Liberty, May 24, 1776, in the Belknap Papers, 61.c.121, Massachusetts Historical Society.

Quarles, Benjamin. *The Negro in the American Revolution*. Chapel Hill: University of North Carolina Press, 1961.

Quarles, Benjamin. "Lord Dunmore As Liberator." *William and Mary Quarterly* 3d ser. 15 (1958):494-507.

Quinn, David B., ed. *The Voyages and Colonizing Activities of Sir Humphrey Gilbert*. 2 vols. London: The Hakluyt Society, 1940.

Rainbolt, John C. "The Alteration in the Relationship between Leadership and Constituents in Virginia, 1660 to 1720." *William and Mary Quarterly* 3d ser. 27 (1970):411-434.

Ramsay, David. *History of the American Revolution*. 2 vols. Philadelphia: R. Aitken & Son, 1789.

Ramsay, David. *The History of the Revolution of South-Carolina, from a British Province to an Independent State*. 2 vols. Trenton: Isaac Collins, 1785.

Ransom, Roger L. "British Policy and Colonial Growth: Some Implications of the Burden from the Navigation Acts." *Journal of Economic History* 28 (1968): 427-435.

Read, William Thompson. *Life and Correspondence of George Read*. Philadelphia: J. B. Lippincott, 1870.

Regan, Richard J. *Private Conscience and Public Law: The American Experience*. New York: Fordham University Press, 1972.

Richards, Leonard. *Gentlemen of Property and Standing: Anti-Abolition Mobs in Jacksonian America*. New York: Oxford University Press, 1970.

Richardson, Fred L. "Early American Political Authority." Ph.D. dissertation, Brandeis University, 1973.

Ritcheson, Charles. *British Politics and the American Revolution*. Norman: University of Oklahoma Press, 1954.

Ritchie, Robert C. "The Duke's Province: A Study of Proprietary New York, 1664-1685." Ph.D. dissertation, U.C.L.A., 1972.

Robbins, Caroline. *The Eighteenth-Century Commonwealthman.* Cambridge, Mass.: Harvard University Press, 1959; New York: Atheneum, 1968.

Roche, John P. "American Liberty: An Analysis of the 'Tradition' of Freedom." In *Aspects of Liberty*, edited by Milton Konvitz and Clinton Rossiter. Ithaca: Cornell University Press, 1958.

Roche, John P. "Constitutional Law: Distribution of Powers." *International Encyclopedia of the Social Sciences* 3 (1968):300-307.

Roche, John P. "Founding Fathers: A Reform Caucus in Action." *American Political Science Review* 55 (1961):799-816.

Ross, Julie. "Jacob Bailey: Portrait of an American Clergyman in Eighteenth Century Nova Scotia." Honours essay, History Department, Dalhousie University, Halifax, Nova Scotia.

Rossiter, Clinton. *Seedtime of the Republic.* New York: Harcourt, Brace, 1953.

Rothermund, Dietmar. *The Layman's Progress: Religious and Political Experience in Colonial Pennsylvania, 1740-1770.* Philadelphia: University of Pennsylvania Press, 1961.

Rothman, David. *The Discovery of the Asylum, Social Order and Disorder in the New Republic.* Boston: Little, Brown, 1971.

Rush, Benjamin. *Autobiography.* Edited by George W. Corner. Princeton: Princeton University Press, 1948.

Rush, Benjamin. *Letters of Benjamin Rush.* Edited by L. H. Butterfield. Princeton: Princeton University Press, 1951.

Rush, Benjamin. "Of the Mode of Education Proper in a Republic." In his *Essays, Literary, Moral and Philosophical*, pp. 6-20. Philadelphia: Bradford, 1806.

Rush, Benjamin. "Thoughts upon Female Education." In his *Essays, Literary, Moral and Philosophical*, pp. 75-92. Philadelphia: Bradford, 1806.

Sanderson, Howard K. *Lynn in the Revolution.* Boston: W. B. Clarke, 1909.

Sanderson, John and Walm, Robert. *Biographies of the Signers.* 5 vols. Philadelphia: H. W. Brown & C. Peters, 1828.

Sayre, Stephen. Undated proposal in the Earl of Dartmouth Papers, William Salt Library, Stafford, England, D 1778/2/1079.

Scheiber, Harry. "Government and the Economy: Studies of the 'Commonwealth' Policy in Nineteenth-Century America." *The Journal of Interdisciplinary History* 3 (1972):135-151.

Schlesinger, Arthur M. "The American Revolution Reconsidered." *Political Science Quarterly* 34 (1919):61-78.

Schlesinger, Arthur M. *The Colonial Merchants and the American Revolution, 1763-1776.* New York: Atheneum, 1968.

Schlesinger, Arthur M. "The Uprising Against the East India Company." *Political Science Quarterly* 32 (1917):60-79.

Schubert, Glendon. *The Public Interest: A Critique of the Theory of a Political Concept.* Glencoe, Ill.: Free Press, 1960.

Séguin, J A R. *A Bibliography of John Trenchard, 1662-1723.* Jersey City: R. Paxton, 1965.

Séguin, J A R. *A Bibliography of Thomas Gordon, ca. 1692-1750.* Jersey City: R. Paxton, 1965.

Sellers, John. "The Origins and Careers of the New England Soldier: Non-Commissioned Officers and Privates of the Massachusetts Continental Line." Unpublished paper, 1972.

Shils, Edward. "Concentration and Dispersal of Charisma." *World Politics* 11 (1958-59):1-19.

Shils, Edward. "Political Development in the New States: II." *Comparative Studies in Society and History* 2 (1960):379-411.

Shy, John W. *Toward Lexington: The Role of the British Army in the Coming of the American Revolution.* Princeton: Princeton University Press, 1965.

Sirmans, M. Eugene. *Colonial South Carolina: A Political History, 1663-1763.* Chapel Hill: University of North Carolina Press, 1966.

Slaski, Eugene R. "Thomas Willing: Moderation During the American Revolution." Ph.D. dissertation, Florida State University, 1971.

Sloan, Robert W. "New Ireland: Loyalists in Eastern Maine During the American Revolution." Ph.D. dissertation, Michigan State University, 1971.

Smith, Hilrie Shelton, et al., eds. *American Christianity: An Historical Interpretation with Representative Documents.* 2 vols. New York: Scribner, 1960-63.

Smith, Jonathan. *Peterborough, New Hampshire, in the American Revolution.* Peterborough: Peterborough Historical Society, 1913.

Smith, Paul H. *Loyalists and Redcoats.* Chapel Hill: University of North Carolina Press, 1964.

Smith, Paul H. "The American Loyalists: Notes on Their Organization and Numerical Strength." *William and Mary Quarterly* 3d ser. 25 (1968):259-277.

Smith, William Ander. "Anglo-Colonial Society and the Mob, 1740-1775." Ph.D. dissertation, Claremont Graduate School, 1965.

Smith, William R. *History as Argument: Three Patriot Historians of the American Revolution.* The Hague: Mouton, 1966.

Smith, William, Jr. *The History of the Province of New York.* Edited by Michael Kammen. Cambridge, Mass.: Harvard University Press, 1972.

Sorauf, Frank J. "The Public Interest Reconsidered." *Journal of Politics* 19 (1957): 616-639.

Sosin, Jack M. *Agents and Merchants: British Colonial Policy and the Origins of the American Revolution, 1763-1775.* Lincoln: University of Nebraska Press, 1965.

Sosin, Jack M. *The Revolutionary Frontier, 1763-1783.* New York: Rinehart and Winston, 1967.

Sosin, Jack M. "The Use of Indians in the War of the American Revolution: A Re-Assessment of Responsibility." *Canadian Historical Review* 46 (1965):101-121.

Spray, William A. *The Blacks in New Brunswick.* Fredericton: Brunswick, 1972.

Steele, Ian K. *Politics of Colonial Policy: The Board of Trade in Colonial Administration, 1696-1720.* Oxford: Clarendon, 1968.

Stewart, Gordon and Rawlyk, George. *A People Highly Favoured of God.* Toronto: Macmillan, 1972.

Stokes, Durward T. "The Baptist and Methodist Clergy in South Carolina and the American Revolution." *South Carolina Historical Magazine* 73 (1972):87-96.

Stourzh, Gerald. "William Blackstone, Teacher of Revolution." *Jahrbuch für Amerikastudien,* Carl Winter Universitätsverlag, Heidelberg, Band 5 (1970):184-200.

Stourzh, Gerald. *Alexander Hamilton and the Idea of Republican Government.* Stanford: Stanford University Press, 1970.

Sussman, Gail. "A Christian Duty: Social Responsibility and Control in New Haven, 1638-1662." Unpublished essay, Yale University, 1972.

Sydnor, Charles. *Gentlemen Freeholders: Political Practices in Washington's Virginia.* Chapel Hill: University of North Carolina Press, 1952.

Syrett, David. *Shipping and the American War, 1775-1783: A Study of British Transport Organization.* London: University of London, Athlone Press, 1970.

Talman, James John, ed. *Loyalist Narratives from Upper Canada.* Toronto: Champlain Society, 1946.

Taylor, Robert J. *Western Massachusetts in the Revolution.* Providence: Brown University Press, 1954.

Taylor, William L. *A Productive Monopoly: The Effect of Railroad Control on New England Coastal Steamship Lines, 1870-1916.* Providence: Brown University Press, 1970.

Thorne, Dorothy G. "North Carolina Friends and the Revolution." *The North Carolina Historical Review* 38 (1961):323-340.

Thorpe, Francis N., ed. *The Federal and State Constitutions, Colonial Charters, and other Organic Laws of the United States of America.* 7 vols. Washington: Government Printing Office, 1909.

Tully, Alan. "William Penn's Legacy: Politics and Social Structure in Colonial Pennsylvania 1726 to 1755." Ph.D. dissertation, Johns Hopkins University, 1973.

Tyler, Moses C. *The Literary History of the American Revolution, 1763-1783.* 2 vols. New York and London: Putnam, 1897.

Underhill, Frank H. *In Search of Canadian Liberalism.* Toronto: Macmillan, 1960.

Upton, Leslie Francis Stokes. *Revolutionary Versus Loyalist.* Waltham, Mass.: Blaisdell, 1968.

Upton, Leslie Francis Stokes. *The Loyal Whig: William Smith of New York and Quebec.* Toronto: University of Toronto Press, 1969.

Van Every, Dale. *A Company of Heroes: The American Frontier, 1775-1783.* New York: Morrow, 1962.

Van Rensselaer, Mrs. John King. *The Goede Vrouw of Mana-ha-ta: At Home and in Society, 1609-1760.* New York: Scribners & Sons, 1898.

Van Tyne, Claude H. *The Loyalists in the American Revolution.* New York: Macmillan, 1902.

Ver Steeg, Clarence L. *Robert Morris: Revolutionary Financier.* Philadelphia: University of Pennsylvania Press, 1954.

Vincent, Philip. "A True Relation of the Late Battell Fought in New England..." (London, 1638) in *Collections of the Massachusetts Historical Society* 3d ser. 6 (1837):29-43.

Volwiler, Albert T. *George Croghan and the Westward Movement, 1741-1782.* Cleveland: Arthur H. Clark Co., 1926.

Wainwright, Nicholas, ed. "A Diary of Trifling Occurences, Philadelphia, 1776-1778." *Pennsylvania Magazine of History and Biography* 82 (1958):411-465.

Wainwright, Nicholas. "Governor John Blackwell." *Pennsylvania Magazine of History and Biography* 74 (1950):457-472.

Warner, Sam Bass, Jr. *The Private City: Philadelphia in Three Periods of Its Growth.* Philadelphia: University of Pennsylvania Press, 1968.

Waterhouse, Richard. "South Carolina's Colonial Elite: A Study of the Social Structure and Political Culture of a Southern Colony, 1670-1760." Ph.D. dissertation, Johns Hopkins University, 1973.

Waters, John J., Jr. *The Otis Family in Provincial and Revolutionary Massachusetts.* Chapel Hill: University of North Carolina Press, 1968.

Watson, John L. "The Marston Family of Salem, Massachusetts." *New England Historical and Genealogical Register* 27 (1873):390-403.

Webster, Noah. *Dissertations on the English Language.* Boston: I. Thomas, 1789.

Webster, Noah. *Sketches of American Policy (1785).* Edited by Harry W. Warfel. New York: Scholars Facsimiles & Reprints, 1937.

Weir, Robert M. "Bolingbroke, the Politics of Nostalgia, and the American South: A Review Essay." *South Carolina Historical Magazine* 70 (1969):267-273.

Weir, Robert M. "'The Harmony We Were Famous For': An Interpretation of Pre-Revolutionary South Carolina Politics." *William and Mary Quarterly* 3d ser. 26 (1969):473-501.

Wells, William V. *The Life and Public Services of Samuel Adams.* 3 vols. Boston: Little, Brown, 1865.

White, Leonard D. *The Federalists: A Study in Administrative History.* New York: Macmillan, 1948.

White, Leonard D. *The Jeffersonians: A Study in Administrative History, 1801-1829.* New York: Macmillan, 1951.

White, Philip L. *The Beekmans of New York in Politics and Commerce, 1647-1877.* New York: New York Historical Society, 1956.

Whitehead, John S. "The Separation of College and State: The Transformation of

Columbia, Dartmouth, Harvard, and Yale from Quasi-Public to Private Institutions, 1776-1876." Ph.D. dissertation, Yale University, 1971.

Williams, Orlo C. *The Historical Development of Private Bill Procedure and Standing Orders in the House of Commons*. London: H. M. Stationery Office, 1948.

Williamson, Chilton. *American Suffrage: From Property to Democracy, 1760-1860*. Princeton: Princeton University Press, 1960.

Williamson, Chilton. *Vermont in a Quandary: 1763-1825*. Montpelier: Vermont Historical Society, 1949.

Winks, Robin. *The Blacks in Canada*. Montreal: McGill-Queens University Press; New Haven: Yale University Press, 1971.

Winsor, Justin. *Narrative and Critical History of America*. 8 vols. Boston: Houghton, Mifflin, 1888.

Wise, Sydney F. and Brown, Robert Craig. *Canada Views the United States*. Seattle and London: University of Washington Press, 1967.

Wood, Gordon S. *The Creation of the American Republic, 1776-1787*. Chapel Hill: University of North Carolina Press, 1967.

Wood, Gordon. "A Note on Mobs in the American Revolution." *William and Mary Quarterly* 3d ser. 23 (1966):635-642.

Woodmason, Charles. *The Carolina Backcountry on the Eve of Revolution: The Journal and Other Writings of Charles Woodmason, Anglican Itinerant*. Edited by Richard Hooker. Chapel Hill: University of North Carolina Press, 1953.

Wright, Conrad. "Piety, Morality & the Commonwealth." *Crane Review* 9 (1967): 90-106.

Wright, Esmond. *Fabric of Freedom, 1763-1800*. New York: Hill and Wang, 1961.

Wright, Esther Clark. *The Loyalists of New Brunswick*. Fredericton: 1955.

Wright, Louis B. *The Colonial Search for a Southern Eden*. University, Ala.: University of Alabama Press, 1953.

Wright, Louis B. "Elizabethan Politics and Colonial Enterprise." *The North Carolina Historical Review* 32 (1955):254-269.

Wright, Louis B. *Gold, Glory and the Gospel*. New York: Atheneum, 1970.

Wright, Louis B. *Religion and Empire*. Chapel Hill: University of North Carolina Press, 1943.

Zeichner, Oscar. *Connecticut's Years of Controversy, 1750-1776*. Chapel Hill: University of North Carolina Press, 1949.

Zemsky, Robert. *Merchants, Farmers, and River Gods: An Essay on Eighteenth Century American Politics*. Boston: Gambit, 1971.

Zimmer, Anne Young and Kelly, Alfred H. "Jonathan Boucher: Constitutional Conservative." *Journal of American History* 58 (1972):897-922.

Zubly, John Joachim. *An Humble Enquiry into the Nature of the Dependency of the American Colonies upon the Parliament of Great Britain*. (Charleston) 1769.

Zuckerman, Michael. *Peaceable Kingdoms: New England Towns in the Eighteenth Century*. New York: Knopf, 1970.

Zuckerman, Michael. "The Social Context of Democracy in Massachusetts." In *Colonial America: Essays on Politics and Social Development*, edited by Stanley N. Katz. Boston: Little, Brown, 1971.

DATE DUE
